D1253860

De-Facing Power

In this major contribution to the power debate, Clarissa Rile Hayward challenges the prevailing view which treats power as something powerful people have and use. Rather than seeing it as having a "face," she considers power as a complex network of social boundaries – norms, identities, institutions – which define both the field of action and the individual's freedom within it, for the "powerful" and "powerless" alike. Hayward suggests that the critical analysis of power relations should focus on the ways in which these relationships affect people's capacities to help shape the institutions and practices that govern their lives. Using a detailed comparative analysis of the relationships within two ethnically diverse educational settings – one in a low-income, predominantly African-American, urban school, the other in an affluent, predominantly white, suburban school – this book develops a compelling account of the concept of power in terms of networks of practices and relations.

CLARISSA RILE HAYWARD is Assistant Professor of Political Science at Ohio State University.

Contemporary Political Theory

Series Editor
Ian Shapiro

Editorial Board
Russell Hardin   Stephen Holmes   Jeffrey Isaac
John Keane   Elizabeth Kiss   Susan Okin
Phillipe Van Parijs   Phillip Pettit

As the twenty-first century begins, major new political challenges have arisen at the same time as some of the most enduring dilemmas of political association remain unresolved. The collapse of communism and the end of the Cold War reflect a victory for democratic and liberal values, yet in many of the western countries that nurtured those values there are severe problems of urban decay, class and racial conflict, and failing political legitimacy. Enduring global injustice and inequality seem compounded by environmental problems, disease, the oppression of women, racial, ethnic and religious minorities, and the relentless growth of the world's population. In such circumstances, the need for creative thinking about the fundamentals of human political association is manifest. This new series in contemporary political theory is needed to foster such systematic normative reflection.

The series proceeds in the belief that the time is ripe for a reassertion of the importance of problem-driven political theory. It is concerned, that is, with works that are motivated by the impulse to understand, think critically about, and address the problems in the world, rather than issues that are thrown up primarily in academic debate. Books in the series may be interdisciplinary in character, ranging over issues conventionally dealt with in philosophy, law, history and the human sciences. The range of materials and the methods of proceeding should be dictated by the problem at hand, not the conventional debates or disciplinary divisions of academia.

Other books in the series

Ian Shapiro and Casiano Hacker-Cordón (eds.)
Democracy's Value

Ian Shapiro and Casiano Hacker-Cordón (eds.)
Democracy's Edges

Brooke A. Ackerly
Political Theory and Feminist Social Criticism

De-Facing Power

Clarissa Rile Hayward

CAMBRIDGE
UNIVERSITY PRESS

PUBLISHED BY THE PRESS SYNDICATE OF THE UNIVERSITY OF CAMBRIDGE
The Pitt Building, Trumpington Street, Cambridge, United Kingdom

CAMBRIDGE UNIVERSITY PRESS
The Edinburgh Building, Cambridge CB2 2RU, UK   www.cup.cam.ac.uk
40 West 20th Street, New York, NY 10011-4211, USA   www.cup.org
10 Stamford Road, Oakleigh, Melbourne 3166, Australia
Ruiz de Alarcón 13, 28014 Madrid, Spain

First published 2000

Printed in the United Kingdom at the University Press, Cambridge

Typeface Plantin MT 10/13 pt   *System* QuarkXPress™   [SE]

A catalogue record for this book is available from the British Library

Library of Congress Cataloguing in Publication data

Hayward, Clarissa Rile.
    De-Facing power / Clarissa Rile Hayward.
        p. cm. – (Contemporary political theory)
    Includes bibliographical references and index.
    ISBN 0 521 78079 9
    1. Power (Social sciences) – United States – Case studies.   2. Critical pedagogy – Case
studies.   3. Politics and education – Case studies.   I. Title.   II. Series.

HN90.P6 H39 2000   303.3–dc21   00-020470

ISBN 0 521 78079 9 hardback
ISBN 0 521 78564 2 paperback

For Adam, Aidan, and Elias

Contents

Acknowledgments   *page* viii

1 Introduction   1

2 De-facing power   11

3 Power and pedagogy   40

4 "The environment" and the North End Community School   57

5 The "world" of Fair View   111

6 Power and freedom   161

Appendix A: Tables   179
Appendix B: Research methods   187
References   199
Index   212

Acknowledgments

I am indebted to many friends and colleagues whose comments, suggestions, and questions helped shape this book. I would like to thank, in particular, Ian Shapiro, for his invaluable advice and support through every phase of the project. Shapiro, Cathy Cohen, and Rogers Smith read and commented extensively on multiple drafts. The final product has been immeasurably improved as a result of their insights and guidance.

I benefited, as well, from constructive comments and suggestions on all or parts of the manuscript from Joshua Gamson, Bill Liddle, Kevin O'Brien, Karen Rile, Jim Scott, and three anonymous reviewers. Earlier versions of the arguments in chapters 2 and 6 were presented in seminars in the political science departments at the Ohio State University, Stanford University, and Yale University, and at the 1999 Midwest Political Science Association meeting. I gratefully acknowledge the helpful comments of participants in these seminars. Thanks also to Doug Rae, who offered much needed advice and encouragement early on.

I owe a special debt to the teachers, students, and staff members at the schools that, in these pages, I call the North End Community School and Fair View Elementary. They generously invited me into their classrooms and shared with me their time, thoughts, and experiences. Although they might disagree with aspects of the ethnographic accounts in chapters 3, 4, and 5, the arguments presented there owe much to their reflections and wisdom.

I am grateful, as well, for financial assistance from the Ohio State University and Yale University, which helped support research for this project. I would like to express my gratitude for the research assistance provided by Amy Ertel, Heather Mann, and Charles Smith. Thanks are due, as well, to John Haslam of Cambridge University Press for his interest and support, and to Carol Fellingham Webb for her excellent copyediting.

Finally, I want to thank my husband, Adam, whose role in this project went well beyond that of the "supportive spouse" typically mentioned near the end of acknowledgment sections. He was the first to read and to comment on almost every part of the book. It has benefited tremendously both from his literary insights and from his practical understandings, based on his own experience teaching in urban public schools.

Parts of the arguments in chapters 2 and 4 first appeared, in different form, as "De-Facing Power," in *Polity*, volume 31, number 1 (fall 1998) (chapter 2), and "'The Environment': Power, Pedagogy, and American Urban Schooling," in *The Urban Review*, volume 31, number 4 (December 1999) (chapter 4). Thanks to the publishers of both journals for permission to reprint this material.

1   Introduction

On a mid-September afternoon, I rode the indirect route that public transportation provides to the core urban North End Community School.[1] The trip from the middle-class neighborhood that borders North End – two or three miles at most – takes multiple bus rides, and more than half an hour. The bus dropped me about a block and a half from the school, outside the public housing project where many North End students live.

Approaching the school building, I was surprised to see that the vast majority of the children playing outside wore uniforms: plaid jumpers with white blouses for the girls, gray pants, white shirts, and red ties and jackets for the boys.

I had come for an interview with the principal, Natalie Carson, to arrange to conduct participant-observation research in a fourth grade classroom throughout the academic year, and to work as a volunteer at the school.[2] Our meeting was short. Carson asked what I expected to learn while at North End. She asked which days I wanted to come, and which hours. She asked me for references, and she told me that the central district office would require me to undergo a security check.

Leaving Carson's office, I saw in the hallway a group of students who looked like fourth or fifth graders. They were standing in line, some pushing each other, some dancing. A teacher spoke in a raised voice, correcting children who talked and those who stepped out of line.

About two weeks later, I received a message on my answering machine from Monica Segal, a fourth grade teacher at Fair View Elementary, which is a public school in the affluent suburban community of Fair View, Connecticut.[3]

---

[1] Unless otherwise indicated, the proper names of schools, school districts, and individuals in schools are pseudonyms. As a condition for access to the classrooms I studied, I agreed not to disclose these identities. For demographic and other data on the North End Community School and the North End neighborhood, see pages 59 and 62–3 and Appendix A, tables 1–3.   [2] On my participant-observation research, see Appendix B.
[3] For demographic and other data on Fair View Elementary and the town of Fair View, see pages 114–16 and Appendix A, tables 1–3.

When we spoke, Segal told me a little about the school. There was a new principal this year, she said. She referred to her as "Anita."

She told me that the fourth graders were divided into five classes. At the end of each year, she explained, third grade teachers met and decided how to arrange the students for the following year, aiming for a balance in academic ability and classroom behavior.

Segal said that this year would be the first that the school did not offer an advanced math class, a change that, she reported, was currently at the center of a controversy. Parents of "gifted" children were unhappy with the decision to eliminate the class.

And Segal told me about her own classroom. She said that she had removed all the desks and replaced them with tables and chairs, as well as a couch and other comfortable furniture. She said that her students did most of their work independently, at their own speed. She told me that this year she was "letting the children make all of the decisions in the classroom." In fact, she said, it was the students who had decided that I could come in once a week to observe and help out.

The study of power

I arranged to participate in and to observe classes at North End and at Fair View, because I wanted to study a social phenomenon known as "power." Schooled in the political theories of power that developed in the United States in the second half of the twentieth century, I had learned that power takes many forms or, in the language of the political science power debate, wears many "faces." *The powerful*, I had learned, *have power* in the form of resources, the control of political agendas, or strategic advantage conferred by social structures. They *use power*, I had further learned, interfering with choices that the powerless would make, but for power's exercise. The powerful coerce the powerless. They manipulate them in ways that change their conduct. They teach them to anticipate defeat, and therefore not to challenge the *status quo*. At times, they even induce the powerless to misapprehend their own preferences and to act in ways contrary to their interests.

Political theories of power's many faces suggested questions that I should ask at the North End Community School and at Fair View Elementary. How is power distributed at each site? Who has power, who lacks power, and in what do power's mechanisms consist? How do powerful agents use the power they have? And how do their actions on power's mechanisms affect powerless actors?

What is more, sociological studies and educational theories of the role power plays in schools suggested explanatory hypotheses. At North End, where students are members of marginalized racial, ethnic, and economic groups, teachers, administrators, and other powerful agents might use power to induce children to alter their behavior, desires, and attitudes, in ways contrary to their interests. At Fair View, by contrast, powerful teachers might *empower* privileged students, enabling them to realize their chosen ends, or their authentic interests and desires.

My aim in this book is to make the case, not only that the hypotheses suggested by studies of power in the classroom are wrong, but also that the questions informing these hypotheses are, in important ways, misguided. At North End power is located, not only and not principally in mechanisms that teachers and other people who seem "powerful" possess or direct (such as rules requiring children to wear uniforms and to stand in line), but also in boundaries to social action that no actor "has" or "uses." Key political mechanisms include the bus route that makes it impossible to ride public transportation directly to and from North End and the middle-class neighborhood adjacent to it. They include the zoning, the housing, and the other laws and policies that shaped the decision to site public housing units in this particular urban neighborhood. They include the institutional rules that render the city in which North End is located a municipality and a school district, distinct from suburban municipalities and districts.

Power's mechanisms shape social action at North End, what is more, by constraining and enabling the forms of action that are possible for *all* actors here. They affect the fields of action, not only of students, who seem relatively "powerless," but also of teachers, administrators, and other actors who, by the prevailing view, "have" and "use" power.

Furthermore, the privileged world of Fair View is not a site of unambiguous "empowerment." In this resource-rich suburban school, the fields of action of teachers, students, and other agents are not only enabled, but also constrained by boundaries that include social definitions of what it means to be "gifted" and the social standards Segal relies on to define academic ability and to distinguish good classroom behavior from bad. Children in Segal's classroom do not, in fact, decide everything. What is more, what they do not decide – the particular norms and the particular standards that are placed beyond students' reach at Fair View – delimit and circumscribe social possibility in ways that warrant the attention of those who would critically analyze power relations.

In the pages that follow, I argue that students of power should *de-face* this concept. We should define power, not as an instrument some agents use to alter the independent action of others, but rather as a network of boundaries that delimit, for all, the field of what is socially possible. This alternative conceptualization rejects the unsustainable definition of freedom, implicit in accounts of power's various "faces," as a state in which action is independently chosen and/or authentic. It directs attention toward a series of relevant empirical questions that students of power-with-a-face tend to overlook. And it suggests conceptual and normative links between theories of power and theories of democracy. Power relations that warrant criticism, my view suggests, are those defined by practices and institutions that severely restrict participants' social capacities to participate in their making and re-making.

Social action, social boundaries

The argument is, of course, not divorced from other social theorizing about and empirical work on power relations. As a preface to elaborating my critique of definitions of power-with-a-face, and my positive claims about power, I want to comment briefly on similarities between my view and what I take to be three kindred approaches to conceptualizing the relation between social boundaries and social action.[4]

The first is captured in work by social scientists who, beginning in the late 1970s, contributed to literatures often grouped together under the banner of the "new institutionalism." New institutionalists told stories about the "why" of social action, which they opposed to purely behavioral accounts that bracket questions of how strategies, goals, preferences, and identities are socially shaped. Rather than taking desires, aims, ends, and interests as starting points, that is to say, asking only how these affect policy decisions and other political outcomes, new institutionalists emphasized that, and explored the ways in which, institutions shape what actors can do in particular social contexts, what they want to do, and the ways in which it is strategically rational for them to pursue particular aims, ends, and interests.[5]

Theorists of power's so-called "third face" studied the ways in which power's mechanisms shape desires and preferences.[6] Structural power theorists viewed power relations as shaped by institutional roles and relations.[7] But these and other students of power-with-a-face were united by

---

[4] Throughout this book, I use "action" broadly, to mean not only how individual and collective actors conduct themselves, but also what they believe and perceive, what they want, and with whom they identify.

[5] This brief description does not do justice to a complex literature composed of what some have characterized as divergent historical, sociological, and rational choice variants. See Hall and Taylor (1996) and Smith (1992).

[6] Gaventa (1980) and Lukes (1974 and 1976).

[7] Ball (1975a, 1975b, 1978, and 1992), Barnes (1988), Benton (1981), Isaac (1987a and 1987b), and Wartenberg (1990 and 1992).

the assumption that elaborating normatively compelling arguments about power requires dichotomizing, both between agents who have power and actors who are powerless, and between actions agents choose or authentically desire, and those that are socially constrained: impeded or otherwise altered by the actions of others.

To de-face power is to emphasize, with the new institutionalists, that social boundaries to action circumscribe *all social action*. Mechanisms of power – boundaries that, by my view, include but are not limited to institutional rules, norms, and procedures – define and delimit fields of action. They do so, not only for those who seem powerless, like students, but also for teachers, principals, and other apparently "powerful" agents. Power's mechanisms influence what these actors want to do in the school and the classroom, what they believe they need to do, and should do. And they delimit options for realizing pedagogic aims and ends.

A second approach to conceptualizing the relation between social boundaries and social action that has important affinities with my own is that outlined by Michel Foucault in his historical writings and programmatic statements on power, and expanded on by some poststructuralist theorists and philosophers.[8] Although Foucault and those who drew on his work tended to emphasize, as key political mechanisms, less institutional rules and procedures than discursive norms and social identities, they shared with new institutionalists, and with my own view, the rejection of the premise that power is directed by agents who "have" or "use" it. In a frequently cited passage, Foucault asserted that power "comes from below . . . there is no binary and all-encompassing opposition between rulers and ruled at the root of power relations."[9]

But Foucault and Foucaultians pushed even further than the new institutionalists – and usefully so – this claim that (at least some forms of) power "[circulate] without voice or signature."[10] The difference was the product of Foucault's Nietzschean ontology. Whereas many new institutionalists began with Giddens's theory of "structuration,"[11] assuming that agents act upon, and are simultaneously constrained by social limits to what they might do, be, and desire, those who adopted a Foucaultian view emphasized, as key political mechanisms, boundaries that define the agent itself, this social being that does, that is, that wants. Power does not simply act *upon* a (pre-political) agent, that is to say, constituting its preferences and delimiting how it might rationally act to realize them. It also produces this agent. It forges a coherent, responsible, rational, modern

---

[8] Foucault (1970, 1979, 1980a, 1980b, and 1982), Brown (1995), Butler (1997), Connolly (1991 and 1995), Honig (1993), and Wolin (1996).   [9] Foucault (1980a: 94).
[10] Butler (1997: 6).   [11] Giddens (1976, 1979, 1981, and 1984).

subject out of a human "material" that does not fit this or any identity without "remainder."

Although these claims are not demonstrably true, any more so than are Giddens's ontological presuppositions, or for that matter those that sustain behavioralism, they are arguably Foucault's most important claims about power. The significance of the archaeological[12] and genealogical[13] arguments that power is "productive," that human agents are not only its targets but also its "effects,"[14] lies in the fact that, in refusing (with Nietzsche) to assume that some essence is at the root of human subjectivity, they raise the possibility that *every* ordering of social relations, and *every* ordering of social selves (every inter- and intrasubjective power relation) bears some cost in the form of a violence it does to "what might be" in the self and in the social world.[15]

Foucault provides a good starting point for critical analyses of power relations. It is a point, however, from which I start an analysis that neither Foucault nor his more recent appropriators likely would endorse. This is the case because I am largely persuaded by arguments by Jürgen Habermas and others[16] that archaeology and genealogy *alone* are conservative forms of political criticism, that resistance to and transgression of extant social boundaries *alone* define an unnecessarily constrictive vision of political change. My argument shares with the Foucaultian view the "hypothesis" that "power is co-extensive with the social body; there are no spaces of primal liberty between the meshes of its network."[17] Yet it is decidedly un-Foucaultian in its effort to elaborate critical arguments about particular relations of power and to draw distinctions grounded in democratic norms and values.

These departures from the Foucaultian tradition point to a third understanding of the relation between social boundaries and social action that bears affinities with the argument for de-facing power: discourse theoretic models of politics as the collective definition of social possibility. Work by Habermas and those who drew on his theory of communicative action[18] has the advantage over Foucaultian archaeological and genealogical analyses of emphasizing that legal and other boundaries to social

---

[12] That is, the claim that the modern subject was an epistemological impossibility prior to modernity, that only with Kant and the dawn of the "Age of Man" did it become possible to conceive "a being whose nature . . . is to know nature, and itself, in consequence, as a natural being" (Foucault 1970: 310).

[13] That is, the historical argument is that there emerged around the time of the French revolution a regime of "bio-power" that grew up around the "modalities" of disciplinary control of the individual body and control of the life of the population (Foucault 1979 and 1980a).   [14] Foucault (1980b: 98).   [15] Connolly (1993).

[16] Habermas (1986 and 1987b: chs. 9 and 10). Other important expositions of this line of criticism are Fraser (1981) and Walzer (1983).   [17] Foucault (1980b: 142).

[18] Habermas (1984, 1987a, and 1998).

action constrain *and* enable. Foucault's reversal of Clausewitz's slogan (his assertion that politics is "war by other means"[19]) is, then, an over-statement. Norms can be the product of, not only strategic action, but also what Habermas called action "oriented toward mutual understanding."

It is not enough to demonstrate that particular mechanisms and relations of power "might be otherwise." In addition, social critics need to elaborate criteria for distinguishing better from worse forms of power relation, or, more specifically, relations that promote participants' political freedom – that is, their capacity to act in ways that affect norms and other political mechanisms defining the field of the possible – from those that approximate states of domination. To this end, Habermas relied almost exclusively on the discourse principle (to which he referred as "D"): "Just those action norms are valid to which all possibly affected persons could agree as participants in rational discourses," where rational discourses include "*any* attempt to reach an understanding over problematic validity claims insofar as this takes place under conditions of communication that enable the free processing of topics and contributions, information and reasons in the public space constituted by illocutionary obligations."[20] Privileging law, however, when analyzing boundaries that define and delimit social action, functioned as a crutch that enabled Habermas and others to wish away the constraining effects of the deliberative and discursive norms "D" presupposes.[21] Power's mechanisms include social standards, such as standards of discursive competence and rationality. They include socially valued ends and social identities. Habermas and deliberative democrats, then, tended to skirt hard questions about how best to organize power relations in polities, economies, communities, families, schools, in selves, if these relations involve irreconcilable conflict, if every possible order involves some element of coercion.

None the less, I want to emphasize – and this I see as a central point of agreement between my view and Habermas's – that power relations might, to a greater or lesser extent, enable those they position to act in ways that affect their constitutive boundaries. Students of power should consider the extent to which, and investigate the ways in which, particular relations of power enable and promote this social capacity for action *upon* boundaries to action.

[19] Foucault (1980b: 90).   [20] Habermas (1998: 106–7), emphasis as in original.
[21] On the differential constraining effects of communicative norms and standards of rationality, see Fraser (1992) and Young (1996).

Outline of the argument

De-facing power is a matter of conceptualizing political mechanisms as boundaries, at least in part the product of human action, that facilitate and limit action for all actors, in all social contexts. Power's mechanisms include laws, norms, standards, and personal and social group identities. They demarcate fields of action. They render possible and impossible, probable and improbable, particular forms of conduct, speech, belief, reason, and desire. Freedom, by this view, is not "negative freedom," a state or a "space" in which action is chosen, independent of the action of others.[22] Instead, it is political freedom: a social capacity to act, alone and with others, upon the boundaries that define one's field of action. Power relations enable and constrain participants' freedom, to varying degrees and in varying ways. Therefore, developing critical accounts of power relations, accounts that might inform strategies for changing them in freedom-promoting ways, requires attending to the ways in which power's mechanisms enable and disable this capacity for "action on" power.

I begin making the case for de-facing power by critically engaging the power debate in political science. I argue that participants in this debate arbitrarily excluded from their analyses some realm of social action they defined as "free," the effects of power on the action of agents they defined as "powerful," and the ways power is exercised in the absence of interaction and other clear connections between the "powerful" and "powerless." I argue that students of power relations should ask, not "How is power distributed?" and "Do the powerful interfere with the free action of the powerless?" but "How – that is, through which mechanisms and through which political processes – do people define and order collective value and meaning?"

I then take up the example of power relations in the classroom and the school, to make the case that difficulties with definitions of power-with-a-face extend beyond the conceptual problems that plague debates among political theorists. I consider critical pedagogy, a literature that applied definitions of power-with-a-face to the specific case of power relations in schools. My central claim in chapter 3 is that viewing power as an instrument powerful teachers have and use to interfere with the free action of powerless students introduces into empirical analyses assumptions that deflect attention from questions crucial to developing critical accounts of power relations in the classroom.

What alternative account might a de-faced view provide? In chapter 4, I draw on participant-observation and other data from the North

---

[22] Berlin (1969).

End Community School to argue that power shapes freedom there in significant part via rules, norms, social group identities, and other boundaries defining pedagogic practices and municipal and educational institutions, boundaries that no agent has, uses, or directs. Institutional and other limits to action work together to define for adults at this core urban school a set of immediate problems to which some refer as "the environment." Power shapes fields of possibility by requiring these actors (who by the prevailing view "have power") to respond to problems that threaten their students' basic well-being, and to do so before they address other, perhaps equally valued, pedagogic ends. Power's mechanisms define, as well, a limited set of possibilities and strategic options for responding to these problems. And they do so in ways that render locally *enabling* what some critics label "authoritarian" approaches to teaching and disciplining children.

In chapter 5, I turn my attention to Fair View Elementary. My account of power relations there highlights striking differences, not only in resources but also in pedagogy, between North End and Fair View. These include the more participatory and internalized disciplinary style at Fair View, the emphasis there on independent work and active participation in what some teachers call "the learning process," and the stress on student self-motivation and self-regulation. These differences, my account suggests, contribute to inequalities of access to skills and dispositions that are rewarded with recognition, status, and highly compensated and relatively autonomous jobs. That greater rewards are attached to the actions and attitudes cultivated at Fair View does not, however, mean that actors there choose freely, or have a wider range of actions and attitudes from which to choose, than do actors at North End. The central claims advanced in chapter 5 are three. First, depoliticized standards of conduct and character, ends of learning, and social identities, which help define power relations at Fair View, are as firm limits to action as are the hierarchically imposed and enforced rules at North End. Second, transgressions of these limits are punished at least as severely, if not more so, at Fair View. And third, the depoliticization of key norms, identities, and other boundaries defining pedagogic practices at Fair View reproduces and reinforces inequalities, both within and beyond the bounds of the community.

The analysis of power relations at these two sites points, then, to a distinction between being privileged and being socially enabled to act in ways that contest and change the power relations in which one participates. Fair View actors, although privileged, are not so enabled. This claim does not, however, translate into the assertion that all power relations are equivalent. In the concluding chapter, I ask, "If we de-face power – if we expand the definition of power to include mechanisms no actor possesses or manipulates, boundaries that affect the action of even actors who seem 'powerful' – then how might we criticize particular power relations?" I argue that students of power de-faced should criticize relationships that prevent or discourage participants from acting in ways that affect their constitutive boundaries to action. Such criticism requires asking (with Habermas) whether power relations defined by social prac-tices and institutions enable those whose action they affect to participate in determining the norms that comprise them. It requires asking (with Foucault) whether some collective norms are depoliticized in ways that legitimize the discipline and punishment of those who transgress them.

By the view that predominates in political theory, and in political science generally, power is directed by the teacher who raises her voice at the North End Community School, inducing her students to be quiet, to stand in line. It is directed, as well, by the Fair View Elementary teacher who empowers her students, letting them "make all of the decisions in the classroom." Power, most theorists and most empirical researchers who studied the concept agreed, is a tool people either have or lack, an instru-ment that some agents use to interfere with the free action of others. In the pages that follow, however, I make the case that those who would crit-ically analyze the ways in which human agents enable and constrain polit-ical freedom, understood as the social capacity to help shape the terms of one's life with others, must reject this assumption that power wears the "face" of agents who use and direct it.

2   De-facing power

When Robert Dahl wrote, "*A* has power over *B* to the extent that he can get *B* to do something that *B* would not otherwise do,"[1] he posed a problem that long outlasted the debate in which he was engaged. His argument was, in large part, a critique of elite theories of community power,[2] which he and his fellow pluralists effectively discredited as ideologically motivated and methodologically lax.[3] But Dahl's larger ambition – to explicate, systematically, "the central intuitively understood meaning" of the concept of power[4] – survived the dispute. In the decades following, most political theorists who studied power adopted Dahl's formulation of the problem of how power shapes freedom. The result is a considerable literature consisting largely in debates about how best to answer the question, "What do we mean when we say that *A* has power over *B*?" Contemporary theorists challenged nearly every element of Dahl's answer to this question, including his explication of the scope of responses by *B* that *A* can affect, and the means by which *A* might exercise power over *B*, as well as his behavioralist and logical empiricist epistemological assumptions and his pluralist ideological conclusions. They devoted almost no critical attention, however, to his definition of the problem itself.

In this chapter I challenge the view that Dahl's question is the best question to ask when studying power. Against the prevailing conceptualization of power as a social phenomenon that necessarily wears a "face" – against, that is, the presumption that power is an instrument powerful agents use to alter the free action of the powerless – I argue for *de-facing* power by reconceptualizing it as a network of social boundaries that constrain and enable action for all actors.

I begin with an overview of debates among contemporary political

---

[1] Dahl (1957: 202–3).
[2] Dahl's critique was directed at Hunter (1953) and Mills (1956). See Dahl (1958). For overviews of the community power debate, see Clark (1972) and Ricci (1980). Leif (1972) and Hawley and Svara (1972) provide extensive bibliographies.
[3] Polsby (1960 and 1968) and Wolfinger (1971).   [4] Dahl (1957: 202).

theorists who studied power. These debates, I suggest, grew out of early efforts by Dahl and others[5] to formulate, in terms amenable to scientific study, the common-sense understanding of power as an instrument powerful agents use to alter the free action of the powerless.[6] Although contributors to the power literature gradually tested and expanded Dahl's demarcation of the boundaries defining forms of social constraint on freedom that count as "political," definitions of power-with-a-face provided the consensus within which their, at times heated, debates took place. I challenge this predominant conceptualization, arguing that it introduces into the study of power relations assumptions that deflect analysis from a series of questions relevant to developing critical accounts of how power shapes freedom. I propose reconceptualizing power's mechanisms, not as instruments powerful agents use to prevent the powerless from acting independently or authentically, but as social boundaries (such as laws, rules, norms, institutional arrangements, and social identities and exclusions) that constrain and enable action for all actors.

The many "faces" of social power

Setting the terms of debate: Dahl's "intuitive notion" of power

In a series of writings published over the course of a decade beginning in the late 1950s, Robert Dahl attempted to explicate, in terms amenable to scientific investigation, the common-sense understanding of the concept of power.[7] His starting point was what he referred to as "one's intuitive [notion]" of power,[8] a conceptualization that he claimed had guided "practically every political theorist for several thousand years"[9] and was an important part of the subjective understandings of all social beings. Power, by this view, is an instrument actors possess, to varying degrees, and wield over other actors. Hence Dahl began his classic 1957 article with this assertion: "That some people have more power than others is one of the most palpable facts of human existence."[10] The purpose of studying "the Thing," he claimed, is to determine how it is distributed

---

[5] For example, Lasswell and Kaplan (1950), March (1955), and Simon (1953).

[6] This conceptualization of power is not unique to contemporary political theory. Its origin in contemporary social theory is Weber's (1947: 152) definition of power (*Macht*) as "the probability that one actor within a social relationship will be in a position to carry out his own will despite resistance, regardless of the basis on which this probability rests . . ." Its roots in modern political thought extend at least as far back as Hobbes's claim: "For whensoever any agent has all those accidents which are necessarily requisite for the production of some effect in the patient, then we say that the agent has the *power* to produce that effect, if it be applied to a patient . . ." (Hobbes 1966: 127; emphasis as in original).

[7] These include Dahl (1957, 1958, 1963, 1965, and 1968).

[8] Dahl (1957: 202).   [9] Dahl (1968: 407).   [10] Dahl (1957: 201).

among actors within societies.[11] And, because "power comparability" is an empirical problem that can be investigated scientifically, the job confronting the modern political theorist is that of defining it systematically, enabling researchers to operationalize it in ways that conform to prevailing norms of social scientific analysis.

Three aspects of this effort to formulate a scientific theory of power deserve special attention because of the central role they played in debates among critics and defenders of early pluralist theories: the epistemological premises of behavioralism and logical empiricism, and the ideological conclusions associated with pluralism in the United States in the 1960s.

Behavioralism was, during the period when Dahl first wrote on power, the reigning orthodoxy in political science and in the social sciences generally. Dahl's aim in his early work was to define power in terms that could be measured exclusively with reference to the behavior of the powerful and its effect on the behavior of the powerless. In later writings he moved away from the premise that observed behaviors provide the only valid data for scientific claims. Yet, as late as 1965, he asserted: "When one says that the President has more power to influence foreign policy than I have, then I think one means that the President can cause behavior in the State Department or Congress or in Germany or elsewhere that I cannot cause."[12]

To subscribe to behavioralism was, necessarily, to be a logical empiricist. Early references to Hume underscored Dahl's conviction that the scientific analysis of power involved explanation with exclusive reference to data knowable through direct experience. In response to the methodological looseness of researchers who claimed that a "power elite" controlled American politics, he asserted that any scientific statement about power must be amenable to confirmation or disconfirmation by the empirical data that experience reveals.[13] He further identified power as a causal relation, defined in terms of the constant conjunction of cause and effect,[14] and argued that its scientific explanation involved "the subsuming of a particular event or class of events under a more general law."[15] "For the assertion 'C has power over R,'" he wrote, "one can substitute the assertion, 'C's behavior causes R's behavior.' If one can define the causal relation, one can define influence, power, or authority, and vice versa.[16] Power relations, by this view, are empirically verifiable causal relationships amenable to explanation in the form of a covering law.

[11] Ibid.: (205).   [12] Dahl (1965: 93).   [13] Dahl (1958).
[14] Dahl (1965: 87 and 94).   [15] Ibid.: (75).
[16] Dahl (1968: 410). However, he did qualify this claim with reference to the "analogy" between power relations and causal relations.

It is unlikely that this theory's epistemological underpinnings would have received as much critical attention as they did had they not sustained a series of ideological claims about the actual distribution and function of power in liberal democracies. The empiricist assumption that data for scientific explanation should be limited to those capable of being observed and measured, combined with the further behavioralist stipulation that power be defined in terms of concrete behaviors, led those who embraced them to reject as evidence of power's exercise unobservable and non-behavioral phenomena. Thus, in a frequently cited passage, Dahl asserted that to "[*establish*] *the dominance of a specific group in a community or a nation*" requires "*basing . . . analysis on the careful examination of a series of concrete decisions.*"[17] His theoretical work on power, along with his empirical study of New Haven politics, lent credence to the pluralist defense of postwar liberal democracies as relatively open, democratically accountable political systems. In the latter study, in particular, he depicted access to influence over government decision-making as unbiased, and argued that city politics was characterized not by elite dominance, but by competition and power sharing.[18] This claim was ideological to the extent that it served as a Cold War era defense of liberal democracies as both responsive to voters and neutral among political interest groups.[19]

Contributors to the power debate that grew out of these early formulations challenged both Dahl's epistemological assumptions and his ideological conclusions. In the following sections I focus on three points of contention: the definition of the scope of power; claims about the role of conscious knowledge, intentional action, and volition in power's exercise; and the logical empiricist underpinnings of early explications of the means of power. I argue that, although later contributors to the debate rejected Dahl's definition of power strictly in terms of its first, or decision-making face, they embraced his more basic premise that power necessarily wears *some* face, that it is an instrument powerful agents use or direct in order to alter the free action of the powerless.

Central to this debate about the nature and function of power was an implicit definition of freedom as a state in which action is independent of the influence of others. A commitment to negative liberty lent normative

---

[17] Dahl (1958: 466; emphasis as in original). See also Curtis and Petras (1970), a meta-analysis of community power studies, in which the authors argue that the methodological assumptions of decision-making analysis generate pluralist conclusions.

[18] Dahl (1961).

[19] On the ideological dimensions of this and later work by Dahl and other "empirical theorists of democracy," see Skinner (1973).

force to debates about power understood as an instrument powerful "A"s use to constrain, distort, or otherwise alter the free action of powerless "B"s. Definitions of power-with-a-face ultimately hinged on a distinction between free action and action shaped by the action of others. At the heart of the power debate lay disputes over where and how to draw this distinction.

Expanding the boundaries of the political: the scope of influence and the three "faces" of power

Among the best-known challenges to Dahl's explication of the concept of power were those advanced by theorists of power's "three faces" in the 1960s and 1970s. Peter Bachrach and Morton Baratz began the debate with a critique of Dahl's definition of the scope of power as the set of behaviors *A* can elicit from *B*. Although Dahl and proponents of his decision-making approach defended the definition in terms of its relative scientific rigor,[20] Bachrach and Baratz argued that it had a critical weakness: to the extent that researchers limited inquiry to the study of "concrete decisions" about "key political issues," they assumed that failure to participate in politics results from apathy, indifference, or complacency, and overlooked the possibility that non-participation itself is an effect of power.[21] Bachrach and Baratz argued that power's scope is wider than suggested by its "public face": the dominant can influence the subordinate not only by prevailing in the event of manifest conflict, but also, and more significantly, by preventing conflict from arising at all. The powerful, through failure to hear or to respond to the expressed demands of the powerless, or alternatively through less direct mechanisms, such as the law of anticipated reactions,[22] or the mobilization of bias,[23] can "[limit] the scope of decision-making to 'safe' issues," that is, to those that pose no challenge to the political *status quo*.[24] Powerful actors use their communities' dominant myths, values, and institutions to their political advantage,

---

[20] The claim was that only the behavioralist definition of power's scope, and only the decision-making methodology, enabled the researcher to avoid speculation about unobservable phenomena. See Polsby (1960 and 1968).

[21] Bachrach and Baratz (1962 and 1963).

[22] The phrase refers to the phenomenon of *B* conforming to what she believes to be *A*'s wishes without *A* explicitly expressing her desires (Friedrich 1963: ch. 11).

[23] Bachrach and Baratz borrowed this phrase from E.E. Schattschneider, according to whom, "All forms of political organization have a bias in favor of the exploitation of some kinds of conflict and the suppression of others because *organization is the mobilization of bias*. Some issues are organized into politics while others are organized out" (Schattschneider 1960: 71; emphasis as in original).

[24] Bachrach and Baratz (1963: 632).

and, in exercising power, they shape and reinforce these "rules of the game."[25]

Bachrach and Baratz's epistemological critique of decision-making analysis not only had methodological implications for the study of community power, but also informed a substantive challenge to pluralism's ideological claims. By limiting the study of power to the analysis of conflict, they argued, Dahl and his followers overlooked power's hidden "second face." Their behavioralist definition of power's scope ensured that, where nondecision-making influence was at work, pluralists would see political consensus. Critics of Bachrach and Baratz's "neo-elitist" argument counter-charged that it was based on unsubstantiated assumptions,[26] that it was "unresearchable,"[27] and methodologically irrelevant.[28] Nevertheless, they conceded that Bachrach and Baratz had drawn attention to a significant phenomenon that early pluralists had overlooked. They framed their objections to power's second face less in terms of its political claims than its appeal to unobservable "nonissues" and "nonevents."

A more substantive challenge came from Steven Lukes, who, while not denying that power had a hidden, second face, argued that its scope was even wider than Bachrach and Baratz acknowledged. According to Lukes's "three-dimensional" account, power not only influences whether social actors behave as they want and determines whether they participate in politics to express their preferences, but also shapes the ways in which they perceive their wants, desires, and interests. In *Power: A Radical View* Lukes asked rhetorically: "is it not the supreme and most insidious exer-

---

[25] Bachrach and Baratz waffled on whether the mobilization of bias is, in Dahl's terms, a power "resource," or whether the exercise of power serves to maintain and reinforce the mobilization of bias. In their response to Debnam (1975), they argued that the mobilization of bias was not a form of nondecision-making, that rather nondecision-making was the primary means by which the powerful sustain the mobilization of bias. Bachrach and Baratz (1975: 902).

[26] The term "neo-elitist" is from Merelman (1968). He attacked Bachrach and Baratz's "false consensus" argument as "deductive, non-falsifiable, and ridden with undemonstrable assumptions." Raymond Wolfinger (1971) pointed in particular to their unsubstantiated assumptions about mass attitudes and values, which, he argued, were contradicted by empirical research.

[27] Wolfinger claimed that nondecisions and nonevents were impossible to operationalize. Because of what he perceived to be insurmountable difficulties in identifying and isolating nondecisions, and determining whether non-participation was caused by power or by other non-political variables, he concluded: "neo-elitist thought is not readily reconciled with empirical research" (Wolfinger 1971: 1076). However, see Bachrach and Baratz (1970) and Crenson (1971) for empirical studies of nondecision-making power.

[28] Geoffrey Debnam argued that the second face of power could be studied using the conceptual tools and methods of decision-making analysis. Not only did nondecision-making analysis present insurmountable methodological problems, it also added nothing to the study of community power (Debnam 1975).

cise of power to prevent people, to whatever degree, from having grievances by shaping their perceptions, cognitions and preferences in such a way that they accept their role in the existing order of things . . . ?"[29] Claiming for his argument the status of "a *thoroughgoing critique* of the *behavioral focus* of the first two views,"[30] he redefined the power relation, in terms of, not decision-making and nondecision-making, but actors' objective interests. "*A* exercises power over *B* when *A* affects *B* in a manner contrary to *B*'s interests,"[31] Lukes asserted, introducing to a debate, which until that point had accepted preferences as politically unproblematic, contemporary Marxian conceptions of ideological domination and hegemony.

If the second face of power struck behavioralists as difficult to operationalize, this "third face" seemed even harder to study and to test empirically. Critics suggested that Lukes had led the debate into the terrain of metaphysics. The third face of power, they argued, was of little or no use to students of real power relations.[32] John Gaventa effectively refuted this challenge with his study of power relations in a Central Appalachian mining community. Using historical, comparative, and participant-observation analysis, he overcame methodological obstacles to the study of power's hidden faces, demonstrating the ways in which nondecision-making power functions and revealing the processes by which dominant actors manipulate myths, rumors, and symbols to exercise third-dimensional power.[33]

It would seem, then, that theorists of the second and third faces of power had won their battle against the pluralists. By the time Gaventa published *Power and Powerlessness*, few students of power relations would argue against a broad conceptualization of power's scope.[34] The power debate had shifted toward a relatively expansive definition of the politically relevant dimensions of *B*'s action, one that included not only *B*'s conduct, but also her perception of her needs and desires and her capacity to deliberate about and act to attain her ends. It had moved, as well, toward an expansive definition of politically relevant constraints on *B*'s freedom, one that included not only actions by *A* that alter *B*'s behavior, but also those that inhibit or distort *B*'s ability to identify her true interests, needs, and wants. Yet, despite Bachrach and Baratz's tentative

[29] Lukes (1974: 24).
[30] Ibid.; emphasis as in original. However, Lukes acknowledged in a footnote that his account was "behavioural" "in the widest sense," in that he viewed "action and inaction, conscious and unconscious, actual and potential" as "evidence . . . for an attribution of the exercise of power." Ibid.   [31] Ibid. (27).
[32] See, for example, Bradshaw (1976).   [33] Gaventa (1980).
[34] See, however, Polsby (1980), the second edition of his 1963 *Community Power and Political Theory*.

suggestions to the contrary,[35] Dahl's statement of the question that informed the study of power remained unchallenged. Most theoretical and empirical work on power was, in 1980, as it had been in 1957, governed by the goal Dahl termed "power comparability." Political scientists aimed to understand the distribution of power and to identify, now via the mechanisms of first-, second-, and third-dimensional power, how *A* prevails over *B*. Although they challenged Dahl's demarcation of the boundary between free action and action influenced by the action of others, theorists of power's second and third faces maintained this distinction as central to their understanding of how power shapes freedom.[36]

Preserving the role of responsible agency: intention, conscious knowledge, and volition in power's exercise

During the 1970s the terms of the power debate shifted, as a second group of critics challenged the role of intention, conscious knowledge, and volition in early definitions of the exercise of power. Dahl had defined the means of power as an action by *A* involving the use of, or the threat or the promise to use, *A*'s base of influence or power resources.[37] He further had distinguished between the possession of power, which he claimed did not necessarily involve deliberate action or conscious knowledge and the intention to affect another actor, and its exercise, which, he asserted, did.[38] The latter claim derived from his "intuitive" notion of the concept. To the extent that one viewed power as an instrument the powerful use against the powerless, common sense suggested that those who wield it must know that they have it, understand its effects, and choose to act on that understanding. In so defining power's exercise Dahl expressed a widely held view, one that accorded with, among others, Bertrand Russell's definition of power as "the production of intended

---

[35] In later statements of their position, Bachrach and Baratz qualified it by claiming that *A* can unconsciously exercise power, or exercise power to produce unintended effects, and that for *A* to exercise power over *B*, *A* and *B* need not be aware of each other (1970 and 1975). Their revised argument was that power is "relational" in the sense that its successful exercise "is dependent upon the relative importance of conflicting values *in the mind of the recipient* in the power relationship," and requires: (1) that a conflict of values exists between two or more agents; (2) that the subordinate agent complies; and (3) that the dominant agent is able to invoke sanctions against the subordinate (1970: 19 and 21; emphasis as in original).

[36] Not all theorists writing on power during this period endorsed the faced perspective. Important exceptions were some functionalists and some Marxists, who emphasized the systemic nature of power, and in particular its constraining effects on those who, by the predominant view, "have power." See Parsons (1969), and note number 84, below. See also Poulantzas (1968: 99–119), in particular his critique of the voluntarism and individualism of the theories of power advanced by Lasswell and Kaplan, Dahl, and others writing during these years.   [37] Dahl (1957: 203).   [38] Dahl (1968).

effects,"[39] and one that would remain central to later arguments that informed choice and intentional action are necessary conditions for the exercise of power.[40]

In the context of ideological disputes over the boundaries of the power relation, however, pluralist assumptions that, for *A*'s action to qualify as an exercise of power over *B*, *A* must choose to act to produce foreknown effects on *B*, drew attention to the politically conservative implications of this view[41] and fueled a series of challenges by those who would expand the definition of political constraint on human freedom. Jack Nagel, for example, concerned that to define the exercise of power as necessarily intentional was to preclude attention to the role played by anticipated reactions, defined power as a causal relation resulting from the preferences, rather than the intentions, of powerful agents.[42] Similarly, Bachrach and Baratz modified their earlier position to include the non-intentional and unconscious exercise of power, asserting: "Power is operative even when *A* *unconsciously* exercises it or when he is aware of exercising it and produces unintended effects."[43] Increasingly sophisticated treatments of the role of conscious choice, knowledge, and intentionality in power's exercise suggested that this was not an either/or question, that subtle distinctions should be admitted to the debate. D.M. White, elaborating one such account, claimed that "states of mind and heart" are complex, that the job of appraising them cannot be reduced to that of determining whether action is, or is not, intentional.[44]

Generally, after the early 1970s, theorists who studied power qualified the claim that, for an action to count as an exercise of power, the agent who performs it must understand and intend its effects. Even Dennis Wrong, who consciously staked out a position that departed from those of many of his contemporaries in maintaining a central role for intentionality in the definition of power's exercise, granted that, to qualify as political, the effects of an action need not be desired by *A*, but only the foreseeable results of an action *A* chooses to take.[45] At the other extreme, some held that, to exercise power, *A* need not intend or even understand

---

[39] Russell (1938: 35).

[40] Dennis Wrong, for example, argued that what distinguishes power from "social control in general" is that the former involves intended influence. It is important, according to Wrong, "to distinguish the diffuse controls exercised by the group over socialized individuals from direct, intentional efforts by a specific person or group to affect another's conduct. Power is identical with *intended* and effective influence. It is one of two subcategories of *influence*, the other empirically larger subcategory consisting of acts of *unintended* influence" (1980: 3; emphasis as in original).

[41] See Wolfinger's (1971) efforts to draw a line between "power" and "routine" and Debnam's (1975) argument that what is customary cannot be an effect of power.

[42] Nagel (1975).   [43] Bachrach and Baratz (1975: 903; emphasis as in original).

[44] White (1971).   [45] Wrong (1980: 5).

the effects of her actions, as long as she acts voluntarily and in a way that serves her interests.[46] Most fell between these extremes, reserving for "intentions, hopes or desires" some definitive role.[47] In this sense the controversy over intention, conscious knowledge, and volition differed markedly from the three faces of power debate. Whereas the latter seemed to be driven by an impulse to expand the boundaries of constraints on human freedom that count as "political," this later debate was marked by an inhibition, a reluctance to widen the definition of power's exercise to include unconscious, unintended, and involuntary influence.

This reluctance was puzzling in that participants in the debate tended to defend their positions obliquely, relying almost exclusively on references to intuitive understandings and illustrative examples. Typical was White's argument against a strictly intentional definition, which largely amounted to appeals to hypothetical examples and normative intuitions. To defend his claim that some set of cognitive and emotional states on the part of the powerful was relevant to the definition of power's exercise, he resorted to an appeal to a "fundamental" distinction between power and cause. "[A]nd part of 'fundamental' in this context," he wrote, "is that one cannot advance any ultimate justification for the distinction."[48]

Although most students of power relations stopped short of elaborating a defense of the claim that knowledge, intention, or volition is a necessary characteristic of power's exercise, there were exceptions. Steven Lukes and William Connolly argued that the exercise of power must be, to some meaningful degree, the product of choice, because a normatively compelling definition must preserve the relation between power and responsibility. According to Lukes:

> The reason why identifying . . . [the exercise of power] involves the assumption that the exerciser(s) could have acted differently – and, where they are unaware of the consequences of their action or inaction, that they could have ascertained these – is that an attribution of power is at the same time an attribution of (partial or total) responsibility for certain consequences. The point, in other words, of locating power is to fix responsibility for consequences held to flow from the action, or inaction, of certain specifiable agents.[49]

The argument, expounded in greater detail in Connolly's *Terms of Political Discourse*, was that debates about power are premised on a positive valua-

---

[46] An example is Stone (1980) who argued that "upper strata interests" influence public officials disproportionately relative to "lower strata interests" via "systemic power," which predisposes public officials to cooperate with the former more than the latter by shaping their perception that the economic, organizational, and cultural resources they need are controlled by members of the "upper strata." Agents with economic, organizational, and cultural resources do not exercise systemic power directly, then, and they need not exercise it intentionally. What makes them powerful is that they exercise power indirectly, through public officials, who respond to them in ways that serve their interests.

[47] White (1971: 758).   [48] Ibid.   [49] Lukes (1974: 55–6).

tion of individual freedom, a judgment that renders suspect all forms of constraint by one agent on the independent or authentic action of another, whether in the form of coercion, manipulation, or the distortion of true preferences, interests, desires, or wants. When A compels B or alters B's perception of her interests, A's action interferes with the choice B would have made and the action B would have taken were B free from power's grasp. Attributions of power, according to Connolly, are equivalent to moral accusations. To claim that A has power over B is to claim that, should A exercise that power, A would act as an agent morally responsible for its effect. It is to imply that A chooses to act in a way that limits B's ability to choose and to act, that A understands and intends the political effects of her action, or at least that they are its unintended, yet predictable, consequences.[50]

Debates about the role of intention, conscious knowledge, and volition in power's exercise revealed, then, that central to definitions of the various faces of power was an understanding of humans as essentially agents with true desires, interests, and wants, and/or the capacity to choose their ends and to act to attain them. Human agents are, in Connolly's words, "capable . . . of autonomous action, self-restraint, and coherence, and worthy, because of these capacities, to be treated as responsible agents."[51] This understanding of the nature of human being informed and sustained the definition of freedom implicit in the power debate. Most power theorists conceptualized freedom as negative, a matter of being left alone by other agents to act to realize chosen or authentic ends.

A positive valuation of freedom thus understood gave normative weight to studies of the distribution and exercise of power. It also introduced a tension into debates about the role of intentionality in power's exercise. Consider two distinct normative judgments implicit in the claim that A exercises power over B. First, the fact that A exercises power <u>over B</u> is suspect, because exercising power over B means interfering with her free action. Second, the fact that <u>A exercises</u> power over B is suspect, because A is responsible for the political effects her action causes. The first judgment made it difficult to defend the claim that social constraints on B's action are not effects of power, and therefore not the appropriate targets of political analysis and criticism, unless they are understood, intended, and/or willed by a second party. But the second made it difficult to designate as a powerful A an agent whose actions do not meet some set of minimum conditions for personal responsibility.

Hence debates over the role of intention, conscious knowledge, and volition were marked, on the one hand, by the impulse to expand the

---

[50] Connolly (1983, esp. pp. 86–133).
[51] Ibid. (213). Connolly departed from this position in later work.

definition of power to include all significant social constraint on *B*'s free action, and on the other, by a sense that only informed, intentional choices to exercise power "seem[ed] to be the kind . . . that [would] be of central interest . . . to society or to those who would understand its operation."[52] The tension between these impulses was not explicit in most contributions to the power debate. Nor was it resolved. Instead, it was largely obscured, as theorists and empirical researchers focused on relations in which actors who appear to meet the moral qualifications for being designated powerful "*A*"s (the coal-mine owners in Gaventa's study, for example) affect the action of those who seem obvious candidates for powerless "*B*"s (the Appalachian coal-miners) in ways that conform to prevailing intuitions about power, freedom, and responsibility.

Challenging logical empiricism: structural accounts of power-with-a-face

This tension between the desire for an expansive definition of political constraint on freedom and the "intuitive sense" that power's exercise must be the product of choice by a responsible agent led some theorists in the 1980s and early 1990s to elaborate what they referred to as structural accounts of social power.[53] These usefully challenged the logical empiricist underpinnings of earlier debates among theorists of power's various faces, while engaging the problem of the relation between human agency and social structure in power's exercise. Scientific realists such as Roy Bhaskar, Rom Harré, and E.H. Madden provided the epistemological critique of the logical empiricism of earlier accounts of power-with-a-face,[54] while Anthony Giddens's theory of "structuration" provided the ontological critique of what Giddens called the dualism of agency and structure.[55] In this section I consider three distinct, yet compatible, structural responses to the question, "What do we mean when we say that *A* has power over *B*?": those advanced by scientific realists such as Jeffrey Isaac and Ted Benton, Thomas Wartenberg's account of "situated" power, and Barry Barnes's theory of intersubjective social power. These and other structural theories extended analysis of the power relation beyond the dyadic relationship between the powerful *A* and the powerless *B*. They broadened the definition of power's exercise beyond the discrete event in which *A* affects *B*'s free action. Yet they maintained that social

---

[52] Rae (1988: 32–3).
[53] Ball (1975a, 1975b, 1978, and 1992), Barnes (1988), Benton (1981), Isaac (1987a and 1987b), Wartenberg (1990 and 1992).
[54] Bhaskar (1979), Harré (1970), and Harré and Madden (1975)
[55] Giddens (1976, 1979, 1981, 1984).

power wears a "face": that, within structured roles and relations sustained by agents peripheral to the dyad, powerful agents choose to use or to direct social power to constrain the free action of the powerless.

Scientific realists writing on power prefaced their positive arguments about the relation between power and freedom with a critique of the logical empiricism of those who preceded them in the debate.[56] Specifically, they challenged the empiricist ambition to develop an explanatory account of power that accords with a Humean view of causation, and the deductive-nomological project of constructing an account in the form of covering-law explanation. They proposed, instead, that the goal of the study of power be explanation in terms of causal mechanisms or "causal powers," which produce social outcomes in much the same way that the intrinsic properties of copper cause it to conduct electricity.[57] The social world, by this view, can not be explained with reference to covering laws. Because causal powers function in the context of external impediments, which render their effects unpredictable, students of power should aim to develop explanatory models of the real social world by "reasoning from empirical phenomena to their causal mechanisms."[58]

The substantive claim of scientific realists writing on power was that to attribute power to an agent is to make a statement about her "intrinsic nature," that is, about capacities and dispositions that, given certain extrinsic conditions or circumstances, cause social outcomes. According to Harré, "X has the power to do A = if X is subject to stimuli or conditions of an appropriate kind, then X will do A, *in virtue of its intrinsic nature*."[59] To make room for human agency, realists modified this claim when they applied it to the study of social life. Thus, Harré amended the above statement with the assertion: "In ascribing power to people 'can' must be substituted for 'will' in the apodasis of the hypothetical component. Whether he will or no is up to him."[60] Nevertheless, the aim of explanation in the natural and the social sciences, realists argued, is essentially the same. The study of social power is analogous to the study of causal powers in the natural world. Its purpose is to explain political outcomes in terms of the causal powers of agents.

Scientific realists reconciled an expansive definition of political constraint on free action with an account of moral responsibility in power's exercise by distinguishing between, on the one hand, the agent's "social powers," or those capacities and dispositions she has as a result of her

---

[56] Thus, according to Isaac (1987a, 1987b), while theorists of the power's second and third faces claimed to reject Dahl's behavioralism, none rejected its empiricist foundations. However, for the claim that Gaventa adopts a scientific realist approach, see Shapiro and Wendt (1992).   [57] Harré (1970), and Harré and Madden (1975).
[58] Isaac (1987a: 158).   [59] Harré (1970: 85; emphasis as in original).   [60] Ibid.

participation in relatively enduring social relations, and, on the other, her "human powers," or those capacities and dispositions she has as a result of her human agency and her personal characteristics.[61] The claim was that, if A has power over B, A's power depends not only on the powers she has as an agent capable of choice and as an individual with personal talents, abilities, and desires, but also on her social powers, defined as those differential capacities for action and dispositions to act that derive from her participation, with B, in a relatively enduring social relationship. A might choose to act in one way rather than another within her socially structured role, and to the extent that she does, she is responsible for the effects of her action. But regardless of the choices she makes and her knowledge and intention with respect to their effects, A, and ultimately the social structure that distributes differential powers to A and to B, is causally responsible for constraint on B's free action.

Isaac offered as an example of a relatively enduring social relation the relationship between a teacher and her students. All agents in the classroom, dominant and subordinate, negotiate their actions within their roles and relations, but "the structure of education" distributes to teachers and students differential sets of social powers. Educational structures endow teachers with the capacity to assign grades, for example, and students with the disposition to work to earn high marks. Although a particular teacher might choose to use her capacity to assign grades in an arbitrary or an authoritarian manner, while another might downplay the significance of grades or even dispense with grading altogether, it is the asymmetrical distribution of this capacity, along with other social powers, that renders teachers powerful and students powerless. Hence to study and understand "power over," one must attend to the social distribution of "power to."[62] All constraints on B's free action caused by A's greater social power are the result of the power A has over B. Whether A is morally responsible for B's constraint may be an important question, then, but it is a separate one.

In his account of "situated" power, Thomas Wartenberg elaborated a model compatible with Isaac's, but one that stressed that structures are only *relatively* enduring, that is, that they are constituted and subject to change by social agents who shape, without directly participating in, the dyadic power relationship. In Wartenberg's terminology, the power A has over B is the result of a "social field" within which each agent is located. This field is constituted by "peripheral social agents": individual or col-

---

[61] "Social power" and "human power" are from Benton (1981), for whom agents' "extrinsic" causal powers derive from their participation in social relations. Isaac used the term "intrinsic nature" to identify agents' "social identities as participants in enduring, socially structured relationships" (Isaac 1987a: 74–5).   [62] Isaac (1987a and 1987b).

lective actors who grant A the power she has over B by treating B differentially based on choices A makes and actions A takes. Like Isaac, Wartenberg illustrated with the example of the power a teacher has over her students. The teacher's power is "a feature of the structure of [the teacher/student] relationship,"[63] one constituted by the actions of peripheral agents such as parents, university admissions officers, and firms, agents who regulate access to goods students need or desire with reference to the grades teachers assign.[64]

In the absence of supporting social structures, and in particular relations with "peripheral agents" who are external to, but constitute, the dyadic power relationship, the powerful teacher's intentions, choices, and actions in assigning her students grades would have little or no effect on their actions. The intentions and desires of the dominant agent, then, are not the principal cause of her power over the subordinate agent. Even absent intention, conscious knowledge, and volition, powerful agents might have and exercise power over the powerless. For example, men have power over women in marriage, Wartenberg suggested, because of the ways in which various peripheral agents, such as banks and businesses, reward married women and punish women who are single. A husband might choose to use the power he has over his wife by virtue of his role. But even if he does not want to exercise power over her, he does, by virtue of the fact that peripheral agents' actions give his wife incentives to stay married to him.[65] When A exercises power over B, A is not "fully responsible," then, because the effects of her action are in part the result of the actions of agents external to the power relation.[66]

Like Isaac and Wartenberg, Barry Barnes viewed the power relation as structured by social roles and relations peripheral to it. His account departed from theirs, however, in defining *social* power as the added capacity for action created by a shared distribution of knowledge. Acting together, Barnes argued, individuals have more power than the sum total of their individual capacities. When one says that A has more power than B, or that A has power over B, he claimed, one means that A is more able than B to direct the additional capacity for action produced by social organization, institutionalization, and routine, or that A is able to use B's power by virtue of A's "discretion in using . . . routines and . . . organization."[67]

Barnes did not use the example of a power relation involving teacher and student. But if he had, he likely would have argued that the teacher's power derives from the discretion she has in using or directing the

[63] Wartenberg (1992: 82).   [64] Ibid. (83).   [65] Ibid. (96–7).
[66] Wartenberg (1990: 86).   [67] Barnes (1988: 64).

"routine practices and competences"[68] of the society to which she and her students belong. People are not always or even usually reflective. Students might follow instructions in class, or complete assigned tasks, largely as a matter of habit. But when they pause to reflect on their reasons for making the choices they make, they realize that, as long as most people conform to particular routines (as long as they recognize and reward high grades and the specific competencies that, in a given social context, earn them), it is in their interest to conform as well. The teacher's power over her students derives, then, from the distribution of knowledge, which makes possible her discretionary control of the powers of other agents.

In the following section I address difficulties with these structural accounts, and more generally with the understanding of power-with-a-face that informs them. First, I want to emphasize that, although these recent contributions advanced the power debate by siting the dyadic power relationship within socially structured roles and relations that endow A with her capacity to constrain or otherwise alter B's free action, they maintained that power relations are essentially relations involving "powerful" and "powerless" agents, that power's exercise is the "use" A makes of power's mechanisms in order to get B to do (to think, to perceive, to desire) "something that B would not otherwise do" (think, perceive, or desire). Their epistemological and ontological critiques notwithstanding, theorists elaborating structural accounts of the relation between power and freedom remained wedded to the terms of debate set by Dahl and embraced by earlier theorists of power's many faces.

Power de-faced

Debates spawned by Dahl's early writings on power were driven by the impulse to uncover the faces of social power that decision-making analysis obscured. Contributors expanded the scope of power to encompass nondecision-making influence and hegemonic control over the beliefs and preferences of the powerless. They re-defined the exercise of power to include forms of influence the powerful do not fully desire, intend, and consciously understand. And they explained the means of power in terms of the socially structured relation between A and B, rather than their discrete interactions. Participants in the power debate shared a common concern: to reveal and critique social constraint on (negative) freedom. They shared, as well, a conceptualization of power as an instrument powerful agents use to alter the free action of the powerless.

In the discussion that follows I challenge this predominant understand-

---

[68] Ibid. (59).

ing, arguing that it introduces into the study of power a series of assumptions that tend to deflect analysis from questions relevant to developing accounts of how power shapes freedom and criticizing social relations of domination. My challenge centers on prevailing definitions of what counts as *constraint* on freedom, which *differences* in constraint are politically relevant, and what is meant by *social* constraint. I argue that any account that defines the relation between power and freedom as essentially one through which the powerful constrain the independent or authentic action of the powerless draws attention away from the politically significant ways power shapes freedom for all social actors, within and beyond relations in which they participate as relatively powerful and powerless agents. Drawing on poststructuralist insights, which I argue are insufficiently attended to by most contributors to the power debate, I propose *de-facing* power by reconceptualizing it as the network of social boundaries that delimits, for all, fields of possible action.

Constraint: social boundaries to action

By the predominant view, power constrains freedom by interfering decisively with independent or authentic action. Theorists of power's various faces take as their starting point the agent who has access to and can use, or alternatively lacks, power, in the form of mechanisms people might control and direct, or experience as obstacles to choice. When A "exercises power over B," the resulting political effect is to alter B's free action by interfering with its independence (as when A coerces B) and/or its authenticity (as when A distorts B's perception of her true wants, preferences, desires, interests, or needs). Theorists of power-with-a-face proffer various accounts of in what, in Dahl's terminology, the base of A's power might consist: resources, for example, the "rules of the game," myths and symbols, or social capacities and dispositions. They agree, however, that when A acts on these mechanisms, they function as impediments to negative freedom, constraints that interfere with or otherwise alter the free action of the powerless.

This view privileges and insulates from political analysis and criticism some realm of social action, in Dahl's words "something that B would . . . otherwise do." It implies that one might, at least in principle, distinguish free action (ways of behaving, perceiving, and reasoning that are independently chosen or true to the agent's pre-political interests, needs, and desires) from action that is the product of influence by another agent or agents. To illustrate with an example from the three faces of power debate, even self-proclaimed "radical" theorists of power's third face, who defined as political mechanisms social legitimations and other meanings embodied in language and symbol, assumed a distinction between, on the one hand, *B*'s chosen or authentic action, and on the other, action distorted by the influence of some powerful agent or agents. Hence, in a response to a critical essay by Bradshaw, Lukes wrote:

> The basic idea here is that A may exercise power over B, within given structural conditions, by precluding the options that B *would* take up but for the power of A. Of course, other sources of power . . . may intervene, but, unless Bradshaw seriously maintains that *all* our preferences are heteronomous, and the products of some exercise of power, then he must allow that some of A's (actual or hypothetical) preferences and choices are authentically A's.[69]

Structural accounts of power-with-a-face complicated the relationship between social structure and human agency, while maintaining the distinction between free action and action distorted by power. Scientific realists claimed that social powers are political mechanisms that derive from roles and relations, and enable and constrain the action of powerful and powerless actors. Human powers, by contrast, derive from the nature of human beings as agents and from the nature of individuals as unique selves. These are the source of the choices the agent makes and of preferences and desires that are truly hers. Isaac, for one, stressed the importance of distinguishing between the effects on *B*'s action of *A*'s choices, and of the capacities and dispositions that comprise the mechanisms of the power *A* has. In his view, this distinction is crucial because it enables researchers to attend to differences in social limits to action, that is, to differential constraints on negative freedom that derive from relatively enduring roles and relations.[70]

But if one attempts to apply this definition, it becomes difficult to sustain its distinction between free action and action shaped by power. Certainly, the social role is not the only means through which humans socially acquire differential capacities and dispositions, and not only what Benton termed "social powers," but also what he called "human powers," are, in significant part, social. One need not assume that all human action is determined in order to acknowledge that what some scientific realists identified as personal capacities and dispositions (for example, those capacities touted by progressive educationists, such as self-motivation and self-discipline, or the dispositions to value academic success and to work hard to attain it) are acquired socially and in ways that differentially constrain and enable action. Consider again Isaac's example of the power relation involving teacher and student. In elaborating it, he stressed that mechanisms of social power are *unchosen*. Teachers and students have differential capacities and dispositions by virtue of their participation in

---

[69] Lukes (1976: 129; emphasis as in original).   [70] Isaac (1987a: 83–4).

the teacher–student relationship itself. Free action, by contrast, is the product of choice:

I am going to school this afternoon to give a lecture on Dahl, and in doing so, however unintentionally, I am exercising the power of a teacher . . . but tomorrow the students may boycott class and conduct their own teach-in. It is a necessary feature of the existing structure of education that teachers are dominant and students subordinate. But the exercise of these powers, the way this relationship is worked out in concrete practice, is contingent, determined by the way particular individuals and groups choose to deal with their circumstances.[71]

To the extent, however, that the choice of a particular student in Isaac's class to participate in the hypothetical boycott, or more generally her disposition to rebel in certain ways against certain forms of authority, derives from and depends on a range of social influences that themselves are unchosen (her parents' child-rearing practices, for instance, or norms prevailing among her peers at school), and to the extent that such norms and practices vary systematically among groups of students (so that, say, Isaac's middle-class university students are more likely to boycott class and conduct a teach-in than working-class students at the junior college down the road), it becomes difficult to maintain this neat division between "social powers" and "human powers," or actions independent of (differential) social constraint. Even if one were able to make a convincing case that a particular talent, ability, or trait was the authentic personal characteristic of an individual (perhaps that it was genetically based), to the extent that developing that capacity and cultivating the disposition to use it required social action, it would be relevant, according to Isaac's normative argument, whether and to what extent the disposition and the ability to use the developed capacity were asymmetrically distributed.

The point is not to challenge *where* Lukes, Isaac, and other theorists of power-with-a-face drew the boundary distinguishing B's free action from action shaped by social power. In pointing out that the particular capacities and dispositions some theorists identified as "chosen" may be, no less than those defined as "structured," socially shaped, and in ways that vary systematically, I do not mean simply to suggest that agents might be socialized in ways that particular theorists overlooked. Rather, my claim is that any definition of the line dividing free action from action that is, in part, the product of power's exercise itself serves the political function of privileging as natural, chosen, or true some realm of social action. That the capacities and dispositions to function as a responsible agent require social action in the form of enablement and constraint by others and by the self demonstrates the intractability of the problem of identifying a

---

[71] Isaac (1987b: 23–4).

realm of action distinct from, and hence vulnerable to constraint by, power.

Behavioralists defined "choice" in terms of freedom from constraint on conduct. The agent is free from power's grasp, they asserted, if her action is guided only by forces that originate within her self, such as preferences or passions.[72] Postbehavioralist accounts extended the definition of political constraint to include the manipulation of preference, passion, and belief, positing action as free only to the extent that it results from the conscious choice of a self acting independently in its true interest. Once one acknowledges, however, that identity itself is a product of power relations, that fields of action are necessarily bound, for example, through processes of acculturation and identity formation, it becomes necessary to reject a view of power that presupposes the possibility of distinguishing free action from action shaped by the action of others. The ways people act – how they conduct themselves, think, feel, perceive, reason, what people value, how they define themselves in relation to communities to which they experience themselves as belonging, and to those to which they experience themselves as not belonging – are in significant part the effect of social action. To define as "free" a given set of wants, social needs, capacities, beliefs, dispositions, or behaviors is to exclude from analysis a priori a host of ways in which human freedom is shaped.

Power's mechanisms are best conceived, not as instruments powerful agents use to prevent the powerless from acting independently or authentically, but as boundaries that, together, define fields of action for all social actors. Power defines fields of possibility. It facilitates and constrains social action. Its mechanisms consist in, for example, laws, rules, symbols, norms, customs, social identities, and standards, which constrain and enable inter- and intrasubjective action. Actors might act intentionally within or upon particular mechanisms of power. A teacher might invoke a rule of grammar to produce an intended effect on her student's speech and writing. But, as Foucault and others have argued, even conscious social action that effects intended results interacts with and is shaped by norms, conventions, standards, identities, and other institutionalized forms of action: codified actions that are, at times, historically remote, and the effects of which are often unintended. Power's mechanisms are constitutive of even highly strategic forms of action. They function as boundaries, and never simply instruments actors possess and use.

This reconceptualization of power requires modification of the definition of freedom implicit in accounts of power's various faces. For

---

[72] Dahl (1965: 93), for instance, asserted that habit does not involve power when it is "internal," and does when "somebody else can trip off the habitual response."

students of power-with-a-face, freedom is negative: a state in which action is independent of social constraint. For students of power de-faced, by contrast, it is the capacity to act *upon*, or in ways that affect, the boundaries that constrain and enable social action. In chapter 6 I argue that students of power relations should conceptualize freedom as *political freedom*: a social capacity that enables actors, not to escape or to transcend power relations, but to participate effectively in shaping and re-shaping relationships defined by the practices and institutions that govern their action. Here I want to underscore that, although people can act individually and collectively in ways that affect the boundaries defining for them the field of what is possible, these boundaries remain the condition for action in the social world.

Differences in constraint: patterned asymmetries in fields of social possibility

All social actors, then, are situated within relations of power. But to de-face power is not to imply that all social actors are *similarly* situated. Like many other power theorists, I want to make a case for focusing critical analysis on patterned asymmetries in the social capacity for action. At the same time, however, I want to reject the characteristic equation of such asymmetries with states of "powerfulness" and "powerlessness" by proposing a view of relevant differences in social constraint that shifts the normative focus from libertarian to democratic grounds.

For students of power's various faces, differences in the ways power shapes social possibility take the form of states of powerfulness and powerlessness. The power relation necessarily involves a powerful agent (A) and a powerless actor (B). Statements of this definition range from early versions implying absolutely powerful As and powerless Bs, to later accounts, which acknowledged the resistances of the relatively powerless and granted that social limits might constrain the relatively powerful. Thus more sophisticated statements allowed that B can resist even the most insidious forms of domination. B can rebel, ending or reversing the relationship[73] or, alternatively, B's resistance can function as part of the power relation itself.[74] As the literature on power's many faces developed, it became conventional to argue that the absence of choice on the part of the powerless actor is the limit of the power relation. When A's action determines B's action, "power" ends and "force" begins. Some theorists acknowledged, as well, limits to the freedom of the powerful, in

[73] See, for example, Gaventa (1980).   [74] Scott (1985 and 1990).

the form of constraint from above,[75] constraint from below,[76] and lateral constraint.[77] Yet most maintained that power relations involve some A, some agent who, by virtue of her access to power's mechanisms, is able to act freely to alter B's free action.

The difference between A and B, by this view, is not simply that A is able to act upon power's mechanisms to shape B's field of action. Most students of power-with-a-face granted that in many, if not all, cases B can resist. That is, B can act upon power's mechanisms in ways that shape the field of social possibility for A. A further difference marks the qualitative distinction between the fields of action open to powerful and powerless actors, a difference that turns, again, on the distinction between free action and action shaped by the influence of others. Actors who meet prevailing intuitions about what powerful agents are (for example, the coalmine owners in Gaventa's study[78]) act freely on the fields of action of the powerless (for example, Gaventa's Appalachian coal-miners).

Thus, a student of power-with-a-face might argue that what distinguishes the powerful owner from the powerless miners is not only that the former limits the field of action of the latter, but also that in so doing he leaves the miners with choices of which none might satisfy their desires, while satisfying his own true preferences, interests, or wants. The mine owner might want his business to be profitable. He might desire income, wealth, and material goods. The miners, by contrast, cannot plausibly be held to want to slave away at a dangerous and unfulfilling job so that another person can profit from their labor.

Some power theorists focused, not on the authenticity of agents' desires, but on their capacities to function as independently choosing agents. The difference between A and B, by this view, is that A has, and B lacks, a capacity for choice such that, in acting, she functions as an agent responsible for the effects she causes. One might argue, along these lines, that what makes the coal-mine owner an "A" and the miner a "B" is that the severely constraining effects of the owner's actions on the life of the miner are the foreseeable result of a series of choices he makes.

Hence, although theorists debating the role of intentionality in power's exercise disagreed about what conditions A must meet to function as a powerful agent, most agreed that for A to qualify as an "A," and for her relation with B to count as a power relation, she must, in some meaningful

---

[75] Dahl (1968: 408) acknowledged that A might be constrained by a more powerful agent who dominates her just as she dominates B.

[76] Some drew on Hegel's master–slave dialectic and Arendt's (1970) claim that power is based on the consent of the governed to demonstrate that the dominant A is, in significant respects, constrained by the subordinate B.

[77] Wartenberg (1992) claimed that "aligning social agents" play a critical constitutive role in power relations.   [78] Gaventa (1980).

sense, choose to exercise the power she has over B, understand, and/or intend the effects of her action. Structural accounts, which modified earlier definitions of the difference between the powerful and the powerless, also maintained this distinction between A and B as central to the power relation. Barnes, for instance, who claimed that A does not "possess" social power, none the less assumed a qualitative distinction between the fields of action open to powerful and powerless. What makes A powerful, by his view, is that she is able to *use* and to *direct* routinized action and the added capacity for action (social power) that routinization creates.[79] Even theorists who drew on Marx's insight that rules and norms (such as those defining capitalist economic institutions and practices) constrain not only those at the bottom of social hierarchies (like workers) but also those at the top (capitalists), tended to reproduce this dichotomy, characterizing power relations as relationships involving powerful agents, whose interests they serve, and the powerless, whom they disadvantage.[80]

This definition of relevant differences in social constraint, although familiar because it accords with deeply held modern intuitions about the nature of power and freedom, has the disadvantage of taking as given the subjectivity of actors designated "powerful." The premise is either that A's desires are in some deep sense *hers*, representative of who she really is, or alternatively that they are chosen, an expression of her nature as a human agent, combined with virtues and flaws of her character, which influence her to choose one way or the other. These premises are appealing, in that they promise to deliver a kind of moral closure. Lord Acton followed his famous statement, "Power tends to corrupt and absolute power corrupts absolutely," with the claim that "Great men are almost always bad men."[81] A definition of relevant differences in social constraint that centers on A's authentic or independent action satisfies the desire to point a finger of accusation at the "great man" who, by virtue of his evil desires or bad character, is responsible for significant restrictions on human freedom.

At the same time, however, it directs attention away from at least two sets of questions relevant to critical analyses of how power shapes freedom. First, it tends to deflect attention from questions about how the fields of action of actors who seem "powerful" are socially shaped. Gaventa, for instance, argues persuasively that the miners' perceptions of their needs, desires, and interests are influenced by social power, that their capacities to function as responsible agents are severely circumscribed. But he does not ask how the mine owner's desires are socially formed and maintained, how the owner is made into an agent who goes to

---

[79] Barnes (1988: 64–5).   [80] Hartsock (1985).   [81] Dalberg-Acton (1949: 364).

such lengths to discipline himself, dominate others, and destroy the natural environment, all in order to secure a profit.

Second, this definition deflects critical attention from social relations that do not involve individual or collective actors who meet prevailing intuitions about what "powerful" agents are. In the study of power's various faces this exclusion operated, for the most part, at the level of problem definition. Researchers tended to focus on cases, like Gaventa's, in which it seemed obvious who the "powerful" agents were, and who were "powerless." Debates about volition, conscious knowledge, and intentionality made apparent, however, that the limit of the power relation, by this view, is the "A," the agent who chooses, wills, desires, or benefits from the political effects she causes. Thus, according to White, an actor with no "attitude or state of mind . . . toward . . . given effects of [her] behavior" cannot be conceived as a powerful agent, even if she acts in ways that shape the fields of action of others. He offered this example: "We wouldn't say that a mother who had no intentions, hopes or desires for her child exercised power with respect to the political attitudes he obtained as a result of the way she brought him up."[82] Similarly, Raymond Wolfinger asserted that, unless the criteria of interest and effective cause coincide, no powerful A can be identified and therefore no power relation obtains.[83] Although theorists of power-with-a-face disagreed about which social and personal characteristics qualify actors to be designated "powerful," they tended to concur with respect to the limit case. If no agent wills, intends, desires, or benefits from social constraints that her action causes, this is not the proper subject matter of the study of power.

If debates about power were no more than debates about how best to define a political concept, it would matter little which terminological convention most theorists accepted. But they were not. They were normative debates, driven by a commitment to human freedom that informed critical empirical analyses of differential social limits to people's capacities to act in relatively autonomous ways. Such limits, I want to emphasize, are often institutionalized. They are often codified, for example in socially constructed racial and gender identities. They are not necessarily channeled through the actions of "powerful" agents who understand them or will them or benefit from them.

Students of power de-faced, then, reconceptualize the power relation as any relationship involving two or more actors positioned such that at least one can act on power's mechanisms in ways that shape the field of action

---

[82] White (1971: 758).

[83] One of his criticisms of Bachrach and Baratz's argument is that it could lead to identifying as powerful agents those who act in ways that are to their own disadvantage (Wolfinger 1971: 1074).

of the other. In White's hypothetical case, a power relation involving parent and child obtains to the extent that, for example, the mother is capable of reinforcing for her child or, alternatively, problematizing prevailing standards of merit and desert. Without demonstrating any particular cognitive or affective state on the part of the parent, and without showing that she promotes her true interests by influencing her child, a researcher might identify a power relation in which the parent influences her child's "political attitudes," say, by teaching him that people deserve the market wage for the work they perform.

By this view the appropriate focus of critical analyses of power relations remains patterned asymmetries in the social capacity to act. But students of power de-faced do not reduce these to qualitatively distinguishable states of "powerfulness" and "powerlessness." Instead of asking how power is distributed in order to criticize relations that constrain negative freedom, they ask, "How do power's mechanisms define the (im)possible, the (im)probable, the natural, the normal, what counts as a 'problem'?" They criticize relationships that do so in ways that undermine political freedom: that is, power relations that avoidably limit the ability of some or all participants to act in ways that affect their constitutive boundaries.[84]

Social constraint: action upon action[85]

The subject of the study of power's various faces is not *any* form of constraint on free action that results from the action of another agent or agents, but more specifically constraint that is the product of what "the powerful" do to "the powerless." The language of the debate – "*A* exercises power over *B*" – suggests that *B* is the target of *A*'s action. Some "connection," to borrow Dahl's term, establishes this relation by linking *A* to *B*. Generally, this connection takes the form of interaction or communication. But in any case, some form of contact, whether direct or indirect (for example, through a third party), multi-directional or unidirectional (for example, through television or other mass media), a

---

[84] This is an important point of departure between my view and functionalist views, such as Talcott Parsons's, which parallel each other in other respects. One significant point of agreement between Parsons's positive argument and mine is that both emphasize that even actors with a relatively enhanced capacity for action that affects laws, norms, and other social boundaries are, themselves, constrained by these limits (Parsons 1969). But Parsons stresses that both asymmetries in the social capacity for transformative action and the induration of a "stable institutionalized normative order" (1969: 261) are functional in the sense that they promote stability and enable effective collective action. By contrast, my normative argument (expounded in chapter 6) is that these are appropriate targets of political criticism.

[85] This heading is a reference to Foucault's (1982: 790) suggestion that the exercise of power be defined as "a mode of action upon the action of others."

discrete event or an exchange structured by social roles and relations, renders A's action an exercise of power over B.

Early power studies were explicit and uncompromising on this count. Hence Dahl's claim that, in politics as in mechanics, there is "no action at a distance."[86] Later versions qualified the definition of what counts as a "connection." They allowed that A need not perceive B as the target of her action, so long as the effects A has on B are the foreseeable result of a choice A freely makes. Or, alternatively, they avoided explicit discussion of which forms of "action on action" indicate the exercise of power. Almost without exception, however, they took as their subject cases in which the link between A and B is readily apparent. Even if the "powerful" and "powerless" seldom have face-to-face contact (if, say, the latter is a group absent from town hall because politically inactive, absent from the board room because not represented in the upper echelons of the corporate world, and absent from the public spaces inhabited by the dominant because systematically excluded from their communities and associations), some connection joins the two in the form of, perhaps, an edict targeted explicitly at "the powerless" or a policy or law with a known or predictable effect upon them. Some link renders B the apparent object of A's action.

Perhaps the example of the teacher who exercises power over her student was popular among theorists of power-with-a-face in part because the connection between these actors seems self-evident. Teachers interact and communicate with their students daily. They give them grades, such as grades indicating how precisely they use "proper" English grammar. Even structural accounts, then, which drew attention to the roles "peripheral social agents" play and highlighted the importance of other actors in creating and sustaining the routines the powerful agent directs, located power's exercise, in this case, in the teacher's choice to assign particular students particular grades, and not in, say, the practices of university admissions officers, which help imbue grades with their significance, or those of actors outside the classroom who help define and maintain linguistic conventions.

The teacher exercises power over her students. Absent some further connection, other agents who reward academic success and punish academic failure, or who help reinforce the predominance of "standard English," do not. By the prevailing view, at some point the connection between powerful and powerless becomes too tenuous for A's action to count as an exercise of power over B. The alternative, students of power-with-a-face might suggest, is a sacrifice of explanatory simplicity. If every

---

[86] Dahl (1957: 204).

"action upon action" is potentially politically significant, then to offer an account of how power shapes freedom in a given domain becomes a herculean, if not impossible, task.

I want to suggest, however, that if "no action at a distance" ever was an approximate marker of the limits of power's exercise, it has long since become anachronistic. In contemporary political life, severely attenuated "connections" serve as channels for the significant social constraint of action. Assume that the student to whom Isaac and Wartenberg refer is an African-American male who attends a public secondary school in a core urban neighborhood in an older city in the northeastern United States. Not only and not principally the instruction and the grades his teachers give him, and not only and not principally the sum total of his interactions and communications with other actors, shape this student's present and future possibilities. His field of action is delimited, as well, by a range of actions by actors with whom he has no interaction or communication, by actions distant in time and space, by actions of which he is, in no explicit sense, the target. One well-documented class of such actions consists in decisions by American industrial leaders, who, beginning in the 1970s, responded to declining productivity and profitability and increased international business competition by reducing labor costs, in significant part via the globalization of production.[87] "Deindustrialization" and the rise of the service industries in older industrial urban areas render it significantly more likely that, upon graduation, this student will find only low-wage, non-unionized, and possibly temporary or part-time work.[88]

Plant closings and other forms of industrial disinvestment in the community in which the hypothetical student lives intersect with a range of other actions that shape his field of action. Some are deliberate and intentional. Institutionalized racial discrimination in housing, lending, and insurance, for example, played a pivotal role in confining increases in unemployment and poverty to low-income minority neighborhoods.[89] This example is illustrative, then, rather than a description of all significant actions upon the student's field of action. Yet it demonstrates how the field of what is socially possible can be shaped "at a distance." The absence of interaction, communication, and other readily apparent "connections," as between most graduates of high schools in core sections of older American cities and major transnational firms, itself can be evidence of power's exercise.

How, then, might students of power relations decide, when approaching a particular political problem or a specific social domain, which

---

[87] Harrison and Bluestone (1988).   [88] Levy and Michel (1991).
[89] Massey and Denton (1993).

boundaries to action and which relationships to analyze? Those who would de-face power, I want to argue, should focus attention on political mechanisms that comprise relevant practices, as well as the institutions that sustain and govern these practices. By practice, I mean a complex of social boundaries to action that, together, define an end or set of ends; standards, such as standards of ability, character, or achievement; and a community, group, or other collectivity of individuals who pursue these ends and who accept, adhere to, and/or are measured against these standards.[90] By institution, I mean a system of laws, procedures, norms, routines, and other boundaries that determine and distribute rights, duties, sanctions, and rewards, including material rewards, public recognition, and status.

Because of the pivotal role practices play in delimiting the ways people in specific social contexts might act (the activities, projects, and relationships they might engage in, the careers, broadly conceived, that they might pursue) that are recognized, deemed worthwhile, respected, and praised by some collectivity, the boundaries comprising them, along with the institutional boundaries that sustain and regulate them, deserve a central place in the critical analysis of power. To return to the example of power relations involving teachers and students in American urban public schools, de-facing power requires locating power's exercise, not necessarily in classroom "connections" between teacher and student, but rather in those actions that invoke, reproduce, reinforce, or challenge boundaries defining practices of teaching and learning, and the educational and other institutions that shape these pedagogic practices.

I explore this example in detail in the chapters that follow. Here I want to underscore that conceptualizations of power necessarily depend upon (explicit or implicit) definitions of freedom. An understanding of freedom as negative – a political void where action is independent of social constraint – is untenable. What is more, it directs attention away from questions social theorists should ask if they aim to pursue the critical project that has defined the power debate since the publication of Dahl's early work.

De-facing power expands the field of what researchers might study to include any significant restriction on the social capacity to act upon boundaries defining relevant practices and institutions. It does not deflect

---

[90] This definition recalls Alasdair MacIntyre's (1984: 187–94) in its emphasis on ends, standards, and identities as key elements of practices. Unlike MacIntyre, however, I would not specify a minimum threshold of "complexity," stipulate that practices must be "coherent" or "progressive," or deny that institutions play a decisive role in shaping practices.

attention from some realm of social action defined as "free," from effects of power on the fields of action of actors defined as "powerful," from social relations that do not involve agents who seem powerful, and from the ways power is exercised in the absence of apparent connections, such as communication or interaction.

Expanding the definition of power in the ways proposed makes it necessary to modify the grounds for criticizing power relations. By my view, power relations are not only inescapable, but also necessary for promoting a range of social goods. Students of power relations should distinguish, then, relations that promote political freedom from those that approximate states of domination. The latter involve, as Weber and Giddens suggest,[91] durable and relatively stable asymmetries in the capacity to act. They consist in, as Foucault contends,[92] social boundaries that severely restrict participants' mobility, where mobility is the capacity to maneuver and act to change power relations. One might envision, then, a continuum of power relations on which domination forms one end point. At the opposite end is the fluid relation defined by boundaries that are knowable to all participants, and that allow the maximum possible space for effective transformative action. If political freedom is the capacity to participate in shaping the limits that define what is socially possible, the greater the restriction on freedom within a given power relation, the more the relation approximates a state of domination.

The key normative question students of power relations should ask, then, is not "Do power relations exist?" but "Do power's mechanisms define social possibility in ways that are knowable to those whose action they circumscribe, and in ways that enable those they affect to help modify or transform them?" As I argue in the concluding chapter, de-facing power does not entail rejecting wholesale the critical concerns that informed studies of power's various faces; the subject matter of the study of power relations remains significant social constraint on freedom. It does, however, involve shifting the critical focus. The question of how power shapes freedom becomes a question about, not distribution and individual choice, but the differential impact of social practices and institutions on actors' capacities to participate in shaping the conditions of their collective existence.

[91] Weber (1968: 946) defines domination as "a special case of power," a relation characterized by regular patterns of power inequality. For Giddens (1984: 28–59) domination is a state in which power relations are a relatively stable, structured, established feature of a society.

[92] For Foucault (1989: 418) domination is "only one form of power-relation," the defining characteristic of which is that it positions at least one party in such a manner that she has negligible room to maneuver and to act to change the power relation. See Foucault (1988 and 1989: 416–422).

3 Power and pedagogy

It is an early October morning, and fourth grade teachers throughout Connecticut, having just administered the state's mandatory Mastery Test,[1] are getting down to the business of establishing guidelines for the year. Veronica Franklin, a veteran teacher at the core urban North End Community School,[2] plans to introduce classroom rules to her fourth graders that day. I am a participant-observer/volunteer in her classroom, and she asks me to print, photocopy, and affix to each child's desk a sign that reads:

OUR COOPERATIVE LEARNING PLEDGE
We the students of room 18 want our classroom to be a fun, happy place. Therefore, we agree to do these things:
1. Take turns talking quietly.
2. Listen to each other's ideas.
3. Praise each other's ideas.
4. Help each other when asked.
5. Stay together until everyone is done.
6. Talk about how we worked well together and how we can improve.

Later the same morning, Franklin instructs her students to look at what she refers to as the "rules" that I taped to their desks. She has them read, in unison, the opening statement: "We the students of room 18 want our classroom to be a fun, happy place. Therefore, we agree to do these things."

"This is your classroom," she tells them. "You want it to be a fun, happy place. You have to make everyone happy, including your teacher. Don't act ugly."[3]

She points out that Renee did not log off the computer when she was instructed to.

Franklin proceeds to read to her class, one by one, the rules listed in the

---

[1] Authorized by the state General Assembly in 1984, the Connecticut Mastery Test (CMT) is administered annually to all fourth, sixth, and eighth grade students in Connecticut to assess performance in reading, writing, and mathematics relative to a state-established standard of competency.

[2] For demographic and other data on the North End Community School, see pages 59 and 62–3, and Appendix A, tables 1–3.

[3] Unless otherwise noted, all direct quotes are from my field notes.

pledge, pausing on more than one occasion to point out examples of children who, so early in the day, already have violated regulations. She amends rules to clarify the boundaries of what they permit. The first, for example, she says, means only that children are allowed to talk *about their school work*. She elaborates the consequences of failure to live up to the "pledge," telling the students that "if it gets too bad," she will have to "take over," by which she means to move them from their newly assigned small work groups back to rows of single desks.

When Franklin reads the final rule on the list ("Talk about how we worked well together and how we can improve") she tells the class, "That's what we're going to do at three o'clock." She asks, "Now we are a big *what* in here?"

"*Family!*" holler the students, in unison.

"And we're going to do what?"

"*Work together!*"

Mrs. Franklin tells the children that she and I are the heads of the family, and that all of its members have to cooperate.

It is near the end of the same school day when Franklin announces, "We're going to evaluate our groups and see what we can do to eliminate some of this foolishness." She tells Booker and Asha to switch seats so that Renee and Booker are no longer sitting next to each other. She comments that the "spoiled apple" ruins the bunch, adding, "Everything you do, you always have someone to spoil it."

Her students in their proper places, the teacher initiates a "self-grading" process by asking Charles what mark he thinks his group deserves. Charles says he thinks it deserves an "A."

"Why?" Mrs. Franklin asks.

"We did go to [inaudible] together — "

But she cuts him off. "Aman?" she says, calling on a second member of Charles's group. Aman answers, "B."

"Why?" Franklin asks.

"Sometimes we were being foolish."

She calls on the third group member. "Candy?"

"B."

"Why?"

"Sometimes we was talking, goofing around."

Franklin calls on Tesha, the group's fourth member, who agrees that she and her partners should receive a "B," because at times, she says, they talked and laughed. The teacher asks the rest of her students how many think that the group should receive a "B" for the day's work, and all raise their hands. "Charles," she asks, "do you really think you deserve an 'A'?"

Charles responds, "Yes," but then, after a moment, "no."

Mrs. Franklin repeats the process, group by group, instructing students to grade themselves publicly for their collective efforts, and directing a class vote on each group's grade. Students who award themselves and their groups "A"s justify their evaluations with reference to the rules their teacher gave them, both in writing and orally. For example:

JACLYN: Learned good, followed the rules.
EVETTE: We turned work into you.
KEVIN: Stayed together, worked together, praised each other's ideals [sic].

Those who give themselves "D"s and "F"s explain their critical self-evaluations in terms of rule violation:

KENNETH: Cause they acting silly. We talking and not helping others out.
RENEE: Me and Asha and Booker fooling around.
BOOKER: Because me and Renee was acting up.[4]

The following day I am, again, a participant-observer and classroom volunteer, this time in Monica Segal's fourth grade in the suburban Fair View Elementary School.[5] At the teacher's suggestion, I join a work group at a table with an extra seat.

The day's math lesson involves working with a "hundreds board," a ten-by-ten square with the numbers one through one hundred printed on it. Segal distributes to each group of five or six students a pile of chips and a photocopied sheet of "clues." She instructs them to cut the paper into pieces and to distribute the clues, one per student. The goal of the exercise, she says, is to discover the particular number that is the solution to the puzzle. She gives the class no further instructions.

The group I joined, like others in the classroom, falls quickly into a chaotic state of dissension. Each student wants to read her clue first. Each has her own idea about how to solve the problem. The five children talk at once, raising their voices to drown out those of their competitors.

One member of our group, Jimmy, yells for everyone to "Wait a minute!" He suggests that we each take five chips and surrender one each time we want to talk.[6] The others agree, and we take five chips apiece from the pile in the center of the table.

At this point, the children in the group lower their voices noticeably. They listen, and agree, when a second student suggests taking turns to

---

[4] I deliberately do not translate the students' speech into "standard English." Linguistic conventions, as well as definitions of departures from these as personal or cultural deficiencies, are, at this site, important mechanisms of power.

[5] For background data on Fair View Elementary and the Fair View district, see pages 114–16, and Appendix A, tables 1–3.

[6] Segal previously taught this strategy to the class.

read the clues aloud. They further agree to use the remaining chips to cover all the impossibilities on the board. So, for example, when a clue states that the solution is smaller than 40, together they cover with chips all the numbers from 40 to 100.

As the children work, one girl, Cass, stops to comment, "Wait a minute. Have you noticed how well we're working together as a group?"

The five students solve the problem within minutes, and they solve a second before the time period has ended.

After the exercise, Segal convenes a class meeting to talk about what happened. The aim of the discussion, she explains, will be to come up with a set of guidelines for working together. The students, seated on the floor around their teacher, raise their hands to describe problems they encountered in their groups, and to suggest rules to help address them. Segal gives each child a chance to speak. She copies the students' ideas on to an oversized pad of paper, explaining when she does not write out particular suggestions that she judges to be re-statements of previously recorded rules, and translating several prohibitions into positively worded statements.

At the end of the meeting Segal tells the class that she intentionally did not give them guidelines for the project, because she wanted them to realize that "sometimes we need rules." She detaches the list from the pad and tapes it to the board at the front of the classroom, where it will remain for the rest of the school year. It reads:

> No put downs.
> Cooperate.
> Listen to each other.
> Give everyone an equal chance.
> Share work evenly.
> Talk quietly.

Power and powerlessness: problems with the evidence

How might theorists of power's various "faces" interpret the striking differences in what happens during these two lessons in rule-making? Monica Segal, a student of power-with-a-face might suggest, uses her power over her students to "empower" them. She enables them to use mechanisms of power, including in this instance rules, to make and to act upon choices, or to realize their desires or interests. She allows the children in her classroom an important measure of control over their learning experience, teaches them to participate in collective decision-making, and helps them understand the necessity and the enabling potential of rules. Clearly, the classroom is not without limits. Students are required to raise their hands in order to speak during the group meeting, for example, and they have to follow instructions about the use of the hundreds board. Nor is it devoid of hierarchy. The teacher makes evident her role as leader at various points during the lesson, such as when she decides to omit from the list rules that she judges to be duplicates of others. Almost all would acknowledge, however, that such limits and hierarchy are unavoidable, indeed necessary, in adult–child relations. The order and regulation in Segal's fourth grade classroom, a student of power-with-a-face might emphasize, function as positive guidelines in that they enable children to work effectively and to succeed. Segal makes a series of pedagogic choices that give her students power, in the form of opportunities and capacities that enable them to act independently and authentically.

Veronica Franklin, by contrast, makes pedagogic choices that, by the faced view, constrain students' negative freedom. She teaches the children in her class to produce work for the teacher, to abide by rules imposed by the teacher, and to conform to definitions determined by the teacher, in order to earn rewards and avoid punishment. Her approach to discipline seems to belie the rhetoric of the Cooperative Learning Pledge, itself egalitarian, communitarian, and democratic. Franklin singles out individual students for criticism and blame. She relies on prohibition and threat to maintain order in the classroom. When she introduces the Cooperative Learning Pledge, she translates it from the language of consensual group resolution to that of "rules," from an agreement aimed at making "our classroom" "fun and happy" to a set of codes that restrict student conduct. She uses the metaphor of "family" to signify hierarchy, "cooperation" to denote conformity to imposed rules, and "self-evaluation" to mean adoption of the standards and judgments of the teacher. Employing apparently democratic procedures to reinforce her own judgments, she teaches that rules are prohibitions, prescribed by adults in positions of authority and unaccompanied by explanation or justification. A student of power-with-a-face might suggest that Franklin uses the power she has over students to teach them to value obedience, to reject "foolishness" in the form of non-productive activity, and to understand and accept the dichotomy between ideal statements about democracy and real experiences of "powerlessness." In short, Segal exercises power to empower students to function as powerful members of society, while Franklin exercises power over, inducing her students to do, believe, and value in ways they "would not otherwise."

Such an account would be familiar.[7] But it would leave important

---

[7] At least since Bowles and Gintis's (1976) classic study, educational theorists and empirical researchers have argued that teachers and other "powerful" actors in schools use

explanatory gaps. Relatively early in my study of power relations in Franklin's and Segal's classrooms, I realized that standard accounts of power-with-a-face were unable to capture much of the role power plays there. They could not offer a plausible account of why, if there exist "liberating" or "empowering" pedagogic methods, Segal and other Fair View teachers choose to employ them, while Franklin and others at the North End Community School consistently eschew them in favor of a disempowering "authoritarianism."[8] They deflected attention, what is more, from the ways in which Franklin's emphasis on rule-following enables her students to manage a series of problems they encounter daily, as well as from the ways power's mechanisms subject Segal's privileged students. Standard accounts of the relation between power and freedom, by foregrounding interaction, communication, and other connections among powerful and powerless actors, tended to direct critical analyses away from interrelations among the boundaries defining the field of the possible in these distinct sites.

I argued in the last chapter that there are conceptual difficulties with defining power in terms of relations and interactions among powerful "A"s and powerless "B"s. Now I turn my attention to the practical difficulties such a view presents. I use critical theories of education, which are concerned specifically with the role power plays in the classroom and the school, to demonstrate that the significance of limits to the conventional definition extends beyond debates among political theorists. Reducing the exercise of power to a series of connections through which powerful agents alter the independent or authentic action of the powerless imposes arbitrary limits on both the analytic and the critical content of empirical studies of power relations.

Power and pedagogy: critical educational theory

Critical educational theory, or critical pedagogy, with roots in the "new" sociology of education[9] and the educational thought of American pragmatists,[10] applied a faced view of power to social relations in the

---

power to alter the free action of their "powerless" students, often in ways that reproduce and reinforce social hierarchies. See, for example, Anyon (1980, 1981, and 1997), Apple (1979), Carnoy and Levin (1985), and Mickelson (1980).

[8] I place "authoritarianism" in quotation marks to distance myself from the claim, implicit in the label, that disciplinary approaches termed "authoritarian" constrain and punish, while more "progressive" approaches to discipline characterized by what Delpit (1988: 289) calls "veiled commands" (she offers the example, "Would you like to sit down now?") do not.

[9] For an early review of the new sociology of education, see Karabel and Halsey (1977).

[10] Particularly influential was Dewey's definition of the school, and of the process of education generally, as a "laboratory" for democratic citizenship, understood as active and

classroom and the school. Driven by the call to "politicize the pedagogical,"[11] critical educational theorists set themselves in opposition to mainstream liberal and conservative educational theorists, whom they criticized for treating schooling as "an unproblematic vehicle for transmitting knowledge."[12] By their account, pedagogy[13] is an inescapably political process. Hence their emphasis on the role power plays in the classroom, shaping what happens in schools and helping reproduce and legitimize social hierarchy outside schools. Although significant differences separated early critical reproduction theories of schooling,[14] later resistance theories,[15] and more recent "critical postmodern" accounts,[16] the views of researchers contributing to this literature converged around at least two points of agreement. The first was the explanatory claim that education can, and often does, function as a political "sorting mechanism," reproducing and legitimizing social hierarchy by naturalizing dominant forms of knowledge and subjectivity. The second was the normative claim that "critical intellectuals" should work to transform power relations by empowering marginalized students, and in particular by enabling them to "give voice to" and to critically analyze their "experience," providing them with "a language of possibility" that might inform and promote the transformation of social inequality and injustice.[17]

Like political theorists of power-with-a-face, critical educational theorists tended to define power relations in terms of qualitatively distinct states of powerfulness and powerlessness. Reacting against earlier structural Marxist accounts,[18] which many characterized as reductionist in

footnote 10 (cont.)
equal participation in communal self-reconstruction. Dewey elaborated, especially in later writings informed by his practical work in progressive schools, a pedagogy that promotes a scientific understanding of the (communal) self and aims at increased control over the social experience. By his view, the pedagogic process is "that reconstruction or reorganization of experience which adds to the meaning of experience, and which increases ability to direct the course of subsequent experience" (Dewey 1916: 89–90). See also Dewey (1956 and 1963).   [11] Giroux (1988).   [12] Giroux (1997: 167).

[13] Most contributors to this literature understood pedagogy to mean all aspects of the educational process (including the content and design of both the formal and hidden curriculum) through which particular forms of knowledge and student subjectivity are produced and legitimized.

[14] These include Apple (1971 and 1979), Bourdieu (1974), Carnoy and Levin (1976), Keddie (1971), and Young (1971).

[15] See, for example, Apple (1982 and 1986), Giroux (1981a and 1983a), and McLaren (1985 and 1989).

[16] See, for example, Aronowitz and Giroux (1991), Giroux (1988 and 1990a), Gutierrez and McLaren (1995), and McLaren (1995).

[17] For overviews of the critical educational theory literature, see Aronowitz and Giroux (1993: ch. 4), and Giroux and McLaren (1991).

[18] Particularly influential were Althusser's (1971) claim that the educational state apparatus is the dominant ISA (ideological state apparatus) under mature capitalism and Bowles

their understanding of domination as class domination, they argued that schooling reproduces and reinforces, not only class divisions, but also racial, ethnic, gender, and other social inequalities.[19] The proper target of analysis, by this view, is not just "how working class kids get working class jobs,"[20] but more generally the ways in which, along multiple dimensions, teachers and other powerful agents in the classroom exercise power over students, especially those who are members of marginalized social groups. Like participants in the power debate, many acknowledged that powerlessness is rarely, if ever, absolute. Thus "resistance theorists" criticized the determinism of structural Marxist accounts, in particular their "overemphasis on how structural determinants promote economic and cultural inequality, and . . . underemphasis on how human agency accommodates, mediates, and resists the logic of capital . . ."[21] As the literature developed, it grew increasingly attentive to the oppositional behavior of marginalized students.[22] But it maintained as central to the analysis of classroom power relations the distinction between powerful agents and these relatively powerless actors.

Critical educational theorists distanced themselves, as well, from the structural Marxist assertion that "[t]he educational system serves – *through the correspondence of its social relations with those of economic life* – to reproduce economic inequality and to distort personal development."[23] Arguing persuasively that to document "correspondences" is not to offer an account of how power functions in educational settings, they stressed the importance of attention to what Dahl had termed "connections" involving teachers, students, and other actors in schools. To explain the reproduction of power relations through schooling, they argued, one must not simply identify parallels among social relations in the workplace, the family, the classroom, and other relevant sites. Instead, this task requires analyzing the in-school processes through which, and identifying the specific mechanisms by which, powerful agents reproduce, reinforce, and legitimize relations of power and powerlessness. Pierre Bourdieu's

and Gintis's (1976) subsequent argument that, in the United States, schools serve to reproduce among working- and middle-class students the differential skills, motivations, and values necessary for the reproduction of the capitalist division of labor.

[19] Apple (1986), McRobbie (1980), and Weis and Fine (1993).   [20] Willis (1977).

[21] Aronowitz and Giroux (1993: 68). This critique was directed at, not only structural Marxist theories of schooling, but also Bourdieu's "cultural-reproductive" model, and "state-hegemonic" models that drew on Gramsci's concept of hegemony. See also Apple (1986 and 1993), Aronowitz and Giroux (1991), Giroux (1983a), and Hebidge (1979).

[22] Hence critical educational theorists studied meanings, symbols, signs, and other cultural forms of marginalized groups, as well as tensions and conflicts among cultural sites, such as the school, the home, and the workplace. An early and influential study was Willis (1977); see note 26 below. Other examples are Anyon (1984) and Fine (1991).

[23] Bowles and Gintis (1976: 48; emphasis added).

concept of "cultural capital" was of central importance to this literature almost from its inception,[24] as was Basil Bernstein's theory of the role of sociolinguistic codes in social reproduction.[25] Participant-observation was its preferred methodology, and the literature grew to include descriptively rich empirical work on pedagogy and its effect on gendered, classed, and racialized students.[26] Researchers studied classroom communication and interaction, as well as curricular content. They asked, among other questions, what counts as valid knowledge in particular educational settings, how participation is differentially structured, which voices and experiences are affirmed, and which are silenced.[27]

An additional faced element informing critical theories of schooling was the tendency to view power as constraint on negative freedom. Drawing on Paulo Freire, post-Marxist critical educational theorists defined such constraint, less in terms of economic exploitation, than the "silencing" of the "voice" of the oppressed. Power, the claim was, submerges some students in what Freire had termed a "culture of silence,"[28]

---

[24] Through pedagogy, the claim was, middle-class teachers privilege the cultural capital of dominant groups and de-value that of working-class and other marginalized students. They thus not only reproduce, but also legitimize inequality, "making social hierarchies and [their] reproduction . . . appear to be based upon the hierarchy of 'gifts,' merits, or skills" (Bourdieu 1977: 496). See also Bourdieu (1974 and 1977), and Bourdieu and Passeron (1977).

[25] Bernstein argued that, through socialization in the family, working- and middle-class children gain access to, respectively, "restricted" and "elaborated" linguistic codes. Selective access to elaborated codes enables middle-class students to succeed in educational institutions in which the criteria for success are constructed and maintained by the dominant middle class (Bernstein 1975 and 1977).

[26] A classic ethnography was Paul Willis's (1977) study of working-class British secondary school boys, in which the author demonstrated the ways in which the formal school culture, together with the "counter-school culture" it generated among some working-class adolescents, contributed to the reproduction of a patriarchal identity informed by a valuation of "masculine" manual labor over "cissy" mental work. In another classic study, Ogbu (1974) used his research in the low-income, primarily black and Mexican-American neighborhood of Burgherside in Stockton, California, to argue that teachers and other classroom agents help reproduce hierarchies of school achievement and attainment by reinforcing the perception on the part of "subordinate minorities" (whom Ogbu distinguished from "immigrant minorities") that education affords them only very limited opportunities. See also Anyon (1980, 1981, and 1984), Apple (1979 and 1982), Ball (1981), Fine (1987 and 1991), Mickelson (1980), and Sharp and Green (1975).

[27] Some contributors to the literature analyzed curricular content, for example, Anyon (1980 and 1981), Apple (1979, 1982, and 1986), Apple and Christian-Smith (1991), Brown (1981), and Luke (1988). Others focused on how socialization in schools differentially affects members of dominant and marginalized social groups, for example, Carnoy and Levin (1985: ch. 5), Wilcox (1982), and Willis (1977). Some studied "banking" versus "dialogic" models of teaching. See Fine (1987 and 1991), Freire (1970 and 1987), Kreisberg (1992), Shor and Freire (1987), and Weiler (1988). Others emphasized the ways teachers approach school texts, for example whether they obscure or draw attention to the construction of the "canon," and how they define what it means to be "literate." See Freire and Macedo (1987) and Scholes (1985).   [28] Freire (1970).

distorting their consciousness so that they come to experience repressive needs as their own and to view their position of powerlessness as natural or inevitable. Critical pedagogy, by this view, is emancipatory in the sense that it enables students to find their own voices;[29] frees them from "repressive needs," such as those imposed by the mass media, helping them recognize their radical[30] or their real[31] needs; and "excavate[s] . . . 'repressed' knowledge."[32] Critical pedagogy empowers students, then, by providing them with the skills, knowledge, and other tools they need to understand the causes and effects of their oppression, and by tapping their "hidden utopian desire"[33] for justice and equality.

In short, power shapes freedom in the classroom when "hegemonic intellectuals" present dominant forms of knowledge and cultural capital as objective and neutral, and test and grade students on their mastery of these, helping reproduce and legitimize hierarchies based on social group membership. Empowering education, by contrast, is the work of "transformative intellectuals,"[34] who use emancipatory pedagogies to liberate powerless students. An explicit and central claim of much writing by critical educational theorists was that marginalized students need teachers as their guides to this process of being liberated. An implicit, but equally central assumption was that teachers who have power need only be exhorted to recognize its effects and to use it to challenge, rather than reproduce and legitimize social hierarchies. Typically, Henry Giroux claimed that, "classroom teachers *can* and must . . . work . . . to develop pedagogical theories and methods that link self-reflection and understanding with a commitment to change the nature of the larger society."[35] Similarly, Lilia Bartolome, drawing on Freire's claim that, to be effective, teachers of marginalized students need "political clarity,"[36] asserted, "Teachers working toward political clarity understand that they can either maintain the status quo, or they can work to transform the sociocultural reality at the classroom and school level . . ."[37]

The conceptual underpinnings of critical theories of schooling mirrored those of political theories of power-with-a-face. Social power in the classroom was conceived as an instrument used by individual teachers who make curricular and pedagogic choices that enable or constrain the free action of marginalized students. Some educational theorists elaborated structural accounts of power relations in schools, which paralleled

---

[29] Freire and Giroux (1989: vii).   [30] Giroux (1983b: 22).   [31] McLaren (1995: 77).
[32] Ibid. (54).   [33] Ibid. (49).
[34] Giroux (1986b: 29) defined "transformative intellectuals" as "bearers of critical knowledge, rules, and values through which they consciously articulate and problematize their relationship to each other, to students, to subject matter, and to the wider community."
[35] Giroux (1979: 283; emphasis added).   [36] Freire (1987).
[37] Bartolome (1994: 178).

structural political theories of power-with-a-face. Yet their focus remained the ways in which social structures unequally distribute power, and the processes through which the powerful use power's mechanisms to induce the powerless to do what they "otherwise would not." In one such account, Rachel Sharp and Anthony Green stressed, "What seems to be crucial is whether in the last analysis one can control others and bring sanctions to bear against others . . . "[38, 39]

Implications for empirical analysis

This conceptualization of power influenced the ways critical educational theorists accounted for pedagogic differences like those highlighted by the vignettes at the start of the chapter. Most emphasized teachers' pedagogic choices. Franklin and Segal, those adopting such an approach might stress, make radically different decisions about how to exercise the power they have to make and to enforce classroom rules. Franklin demands an unquestioning obedience to rules that she imposes on her students. Segal, by contrast, enables students to reflect about the pur-

---

[38] Sharp and Green (1975: 34). This was a structural account in that it situated the in-school processes through which teachers "exercise power over" students within relations defined by material and social structures. The argument was that, at the working-class Mapledene Lane School, teachers contributed to social stratification by assigning to students whom they perceived as coming from pathological home backgrounds reified identities (such as "peculiar" or "thick") and by interacting differentially with children based on whether they perceived them to be deficient, normal, or exceptional. By Sharp and Green's view, structural constraints, in the form of resource scarcity and the expectations of other "powerful" agents, are partly responsible for the teachers' reproductive pedagogic effects. Their central claim was that the "child-centered" rhetoric of the school served as a mechanism of power, which teachers used to legitimize the categories to which they assigned students, and to increase their control over the children in their charge.

[39] Note: some more recent critical educational theorists, who identified themselves as "critical postmoderns," aimed, in Giroux's (1997: 218) words, to "appropriate critically the most important aspects of" "modernism, postmodernism, and postmodern feminism." These theorists aimed to attend to poststructuralist insights about the production of knowledge and subjectivity, while retaining a modernist commitment to human agency, reason, and the elimination of oppression. Aronowitz and Giroux (1991), Giroux and McLaren (1991), and McLaren (1995). Although they adopted a Foucaultian language of "power networks" and explicitly disavowed key assumptions sustaining theories of power-with-a-face, in particular, the notion of a pre-political autonomous subject, they tended to adhere to Dahl's "intuitive sense" of how power functions. McLaren (1995: 188), for example, asserted, "we need to resituate the challenge of teaching as a task of empowering the powerless from states of dependency and passivity as both an informed movement for revolutionary social and economic transformation and as a means of achieving what Brian Fay calls a 'state of reflective clarity.'" This is a state of liberation "in which people know which of their wants are genuine because they know finally who they really are, and a state of collective autonomy in which they have the power to determine rationally and freely the nature and direction of their collective existence."

poses rules serve and to participate in deliberating about and determining them. Critical theorists of schooling who emphasized teachers' independent and/or authentic pedagogic choice included some neo-Marxist social reproduction theorists, who viewed teachers as agents of the state or the capitalist class. Teachers differentially socialize working-class and middle-class students, the claim was, to adopt the beliefs, habits, skills, and dispositions that capitalism requires for the reproduction of its stratified labor force.[40] Decisions made by powerful classroom agents were central, as well, to more recent resistance and critical postmodern accounts, which stressed "that any genuine pedagogical practice demands a commitment to social transformation in solidarity with subordinated and marginalized groups."[41]

To adopt an understanding of power-with-a-face is not necessarily, however, to assume that teachers like Franklin choose, desire, or benefit from the pedagogies they employ. The difference between Franklin's teaching and Segal's may be, instead, the product of Franklin's powerlessness. Some critical theorists of schooling focused, then, on differences in the distribution of power among classroom teachers, emphasizing that those who teach marginalized students generally lack key power resources, such as educational resources that vary because of different levels of funding relative to student need; personal resources like talent, skill, or the knowledge necessary to understand the political effects of pedagogy; or professional resources such as access to "progressive" teaching methods and techniques.[42] Contributors to the literature argued that teachers of marginalized students may unwittingly help reproduce domination, then, for example, by invoking an "achievement ideology," which they (mistakenly) believe and (erroneously) judge to be an effective motivational tool.[43]

My own research in Franklin's and Segal's classrooms suggests that work by critical educational theorists captures important truths about how power shapes freedom there. Differences in resources between these sites are significant. Differences in pedagogy are striking. And, as I argue in the chapters that follow, these differences affect the field of what is socially possible for actors at the two schools in ways that are troubling to those with a normative commitment to political freedom.

My analyses highlight, however, important aspects of power relations at North End and Fair View that the faced view tends to obscure. These

---

[40] Anyon (1980 and 1981), Bowles and Gintis (1976), Carnoy and Levin (1976) and Mickelson (1980).   [41] Giroux and McLaren (1991: 154).

[42] See, for example, Apple's (1982) claim, drawing on Braverman's (1974) work on deskilling, that new instructional programs in large urban districts deprive teachers of pedagogic and subject-matter knowledge by transforming them into managers and administrators.   [43] MacLeod (1987: ch. 6).

include patterned and normatively significant restrictions on the fields of action of classroom agents who, by the prevailing view, have and use power. They include the constraining *and* enabling effects of pedagogic practices at North End and Fair View. Generally, my ethnographic accounts of power relations at these schools demonstrate that focusing on the distribution of political resources and the constraining effects of teachers' choices on students' negative freedom diverts attention from key asymmetries in the ways practices and institutions delimit social possibility.

An example will help illustrate. Franklin, articulating her concern about a life-threatening danger her fourth graders face in the form of the temptation of lucrative jobs working as lookouts for local drug dealers, explains to me that she believes it is important that she teach the children in her class that "there is a right way to do things." As I argue in the following chapter, this teacher's adoption of an "authoritarian" pedagogy is, in part, a reasoned response to a range of immediate problems that power's mechanisms – including municipal and other public laws and policies, the institutional arrangements and constitutional laws that govern American public education, and the social identities and exclusions constructed around "race" in the contemporary United States – define in her classroom. Even as Franklin constrains students' possibilities (as in the lesson described above, by requiring unquestioning obedience to authority) she enables them, encouraging the children in her charge to develop social competencies she judges they need in the present (such as those that help them avoid violence in the neighborhood) and will likely need in the future (for example, to secure and keep the relatively scarce industrial, clerical, and low-income service sector jobs available in and around North End, or alternatively to leave North End and survive in white middle-class dominated social institutions).

Monica Segal, I argue in chapter 5, perceives herself much as critical educational theorists likely would define her: as a powerful agent who adopts a progressive pedagogy, which empowers her students. But boundaries defining key practices and institutions shape for this apparently powerful teacher, as well, the terrain within which she reasons about and acts upon the pedagogic decisions she makes. Power shapes freedom at Fair View by defining what some teachers refer to as a social "world" in which the personal characteristics and cognitive and social competencies needed to maintain privilege are insulated from forms of social action that might effectively contest them. My research suggests that pedagogy that, by the faced view, "empowers," restricts political freedom. Even as it enables students to act in ways that are socially valued and rewarded, it depoliticizes local pedagogic ends, standards of excellence, and social identities, legitimizing the punishment of actors who fail to conform.

Implications for critique

A faced view of power influenced, then, critical educational theorists' explanatory accounts of the relation between social power and human freedom. It also shaped their normative and prescriptive arguments. For most contributors to the literature, what warrants criticism in relations such as those described at the start of the chapter is the distribution of power resources, and/or the pedagogic choices made by "hegemonic intellectuals."

An emphasis on the relative powerlessness of those who teach marginalized students suggests that redistribution is the key to reducing domination. Thus some researchers called for redistributing funding and other material resources,[44] while others called for empowering the teachers of the powerless by providing them with the "critical categories" they need to understand and change the ways they exercise power.[45]

An emphasis on the pedagogic strategies "hegemonic intellectuals" adopt suggests that changing teachers' choices is paramount. Some critical theorists of schooling, inspired by Freire's "educational projects," which aimed at "de-mythologizing" the "thematic universe" of oppressed people,[46] urged teachers to politicize, rather than legitimize, the social production of knowledge and subjectivity. They argued that teachers should "decenter authority" (their own, as well as textual authority) and create a "safe space" in which oppressed students might regain their silenced voices.[47] They exhorted teachers to help marginalized students develop the critical and emancipatory elements of their oppositional cultures, and "interrogate critically their inner histories and experiences."[48] Teachers, the claim was, should take on the role of "transformative intellectuals" who provide students with "hopeful images"[49] and a "language of possibility,"[50] in order to promote emancipatory struggles.

Not all contributors to the literature endorsed this prevailing normative and prescriptive bent. Some feminist theorists, in particular, challenged the assumption that critical pedagogies "empower," in the sense

---

[44] Bastian, et. al. (1986).   [45] Giroux and McLaren (1991: 160).
[46] Freire (1970).
[47] Aronowitz and Giroux (1991), Giroux and McLaren (1991), and Giroux and Simon (1989: 220).
[48] Giroux (1983b: 22). See also MacLeod's claim (1987: 160) that teachers of working-class students should, not only de-mythologize the "achievement ideology," but also work with students' "collectivist cultural outlook," which he argued is a source of potential politicization and "class solidarity."   [49] Simon (1992).   [50] Giroux (1986a and 1990a).

that they enable independent or authentic action. In affirming a pedagogy of voice and social and self-criticism, these scholars argued, critical educational theorists obscured the power dynamics at work in the very pedagogies they promoted.[51] These critiques were compelling, especially when read against the relatively few references critical theorists made to their own educational practices. Consider Giroux's description of his efforts to "decenter authority" during the introductory meeting of a graduate education course. After introducing the course, he wrote, he "asked" students to break into groups to discuss "whether the principles and rationale [he] offered were suitable to their own perception of the course, [and] invited the students to suggest specific readings outside of the assigned texts that [the class] might take up . . ." The following is an excerpt from his account of these meetings:

It became instantly clear to me that the students also wanted the class to be participatory, critical, and attentive to immediate and global concerns regarding racial politics, and that they wanted both to provide their own list of readings for the course and to evaluate their performance for a course grade. Gently exercising my authority I mediated their concerns with three qualifications. First, I suggested that the course had to be organized around a series of writing assignments . . .[52]

Here the language of the "gentle" use of authority, of "asking" and "suggesting" that students follow the professor's instructions, and of "mediating their concerns," obfuscates, without changing, what happened during the class meeting described above: an instructor assigned work for his students to complete. That, to Giroux, "it became instantly clear" that students' vision of the course exactly mirrored his own is hardly evidence of the absence of power or the effective "decentering" of authority in his classroom.

De-facing power introduces a normative shift to studies of relations such as those involving teachers and students at North End and Fair View. The main focus of criticism becomes, not distributional inequalities

---

[51] Ellsworth (1989), for example, drawing on her own efforts to implement critical pedagogic practices in a university seminar, argued that key terms in the literature, such as "critical," "dialogue," "voice," and "empowerment," obscure the politics of those who use them. In her own classroom, she claimed, critical educational theory's prescriptions in fact functioned to reinforce race-, gender-, and class-based forms of domination. Kramer-Dahl (1996: 251) criticized the failure of critical pedagogy to attend to the ways in which, in encouraging students to make public their experiences and cultures in allegedly "safe" spaces, teachers might heighten student vulnerability to surveillance and discipline. Promoting such a practice, "skirts the issue of who, in the classroom, has the authority to judge what kind of experience counts as relevant and what kind of reading is 'correct.'" It becomes even more difficult, she argued, to accept such practices as unproblematically emancipatory once one takes into consideration "the impending prospect of interrogation, carried out in the often alienating language of critique . . ."

[52] Giroux (1997: 174).

or pedagogic choices that constrain negative freedom, but restrictions on political freedom defined by educational and other relevant institutions and practices. In the next chapter, I argue that key political mechanisms, including racial identities, tax and zoning laws, and municipal and school district boundaries, work together to define at North End a series of urgent problems associated with concentrated urban poverty and racial segregation in and around the school. These shape pedagogic practice in ways that encourage an emphasis on unquestioning obedience to authority. Like most contributors to the education literature, I am critical of pedagogies that promote unreflective rule-following. I depart, however, from critical educational theory's focus on hegemonic intellectuals as the (knowing or unknowing) agents of social reproduction. Such a focus, my account suggests, overlooks the significance of Franklin's claim that it is crucial that she teach students that "there is a right way to do things." The forms of pedagogy critical educational theorists tended to advocate, which emphasize skills needed for radical democratic citizenship, including the capacity and disposition to question hierarchical authority structures, at times compete with what Franklin and her colleagues refer to as the "survival skills" North End students need in order to function in a highly constrained social environment. Critical theorists of schooling likely would advise Franklin to teach her students to challenge, rather than adapt to, "existing relations of power."[53] But existing relations of power, Franklin might reply, render adaptive strategies her first priority.

Critical theorists of schooling had relatively little to say about power relations in schools like Fair View Elementary. Their faced view of power encouraged them to avert their critical gaze from institutions and practices that appeared to empower students to act in ways they choose, or in ways that serve their interests. It is, of course, possible to advance a faced critique of an "empowering" pedagogy like Segal's on the grounds that it is insufficiently emancipatory. A critical theorist might argue that teachers of privileged children should, not only enable them to act independently and authentically, but also encourage them to think critically about the educational and other social inequalities that work to their advantage. The de-faced view suggests a different line of critique. As I argue in chapter 5, power relations at Fair View Elementary are characterized by significant restrictions on political freedom. Here patterned asymmetries in the social capacity for action take the form of the removal of key boundaries from the reach of collective action. This restriction on freedom is promoted by the political and social practices and institutions that produce the "world" of Fair View. It functions to define as "other" actors

[53] Ibid. (97).

who transgress or exceed standards, identities, and other boundaries comprising local pedagogic practices, encouraging and legitimizing their discipline and punishment, both within and beyond the classroom.

In outlining their normative and prescriptive arguments, then, critical educational theorists tended to pay insufficient attention to limits to the ability of "hegemonic" teachers like Franklin to reshape pedagogic practice in freedom-promoting ways. They de-emphasized, as well, constraints on the actions of teachers like Segal, and the constraining effects of pedagogies that appear to "empower." Drawing on ethnographic research I conducted at the North End Community School and Fair View Elementary,[54] I now elaborate a de-faced account of power relations at these sites, an account centered on patterned asymmetries in the ways institutions and practices shape pedagogic possibility.

[54] For a discussion of my research methods, see Appendix B.

4 "The environment" and the North End Community School

The North End Community School is housed in a one-story brick building that stands opposite an abandoned lot on a busy street in the neighborhood of North End. Like many predominantly minority[1] residential
neighborhoods in core sections of older American cities, North End was
once home to industrial plants that provided relatively stable, union-wage
jobs for its then working-class residents. But the majority of these have
long since closed. The "postindustrial revolution" that transformed
American cities beginning in the 1920s and intensifying after World War
II drove manufacturing jobs in North End, as in similarly situated urban
neighborhoods, to the new suburbs and to the growth regions of the
American South, West, and Southwest, while draining inner-city communities of their working-class residents.

These shifts, heightened by global economic restructuring in the 1970s
and 1980s, were driven in part by federal and local government intervention. Disproportionate military and industrial investment in the new metropolitan areas during and after World War II, federal investment in the
interstate highway system beginning in 1956, tax policies (such as the
favorable treatment of interest payments for home mortgages), housing
policies (such as the veterans mortgage programs), and large-scale local
demolition and clearance projects under urban renewal contributed –
along with private investment practices – to the uneven development of
the city *vis-à-vis* its suburbs, and to core urban residential neighborhoods
like North End *vis-à-vis* downtown business, government, and "third
sector" economies.[2]

The shift from a manufacturing-based urban economy to one centered

---

[1] Some object to the use of "minority" on the grounds that it amalgamates social and
ethnic groups defined as non-white, overlooking differences among and within groups
constructed around "race" and ethnicity. Here I use the term not to imply that there exist
homogenous or fixed racial and ethnic identities, but rather to capture the ways in which
groups constructed as white and the institutions they dominate ghettoize those constructed as non-white, especially African-Americans, Latinos, and the so-called new
immigrants, into physically deteriorating and impoverished core urban neighborhoods.

[2] Mollenkopf (1983).

on corporate, public, and private non-profit service sector jobs polarized the urban occupational structure. It produced high-paying managerial and professional jobs and proliferated clerical and low-paying, low-status service sector jobs.[3] This polarization mapped on to twentieth-century demographic shifts in American cities, changes themselves shaped by both public and private institutions and practices. The incorporation of suburban municipalities with restrictive zoning regulations played a key role, as did codified racial discrimination in housing and lending,[4] and the widespread discriminatory practices in these fields, which persisted even after the passage of the Fair Housing Act.[5] These helped fuel the exodus to the suburbs of the white middle and working classes, while confining in declining urban cores the Southern blacks who migrated to industrial cities in the postwar era, and the Latinos and "new immigrants" who followed. In the 1980s and 1990s, changes in public institutions, including social welfare and drug policy, exacerbated social and economic inequalities between cities and suburbs. Two unambiguous examples are cutbacks in Aid to Families with Dependent Children,[6] and changes in drug laws, which dramatically increased arrest and incarcera-

---

[3] This polarization was not confined to American cites. It was a national phenomenon and one that emerged, as well, in other industrialized nations. See Bluestone (1990), Harrison and Bluestone (1988), Levy and Michel (1991), Levy and Murname (1992), Lorence and Nelson (1993), and Morris, et al. (1992).

[4] Squires (1994: 53) quotes from the Federal Housing Administration's 1939 *Underwriting Manual*: "If a neighborhood is to retain stability, it is necessary that properties shall continue to be occupied by the same social and racial classes. A change in social or racial occupancy generally contributes to instability and a decline in values." Squires (ibid.: 54) also quotes from the National Association of Realtors' 1959 Code of Ethics: "A realtor should never be instrumental in introducing into a neighborhood a character of property or occupancy, members of any race or nationality, or an individual whose presence will clearly be detrimental to property values in the neighborhood." On the discriminatory role of neighborhood "improvement associations" and local real estate boards, and the role of the Federal Home Owners' Loan Corporation (HOLC) in initiating "redlining," see Jackson (1985), and Massey and Denton (1993).

[5] Although the 1968 Fair Housing Act banned discrimination in housing sales and rentals, two major audit studies sponsored by the US Department of Housing and Urban Development (HUD), the 1977 Housing Markets Practices Survey of forty large metropolitan areas, and the 1989 Housing Discrimination Study of twenty-five large metropolitan areas, documented racially discriminatory practices among real estate agents. The latter study identified three stages of differential treatment according to race and Hispanic origin: housing availability, completing a transaction, and racial steering. Overall, in 46 percent of cases, black auditors attempting to rent a unit received unfavorable treatment, compared with the white auditors with whom they were paired. Black auditors encountered discriminatory treatment on 50 percent of occasions when they attempted to buy units. Hispanic auditors encountered discriminatory treatment during 43 percent of attempts to rent and 46 percent of attempts to buy (Turner, et al. 1991). See also Fainstein (1995), Feagin (1994), Massey and Denton (1993: ch. 4), Squires and Velez (1987), and Wienk, et al. (1979).

[6] According to Schram (1995: 167–8), "the median state monthly AFDC benefit for a family of four fell 42 percent in real dollars from 1970 to 1990. Even if food stamps are counted as part of the welfare benefits package, in recent years in the average state they

tion rates among African-Americans, especially among young black men living in cities.[7]

What was the impact at the neighborhood level? Consider census data from North End.[8] Here a relatively small proportion of working people hold managerial or professional jobs. About 17 percent, compared with 19, 21.1, and 30 percent for Bridgeport, Hartford, and New Haven, respectively (Connecticut's three largest cities), and 31.5 percent for the state as a whole. Workers are disproportionately concentrated in technical, clerical, sales, and non-professional, non-managerial service sector jobs. Roughly 55 percent of employed persons hold such jobs, a proportion that is about 23 percent higher than the statewide 44.7 percent. The unemployment rate is approximately 8 percent, slightly lower than that in Bridgeport, Hartford, and New Haven, but about 50 percent higher than the statewide rate of 5.4 percent. Labor force participation rates are somewhat lower, both in North End and in the three cities, than in the rest of the state. Per capita income is roughly one-half the average for Connecticut as a whole, while median family income and median household income are both less than half the state average. The family poverty rate of about 26 percent is more than five times the rate for the state as a whole. Significantly fewer residents of North End have high school diplomas and bachelor's degrees than do residents of Bridgeport, Hartford, New Haven, and the state of Connecticut. The tracts are roughly 90 percent black, although only 8.3 percent of Connecticut's residents are African-American.[9]

To understand the impact these changes have on the North End Community School, it is important to consider them in the context of the political decision-making practices that govern American public

are worth not much more than cash public assistance was alone in 1960 . . . The cash value of food stamps and AFDC combined . . . declined 27 percent from 1972 to 1990. Even adding Medicaid benefits to food stamps and AFDC results in no net gain in benefits from 1969 to 1989 for the average state . . . For much of the 1980s, states allowed the real value of benefits to decline simply by not raising benefits to keep up with the rising cost of living. Now in the 1990s, however, states increasingly are taking the extra step of actually reducing the nominal value of benefits."

[7] See Mann (1993) and Tonry (1995).

[8] Although census tracts do not map exactly on to either neighborhood definitions or school assignments, I estimate data for the North End neighborhood by averaging data from the tract in which the North End Community School is located and an adjacent tract that is close to the school and similar in its demographic characteristics. In all likelihood, however, the economic picture is even grimmer than these data suggest, since, as Bourgois (1995: 4–5) notes, census data on core urban neighborhoods tend to be systematically skewed. Bourgois reports that the Census Bureau misses a significant proportion of people who participate in the underground economy, including, by its own estimate, some 20 to 40 percent of young black and Latino men.

[9] For a more detailed comparison of occupational structure, unemployment, labor force participation, income, poverty status, educational attainment, and racial and ethnic composition, see Appendix A, table 1.

schooling, and the constitutional interpretation of the role of states in providing education. The United States Constitution implicitly grants authority over education to state governments,[10] but a strong tradition of local control extends back through the common school movement of the mid-nineteenth century,[11] to predate the republic itself.[12] By the time of the American Civil War, the majority of states had established public school systems, which were largely funded and administered by local towns.[13] When, during the progressive education movement of the late nineteenth and early twentieth centuries, these were centralized, bureaucratized, and professionalized, the result was the contemporary institutional framework for American public education: a system of state-governed local school districts funded in large part by local property taxes.

A series of twentieth-century constitutional decisions established the limits of what states must do, and what they may do, in providing schooling. The Supreme Court ruled that the due process clause of the Fourteenth Amendment protects the right of families to opt out of the public education system by sending their children to religious or non-religious private schools.[14] It ruled that, although *de jure* racial segregation is unconstitutional,[15] *de facto* racial segregation is not,[16] and that

[10] The Constitution does not mention education, rendering its governance one of "[t]he powers ... reserved to the States respectively, or to the people" by the Tenth Amendment.

[11] Cremin (1980: 174) argues that "the development of state systems must be seen in a nineteenth-century context of localism: neither the ideology nor the technology of political control at the state level had been developed to the point where it was seen as a replacement for political control at the district, town, or county level. Even in Massachusetts, where the vigor of Horace Mann's secretaryship made the authority of the state seem more visible and more forceful than elsewhere, that authority was never conceived to be more than stimulatory and supportive in character ..."

[12] Many identify the origin of this tradition of local control over schooling in the founding of the Boston Latin School in 1635. It was strengthened with the passage, in Massachusetts in 1647, of a school act requiring townships of fifty or more households to "appoint one within their town to teach all such children as shall resort to him to write and read, whose wages shall be paid either by the parents or masters of such children, or by the inhabitants in general" and townships of one hundred or more households to establish grammar schools, "the master thereof being able to instruct youth so far as they may be fitted for the university" (quoted in Cremin 1970: 181–2). Both New Haven and Hartford resolved to establish town schools in 1642. The state of Connecticut enacted, in 1650, a statute identical to the Massachusetts school act (ibid.: 180–2).

[13] However, with the exception of North Carolina, Southern states did not voluntarily establish what were generally perceived as Northern institutions. For the most part, public schools were imposed on Southern states during the postwar years (Cremin 1980).

[14] *Pierce v. Society of Sisters* (1925) 268 US 510.

[15] *Brown v. Board of Education of Topeka* (1954) 347 US 483. The effects of the Court's ruling – that "separate educational facilities are inherently unequal" – were not felt until after the passage of the Civil Rights Acts of the mid-1960s, in particular the 1964 Civil Rights Act, which prohibited federal funding of segregated institutions. But by 1970, Southern schools were the most racially integrated in the United States. See Orfield (1983).

[16] *Keyes v. Denver School District* (1972) 413 US 189.

desegregation efforts may not exceed the boundaries of a segregated district, absent proof that the cause of segregation was action by another district or by the state.[17] The Court ruled, as well, that there is no state duty to equalize educational resources among school districts, even when the structure of local finance, in the face of sizable fiscal inequalities between cities and suburbs, results in gross inequalities in educational spending.[18]

Even in those cases in which state supreme court rulings held legislatures to relatively activist roles in equalizing educational opportunity and reducing racial and ethnic isolation, the basic system of socio-economic segregation that resulted from the mapping of twentieth-century economic and demographic shifts on to nineteenth-century institutional arrangements remained intact. Most states with "foundation" or "equalizing formula" programs failed to eliminate funding disparities, much less to raise spending levels in cities to meet greater student need there, because wealthy districts continued to fund schools at a relatively high level based on property tax revenues. Nor were progressive financing formulae sufficient to halt or to reverse the growing concentration of poverty, poverty-related social problems, and low academic achievement in predominantly minority urban schools.

In Connecticut, for example, in 1977 the state supreme court ruled the local property tax-based school finance system unconstitutional, on the grounds that it denied children from poor districts educational opportunity equal to that available to children from wealthy districts.[19] In 1996, the court further ruled that *de facto* racial and ethnic segregation in public schools violates the state constitution.[20] Yet the state maintained its 1909 definition of school district boundaries along municipal lines[21] and its legal requirement that children attend schools in the districts in which they live.[22] In the 1995–6 school year, Connecticut provided 66 percent of school revenue for Education Reference Group (ERG) I districts, that is, for the seven districts with the lowest socio-economic status (SES)

---

[17] In *Milliken v. Bradley* (1974) 418 US 717, the Court reversed a lower court ruling ordering Detroit suburbs to enter into a metropolitan plan to integrate public schools, on the grounds that the plan was punitive to suburban whites.

[18] The Court ruled that "education . . . is not among the rights afforded explicit protection under our federal Constitution. Nor do we find any basis for saying it is implicitly so protected." *San Antonio Independent School District v. Rodriguez* (1973) 411 US 1.

[19] *Horton v. Meskill* 172 Conn. 615. According to this ruling, financing schools via local property taxes, without state funding equalization, violates Article 1, sections 1 and 20, and Article 8, section 1 of the Connecticut state constitution, which mandate that the state provide, for all, substantially equal educational opportunity via free public elementary and secondary schooling.   [20] *Sheff v. O'Neill* 238 Conn. 1.

[21] Connecticut General Statutes, sections 10–240.

[22] Connecticut General Statutes, sections 10–184.

rankings and highest student need.[23] Only 28 percent of school revenue in these districts came from property taxes and other local sources. By comparison, for ERG A, the eleven districts that ranked highest for socio-economic status (SES) and lowest for student need, more than 95 percent of school revenue was locally generated, and less than 3 percent was provided by the state. Yet disparities in spending remained, with per pupil expenditure in the latter group about 9 percent higher than that in the former.[24]

Parents with financial resources, and especially white parents with financial resources, can relocate out of cities and send their children to public schools in the suburbs, which are inaccessible to the children of the poor as well as to many working-class and middle-class African-Americans. They can move to relatively affluent city neighborhoods and send their children to local public schools there. And they can exit the public school system altogether, by sending their children to private schools. Children of the urban poor, by contrast, and in particular blacks, Latinos, and others constructed as non-white are required by law to attend the only educational institutions available to them: physically deteriorated and financially strapped urban public schools.

What is more, socio-economic segregation relegates these students to schools in which they, along with their teachers, are confronted with a range of social problems statistically associated with concentrated urban poverty. At the North End Community School, where the student population is about 90 percent black, close to 10 percent Hispanic,[25] and about 1 percent white,[26] more than 80 percent of students qualify for free or reduced-price meals. No child at the school met the state goal for reading, writing, or mathematics on the 1995–6 Connecticut Mastery Test.[27] And, although data are not available on the census tract or individual school

[23] The State Department of Education groups 166 school districts and three academies based on three measures of socio-economic status (median family income, percentage of students with at least one parent with a bachelor's degree, and percentage of parents with executive, managerial, or professional jobs) and three measures of student need (percentage of children in single-parent or non-family households, school-age children receiving AFDC as a percentage of public school enrollment, and percentage of children in non-English speaking families), weighted for enrollment.

[24] For data on revenue sources and per pupil expenditure for all seven reference groups, see Appendix A, table 2.

[25] Unlike the US Census Bureau, the Connecticut Department of Education distinguishes "Hispanic" persons from "black" and "white."

[26] This intense level of segregation is not atypical of public schools in Northeastern states. In 1991–2, more than half of black public school students in the Northeast attended schools in which at least 90 percent of students were African-American, Latino, Native American, or Asian (Orfield 1983: 8–9).

[27] See Appendix A, table 3 for comparative data on school racial composition, students qualifying for free or reduced-price meals, and Mastery Test achievement.

level, my research suggests – and city-, state-, and national-level data support this inference – that the North End school and the surrounding neighborhood are the sites of a range of social problems statistically associated with concentrated urban poverty. These include public health problems, such as high rates of HIV and AIDS infection;[28] relatively high rates of crime, including violent crime;[29] and high rates of victimization,[30] arrest, and incarceration.[31]

[28] The year before I conducted my research, a second grader at North End died of AIDS. In Veronica Franklin's classroom alone, two students' parents had recently died of AIDS. Although AIDS infection data are not available at the neighborhood or school level, AIDS cases reported in Connecticut are disproportionately concentrated in urban areas – including the city in which the North End school and neighborhood are located – and, within cities, among racial and ethnic minorities. Thus, although only 3.04 cases of AIDS per 1,000 persons were reported in the state from 1981 through June 1998, 6.1,15.24, and 14.11 cases per 1,000 persons were reported in Bridgeport, Hartford, and New Haven, respectively. AIDS cases are even more disproportionately concentrated among African-Americans in Connecticut's cities. There are 12, 17.4, and 24.61 known cases of AIDS per 1,000 African-Americans in Bridgeport, Hartford, and New Haven, respectively. Source: State of Connecticut, Department of Public Health, AIDS Epidemiology Program. For a more detailed breakdown of AIDS cases in Connecticut and its cities, see Appendix A, table 4.

[29] The FBI, in its Uniform Crime Reports, codes as violent crimes homicide, rape, robbery, and aggravated assault. In Veronica Franklin's classroom alone, one child's parent had been murdered, and at least one child had been raped. Violent crime data are not available on the census tract or school level. However, rates of violent crime are significantly higher in each of Connecticut's major cities – including the city in which North End is located – than in the state as a whole. Homicide rates from 1993 to 1996 average only 5.58 per 100,000 persons for the state as a whole, but 34.57, 26.58, and 19.89 for Bridgeport, Hartford, and New Haven respectively. Rape rates average 23.95 per 100,000 persons for the state, but 44.04, 78.62, and 92.4 for Bridgeport, Hartford, and New Haven. Robbery rates average 179.33 per 100,000 persons for Connecticut, but 794.04, 1,005.73, and 933.51 for Bridgeport, Hartford, and New Haven. Aggravated assault rates average 223.55 for the state, but 626.91, 970.33, and 1,014.94 for Bridgeport, Hartford, and New Haven (United States Department of Justice, Federal Bureau of Investigation 1994, 1995, 1996, and 1997). See Appendix A, table 5.

[30] Victimization data, published by the US Department of Justice, are based on surveys, rather than police reports, and therefore are believed to provide a more accurate estimate of victimization rates for crimes that tend to be under-reported, such as rape. Victimization data show, consistently, that urban residents and African-Americans are disproportionately the victims of violent crimes. From 1987 to 1992, for instance, urban residents were, on average, 58 percent more likely to be victims of violent crime than were suburban residents, and African-Americans were 47 percent more likely to be victims of violent crime than were whites (US Department of Justice, Bureau of Justice Statistics 1994). For violent crime victimization rates among blacks and whites, and urban and suburban residents, from 1973 until 1992, see Appendix A, table 6.

[31] On many occasions throughout the year that I studied the North End Community School, teachers discussed former students, and parents of current students, who were incarcerated. Although incarceration data are not available at the census tract or individual school level, rates in each of Connecticut's major cities – including the city in which North End is located – are more than three times the rate for the state as a whole. In July 1998, the Connecticut Department of Corrections confined 2,115, 2,637, and 2,301 men and women from Bridgeport, Hartford, and New Haven, respectively, or 1,533, 1,981, and 1,846 persons per 100,000 1996 population, compared with 15,909 persons, or only

My central methodological claim in this chapter is that understanding how power shapes freedom in Veronica Franklin's classroom at the North End Community School requires extending analysis to include the effects of mechanisms of power this teacher cannot plausibly be held to have, use, or direct. Key power mechanisms include the political decision-making practices, the laws and policies, the racial identities, and the municipal and educational institutional arrangements discussed above. These play a crucial role in delimiting for Franklin, as well as for her fourth grade students, bounded fields of social possibility. To provide an account of how power shapes freedom at North End requires, then, attention to the effects of power's mechanisms on the fields of action of, not only apparently powerless students, but also teachers, who, to some, seem relatively powerful. Critical educational theorists are right, I argue, to challenge the political effects of "authoritarian" schooling. But they are misguided to the extent that they define these as the product of choices made by "hegemonic intellectuals" who exercise "power over" students. Nor is the problem simply one of the distribution of resources, including material resources and the knowledge necessary to understand the political effects of pedagogy.

My central substantive claim is that power's mechanisms work together to define, for Franklin and other teachers at the North End School, a set of problems, possibilities, and strategic options that render locally *enabling*, pedagogic practices that severely constrain political freedom. I begin by offering an account of what Veronica Franklin does in her classroom. I argue, in the first section, that she adopts what some term an authoritarian style of classroom management, or discipline (that is, she prescribes and enforces rule that she requires students to obey unquestioningly), presents school knowledge as information children should absorb in order to win rewards and avoid punishment, and defines "the responsible student" as the child who authors a successful future by being accountable to adults in positions of authority.

I then consider how students respond to the classroom experience at

footnote 31 (*cont.*)
486 per 100,000 1996 population for the state as a whole. In other words, although Bridgeport, Hartford, and New Haven's total populations comprised only 12 percent of the state's, 44 percent of state prisoners were from these three cities. Sources: Connecticut Department of Corrections, and Gaquin and Litmann (1998: 858). Participant-observation and interview data suggesting high rates of incarceration in the predominantly black North End neighborhood are supported, further, by the disproportionately large number of African-Americans in Connecticut state prisons. In 1994, black persons in Connecticut's state prisons were incarcerated at more than seventeen times the rate of white persons: 2,250 per 100,000 population, compared with 130 per 100,000 whites (US Department of Justice, Bureau of Justice Statistics 1996).

North End. My claim in the second section is that pedagogic practice here limits children's social capacities to act in ways that affect the power relations in which they participate. Students at this school do not critically evaluate or participate in deliberating about, deciding, or enforcing school rules, the purpose of which they tend to define in terms of producing obedience to authority. Nor do they have any significant hand in shaping the terms of their classroom work and learning, which they tend to view as geared toward meeting teachers' expectations, procuring rewards, and avoiding punishment. Further, they tend to view discrepancies between the self and a standard of responsibility, defined as accountability toward those in positions of authority, as deficiencies that cause both personal and social problems.

To stop at this point in the argument (as do many accounts of power-with-a-face in the classroom) would, however, be to miss much of the work power performs at North End. In the final section, I ask why Franklin and other North End teachers do what they do. Pedagogic practice at this school, I argue, is shaped in part by the immediate problems, and the possibilities and strategic options for addressing these problems, defined by what some teachers call "the environment." The local "environment" is produced by the social and political practices and by the municipal, educational, and other institutions outlined above. It is the institutionalized product of human action, amenable to change by human action. North End teachers, however, reasonably perceive it as beyond their immediate control. Therefore, rather than engaging in efforts to change it, they manage it, teaching what some term "survival skills" and a series of what they at times acknowledge to be social myths about individual responsibility.

Pedagogy: observations from Veronica Franklin's classroom

"Classroom management"

Veronica Franklin spends several minutes preparing her students to line up to go to lunch. She sends them, first the boys, then the girls, to the sink at the back of the room to wash their hands. She instructs them to put their crayons away, to place their work on top of their desks, and to sit still so that she can tell that they are ready to line up. "I am waiting for three people," she announces, and then, a minute later, "I am waiting for one person. Can you guess who it is?"

The children shout, in unison, "Booker!"

It takes Franklin's students almost five minutes to line up in a manner that satisfies their teacher. The line must be straight, she announces, and each student must be in line, forming, in her words, a "boy-girl-boy-girl" pattern. When her line is finally ready, Franklin leads it through the hallways, stopping it outside the school cafeteria.

At the North End Community School, the normal lunch-time procedure is for teachers to deliver their students, in lines, to the cafeteria monitors. The monitors inspect the lines. If a line is acceptable, they admit the class to the cafeteria, and the teacher leaves to eat her own lunch in the faculty room. But if a line is unacceptable (if, for instance, it is not "boy-girl-boy-girl"), the monitors refuse to admit the class. As Veronica Franklin waits for the monitors to inspect her line, she reprimands several students who are not standing properly. But she is selectively attentive to these lapses. Sometimes when students step out of line, she scolds them sharply, and other times she says nothing.

When the cafeteria monitors approve Franklin's line, they move her class quickly from hallway to cafeteria. Two monitors speak to the children in raised voices, directing them to a table and instructing them to sit in the order in which they lined up. They send the students from another class out of the cafeteria and order them to re-enter, because in moving from hallway to table, they disturbed their "boy-girl-boy-girl" formation.

As the students are seated (about seventy-five children in total during this fourth and fifth grade lunch period) they talk to each other excitedly, creating a high-pitched noise in the cafeteria. Then Reverend Johnson enters. A short, solidly built man employed as a security guard at the school, Johnson is a neighborhood minister who functions as North End's disciplinarian. "Hands up in the air! Put your hands up!" he says several times, loudly. He calls individual students by name, instructing them to put their hands in the air. Reverend Johnson announces that the children will not eat lunch if they do not obey him. Within a minute or two all hands are raised, and there is nearly complete silence in the cafeteria.

One table at a time, Reverend Johnson permits groups of students who are not speaking, and whose hands are in the air, to go to the service area at the front of the cafeteria to get their food. Just as he is about to direct a table of fifth graders to get their lunches, he stops to reprimand several boys in the group. The whole table, he announces, will now have to wait. One of the girls in the group puts her head in her hands, looking despondent.

As the North End Community School's fourth and fifth graders retrieve their lunches, group by group, and bring them on trays back to their places at the tables, Reverend Johnson and the cafeteria monitors police the process closely. They make sure that no child switches seats after getting her food. Reverend Johnson makes rounds while the children eat, correcting students almost constantly. He calls several children over to his side to reprimand them individually for unacceptable behavior. Watching me watch Reverend Johnson, one of Franklin's fourth graders leans across the table and tells me, "He owns the school."

"What do you mean?" I ask, and she answers, "He *owns* the school."

The emphasis on discipline, and specifically on obedience to authority, at the North End Community School is, if not completely surprising to an observer familiar with ethnographic accounts of the schooling of the working class and poor, none the less striking. From the moment that Franklin's fourth graders enter school in the morning until the moment they line up to leave for home in the afternoon, they are monitored and barraged with a series of reprimands and punishments for rule violations that range from the routine and the trivial to the potentially serious. During the course of one typical day, Franklin's students are reproached for offenses that include speaking during breakfast, missing several days of school, "lip reading," wiping spilled milk from the floor at an inappropriate time, failing to demonstrate readiness to line up at the appropriate time, lining up incorrectly, not doing homework, making excuses for not doing homework, acting insufficiently ashamed of not having done homework, not listening during music class, not singing during music class, singing the wrong song, chewing gum, "calling out," "yelling out," laughing, making too much noise, making jokes during class, claiming that vocabulary words that are in the reading text glossary are not, and threatening to "jump" another child after school.

Almost without exception, activity at the school is governed by rules that are made and enforced by school authorities (the principal, the teachers, and other staff members), and that students are required to obey without questioning. The above account of the lunch period captures the rigid codification and regulation of even such apparently simple activities as walking down the hallway, entering the cafeteria, and retrieving and eating lunch. It further illustrates three sets of characteristics of the practice of what education professionals call "classroom management," or discipline, at the North End Community School.

The first has to do with the way rules are prescribed. One expectation I had before I visited the school was that teachers and other adults at North End would be the authors of the rules. This expectation was confirmed. Not once during the course of the year did I observe a student participate in the process of making or revising a school or a classroom regulation. A second expectation I had was that school authorities would explain the purpose of rules to students with reference to protecting them from harm, or otherwise promoting their well-being. This expectation was disconfirmed. Almost without exception, when adults at North End present rules to children or admonish them for failure to obey, they do so without reference to any purpose that rules serve, or any reason for students to obey beyond the avoidance of punishment or the procurement of rewards. At times, punishments at North End are severe: students are suspended from school on several occasions, and on others, not permitted to attend scheduled class trips. Usually they are relatively mild: a check next to the offender's name in the teacher's roll book, or a verbal rebuke. Occasionally school authorities motivate students not only with punishments, but also with rewards, such as adhesive stars for good behavior. But rewards and punishments are rarely, if ever, accompanied by explanations of the purposes rules serve. Why should students form a "boy-girl-boy-girl" pattern when lining up for lunch? Why, for that matter, should they line up at all? The only answer to these questions a North End student might glean from her daily lunch-time encounters with Franklin, Reverend Johnson, and the cafeteria monitors is that, if she fails to line up and to do so correctly, she will not eat lunch.

The second set of characteristics of discipline at the North End Community School is related to the strategies authorities there use to enforce school and classroom rules. Teachers and other adults at North End employ a variety of rewards and punishments in their efforts to induce students to obey. For example, the music teacher, Constance Ware, has an elaborate system of checks (for bad behavior) and stars (for good behavior) that students can accumulate to earn, respectively, negative reports to the school principal and their parents, or prizes from the "prize jar." Reverend Johnson relies heavily on "punishment papers," that is, tedious written assignments, such as dictionary pages to be copied verbatim, by hand. Franklin regularly punishes and rewards students by detaining "bad" children after school and permitting "good" children to leave the classroom first at the end of the day. What all have in common is that they administer punishments and distribute rewards publicly, drawing group attention to individual failures to obey, and, less frequently, to individual instances of exemplary behavior. "I am waiting for one person. Can you guess who it is?" Franklin asks as she prepares her students to line up for lunch. It is common practice at this school to point out the "bad boy" or the "bad girl" whose conduct prevents the group as a whole from attaining perfect compliance with regulations, and Franklin is relatively effective at producing group expressions of disdain for poor behavior and admiration for good behavior. "Booker!" her fourth graders shout enthusiastically during the exchange described above. Not only does this teacher effectively use the group to pressure the "bad boy" to conform to her standard of conduct, she further generates group identification with authority – with the teacher and her rules – and against disobedience.

The third set of characteristics of disciplinary practice at North End illustrated by the lunch-time vignette has to do with gaps in discipline, inconsistencies in the application of rules, and lapses in what, on the surface, appears to be an uncompromising authoritarianism. Adults at North End tolerate much behavior that, if one's knowledge of the school were limited to the above description of a typical lunch period, one would not expect them to tolerate. For example, although students often are required to stand in lines, and to stand in straight lines forming "boy-girl-boy-girl" patterns, they none the less are permitted to *dance* while in line, and they routinely do so. Discipline is not total. Many activities that appear to disrupt the order of the classroom and the school day are permitted. Nor is discipline consistent. Attention to student rule violations is selective. Thus, when Franklin, waiting outside the cafeteria, scolds students who get out of line and then ignores the same behavior in other students only moments later, she acts in a way that is not atypical for a North End teacher.

The latter pattern suggests that the aim of "classroom management" at North End is other than perfect compliance with school and classroom rules. In fact, although adults at the school stress to children the importance of submitting to authority and obeying rules, at times they show signs of being less than completely convinced by their own authoritarian creed. Thus Franklin frequently speaks disparagingly of district and state educational authorities, and she openly violates rules that she herself perceives to be arbitrary. At the end of the school day, for example, she permits students to take home leftover packaged breakfasts, even though, as she observes aloud on my first day in her classroom, she is required by law to return them to the cafeteria. Nor does this teacher, or many of her colleagues, seem to believe that it is best for children to follow all rules and to obey all authority. On occasion, amongst themselves, teachers sanction student rebelliousness. For example, a group of faculty members expresses approval when fifth grade teacher Bernice Henderson tells them that her students stole stickers from (the almost universally disliked) Constance Ware and returned from music class with adhesive stars covering their bodies.

In many ways, disciplinary practice at North End approximates the authoritarian schooling of the poor and the working class criticized by students of power-with-a-face in the classroom. Discipline is directed almost exclusively at the attainment of rewards and the avoidance of punishment. It is normalizing, in the sense that it typically proceeds by drawing attention to and defining as deviant individuals who violate standards of good conduct. And its emphasis is more on unquestioning obedience to imposed rules than the development of students' capacities for autonomous judgment, or their abilities to understand and to consent to rules. Yet the authoritarianism at North End, it seems, is an authoritarianism with reservations. In the last section of the chapter, I probe North End teachers' ambivalence about the "authoritarian" practices in which they participate. Here my aim is to underscore that practices of "classroom management" at this site define power relations characterized by severe asymmetries among participants in the social capacity to evaluate, to deliberate about, and to help determine the collective rules that bind them.

School knowledge

The lesson in the science text book is about stars, and Veronica Franklin begins by asking her students how many of them look up at the sky at night and see the stars. Almost every child raises her hand. Mrs. Franklin proceeds to call on students, one at a time, instructing them to read aloud from the text. Several children take their turns at reading. When there is a pause in the reading, Charles's hand shoots up in the air. "Mrs. Franklin!" he "calls out," not waiting for the teacher to acknowledge him, "What do stars really look like when you go up in space?"

Franklin responds, "I don't know. I've never been up in space," and she asks another child to continue to read from the text. The student reads a passage according to which farmers used to watch the stars in order to know when to plant their crops. At some unspecified time in the past, the passage continues, travelers used stars to find their way. Stars are important to sailors and to various other workers. Some people watch the stars because they think they are beautiful.

"I do," announces Booker, without raising his hand. "I think they're beautiful."

Franklin ignores the comment. She asks her students what they see when they look at the stars at night.

Booker says, "Light."

Victor says, "Shooting stars."

Nicole says, "Falling stars."

The teacher changes the topic. She asks whether any of the children in her class have visited the planetarium at the local campus of the state college, and she instructs a girl who says that she has been there to describe the planetarium to the class.

It is a big room, the girl says, it is dark, there are stars on the ceiling, and "they" tell you about them.

At this point Booker raises his hand, and when Franklin calls his name, he begins to relate a story about people who, he claims, are trying to destroy the planet Earth from Mars. Several students point out that Booker is summarizing the plot of a movie shown recently on television. Franklin announces that Booker can tell the class that story "at 3 p.m.," adding that right now the students in her class are "talking about real things."

Veronica Franklin asks her students to name the planets. Hands shoot up in the air, and children wave them to demonstrate their eagerness to be called on. The first student whose name the teacher calls says, "Neptune."

The second says, "Puerto Rico."

"Puerto Rico is not a planet," responds Franklin.

"Milky Way," says the third student whose name the teacher calls.

"Milky Way is not a planet."

The next three students Franklin chooses say, "Venus," "Jupiter," and "Earth."

"What planet do you live on?" asks the teacher, and the student whose name she calls responds, "Earth!"

Booker, again not raising his hand, makes a comment about "blowing up the planet earth," to which Franklin does not respond.

At the teacher's bidding, Shante reads from the science text book. She reads a passage about the size of the stars. According to the text, stars look small because they are very far away.

"Mrs. Franklin, why do they have to be so far away?" asks Booker. Franklin does not respond.

Victor raises his hand. "But if a star fell," he says in a raised voice, when called on, "it'd be twenty times bigger than a house."

Franklin replies that she does not know if that is so. She directs Shante to continue reading, and the girl reads a passage explaining that stars are composed of gasses. While Shante reads, Asha works on a crayon drawing of a girl. She prints at the top of the paper, above the figure, "Room 18."

"Very good, Shante," announces Veronica Franklin. The teacher comments that Shante read excellently, and then she repeats a statement from the passage that Shante just finished reading. A gas, according to the science book, "has no shape of its own."

"What does that mean?" Franklin asks her students.

Victor raises his hand and answers that it means that it "has no shape of its own." The teacher points out that Victor has repeated what she just said.

Shante raises her hand and suggests that if you put a gas in a cup, it would take the shape of a cup.

Now Franklin begins to read from the science text book. She reads a description of what the text refers to as a "demonstration," which it suggests students perform in the classroom. Franklin announces that the students in her class can try it at home. The demonstration consists of shining a flashlight on the wall in the dark and then turning on a lamp. The light from the flashlight represents a star, and the lamp, the sun. The point, according to the text, is to show that stars shine all the time, but that, when the sun is shining, people cannot see them. Franklin reads her students a question from the text: "Why," she asks, "don't we see a lot of stars shining in New York City?"

Booker answers, "Because it's a bad town?"

Franklin calls on Aman, who says, "Nothing."

She calls on Jaclyn, who says, "A big city has a lot of lights."

"Yes," replies the teacher, "just like the sun."

After directing another student to read a final paragraph from the text, Franklin passes out question-and-answer work sheets. She instructs her students to find the answers to the questions in the passages from the text that they read aloud, and to copy them on the appropriate blank spaces on the work sheets. The children copy answers for most of the remaining class time. When they have completed their work, Franklin reviews the answers.

Charles raises his hand in the middle of this review. "Why is the Big Dipper shaped the way it is?" he asks his teacher.

Franklin says that she does not know. "The class will have to read about that," she says, and she calls on another student to give the answer to the next work sheet question.

At North End, school knowledge is a possession of authorities – of teachers, that is, and ultimately text books – a possession that students, by definition, lack. It consists of bits of factual information (the names of the planets, dictionary definitions of vocabulary words, mathematical symbols and concepts) and the rules that order facts and govern their use (such as rules of grammar and spelling, or procedures for performing mathematical operations). The lesson described above is typical in that the teacher presents it as a series of tasks for students to accomplish in order to acquire knowledge and to demonstrate that they have acquired it, that they are capable of recalling it, and that they are willing to apply it in the ways in which they are instructed. When Veronica Franklin directs her students to read passages about stars from their science text books, answer factual questions about planets and stars, and copy information from the text on to photocopied work sheets, she structures her lesson in much the same way that other lessons at the school (including lessons taught by Franklin and those taught by several other teachers whose classrooms I visited) are structured. At North End, teaching involves imparting knowledge to students, drilling them on the facts and the rules they are required to master, and correcting their mistakes.

I excerpted from my field notes the description of this particular science lesson, not only because it is, in many ways, typical of a lesson at North End, but also because it highlights several characteristics of pedagogic practice there. The first has to do with the classroom teacher's role as the keeper of knowledge. At North End, teachers function to control student access to school knowledge and to judge whether students have acquired the facts and learned the rules that teachers transmit. Thus Franklin chooses the passages her students read in the text book, directs them as they read, quizzes them verbally, and assigns and then reviews the correct answers to questions about the reading. It is worth noting that when the teacher directs her students to fill in their work sheets, she instructs them to do so by copying from the passages they read in their science texts. At North End, to control access to knowledge means not only to dispense the facts and rules outlined in the prescribed curriculum, but also to induce students to adopt the grammar and the diction of academic texts. At times, Franklin takes this mission so far as to reject as incorrect even close paraphrases of answers printed in her teachers' manual, dictating to students the "correct" answers and instructing them to copy them, verbatim, on to their work sheets. She tends to rely heavily on course texts and teachers' manuals to instruct, to drill, and to test. And she generally assumes that she alone in her classroom is competent to judge whether students have acquired the facts and mastered the skills she teaches. Consider the following exchange with Tesha, after she laughs at a classmate who made a mistake when instructed to count aloud by tens:

Franklin turns to Tesha and tells her to count by twenties. Tesha grins but says nothing.
  "See, you can't do it," the teacher announces.
  Tesha says, "No, I just don't want to."
  Franklin responds, "If you don't show me, you can't." She adds, "No one in this class is so much better than the others. If you were, you wouldn't be here. You'd be in a college somewhere. Don't put each other down, we're all trying to learn."

In this exchange, Franklin communicates a strong egalitarian message: no student "is so much better than the others." At the same time, however, she makes it clear that students are neither knowledgeable nor sufficiently competent to contribute to directing or evaluating their own learning. "If you don't show me, you can't." Tesha does not have school knowledge. Nor can she legitimately assert that she has acquired it. Only the teacher can impart knowledge to students and judge whether, and what, they have learned.

The above exchange between Franklin and Tesha illustrates, not only North End teachers' self-definition as the legitimate judges of student knowledgeability, but also a central element in their understanding of the proper attitude of the learner. Franklin corrects Tesha when she claims that she can count by twenties, but chooses not to. In refusing to demonstrate her knowledge as required by her teacher, this girl outsteps her role as a student. At North End, it is not sufficient for the good student to acquire school knowledge. She must also demonstrate that she has acquired it in the ways in which her teacher and her text require. In Franklin's classroom, it is at least as important for students to follow instructions precisely and unquestioningly as it is for them to master the requisite facts and rules. During one lesson, then, Franklin assigns her class a work sheet on writing "friendly letters." The sheet includes a sample letter inviting a friend to attend a party. Most students write letters inviting a classmate to attend a party, but James writes a letter to Natalie Carson, the school principal, inviting her to attend every class at North End "to stop the fooling around and the fighting." James's novel interpretation of this assignment is, by Franklin's standards, wrong. She instructs him to re-write the letter, insisting that students follow not only the form but also the content dictated by the work sheet.

Franklin demands an intellectual obedience, then, that parallels the obedience she requires to school and classroom rules of conduct. What is more, she uses techniques to enforce intellectual discipline that are similar to those she uses to control deviant behavior. She regularly singles out for public praise or reprimand students who excel or fail academically. She rewards those students who absorb and retain information, and who demonstrate their knowledge in the ways in which they are instructed ("Very good, Shante"). She ignores, dismisses, corrects, or punishes not only those children who demonstrate ignorance ("Puerto Rico is not a planet") or make statements unrelated to the subject matter of the lesson ("Right now we are talking about real things"), but also those who attempt to re-direct the lesson by initiating inquiries or raising questions that, although germane, were not introduced by the teacher or the text ("I don't know, I've never been up in space").

An additional parallel between practices of teaching and disciplinary practices at North End is the near total absence of classroom discussion about why students might find it useful to learn specific facts and acquire particular skills. The science lesson described above is typical in that it skips from topic to topic with no apparent rationale. Reading the text book passages and answering the work sheet questions about them serve no evident purpose beyond that of completing the assigned tasks and winning the teacher's approval. Not once during the school year did I observe Veronica Franklin or another North End teacher encourage her students to discuss or to reflect upon the purposes served by their assignments. Only rarely does Franklin offer students reasons for completing their work as instructed, and when she does, she does so exclusively in terms of "getting it right," receiving rewards (such as good grades on tests and report cards), and avoiding punishment and reproach.

The enforcement of intellectual discipline, however, much like the enforcement of rules of conduct, is characterized by inconsistencies and gaps, and by considerable slack in the requirement of rigid adherence to academic standards. A walk down the hall at almost any time during any school day reveals that teachers at North End regularly tolerate classroom activity that is, in the language of professional educators, "off task." Franklin does not stop to correct Asha for drawing a picture during the science lesson. Nor does she consistently intervene when children engage in activities that distract them from classroom lessons or prevent them from completing assignments. Often this teacher permits class discussions to wander off the subject. For instance, she frequently allows students to take turns relating personal anecdotes only tangentially related to the material she is teaching. In conversations with colleagues, Franklin and other North End teachers occasionally express a sense of futility in attempting to impart to students the knowledge they need in order to meet set academic standards, such as those for competence in reading, writing, and mathematics determined by the state and measured by the Connecticut Mastery Test. Veronica Franklin is persistent in her emphasis on the importance of demonstrating obedience to intellectual authority. Yet she neither requires nor expects students to produce complete and accurate work, to demonstrate total obedience in the classroom, or to acquire all the facts and master all the rules ordained by the school district curriculum.

The responsible student

The children in Veronica Franklin's classroom are eating their breakfasts in silence when the sound of loud voices erupts in the hall. Several people speak at once, but one voice, a child's, distinguishes itself from the din. The child is shouting that Booker has a gun. Franklin gets up from her seat and walks quickly to the hallway, where her voice joins the others. She speaks in hushed tones with another adult. She scolds the children until the clamor in the hallway dies down. Back in the classroom, Franklin's students talk to each other excitedly. Someone says that Booker brought "a weapon" to school.

After several minutes, Booker enters the classroom, his head hung down and his lower lip protruding in a pout. He is followed by his teacher, who speaks to him sharply. "You brought that on yourself," she says. The boy, who I learn later broke school rules by bringing a water pistol to school in his book bag, takes his seat without speaking. He puts his head down on the desk and says nothing while Franklin takes attendance, collects homework, and administers the weekly spelling test.

After the test, the teacher begins the day's reading lesson, which consists of a review of a text book story that her class previously read aloud. She asks questions about the plot and calls on students to answer. The story line, I surmise from the review, is roughly as follows:

One morning the principal of a school announces over the loud speaker that, from that point on, children are forbidden to play soccer at the school. He decided to prohibit the game, he explains, because a student recently was injured while playing soccer. The students in the fictional class express to each other their dissatisfaction with the principal's decision, and they agree to send several of their number to his office to meet with him and to convey their disgruntlement. Among the ambassadors is Julio, a shy boy who, according to the reader, "never said anything in class." Upon entering the principal's office, Julio alone speaks up and makes a case for permitting students to play soccer at school. His classmates feel intimidated in the presence of the principal, but Julio advances a number of compelling arguments, ultimately convincing the principal.

When Julio and his classmates return to their classroom, Cricket, a girl who was present at the meeting, but did not speak, tries to gloss over the fact that Julio alone addressed the principal. "The matter is all arranged," she announces, implicitly taking credit for the meeting's success. But Lucas, who was also present during the meeting, explains to the others that Julio is responsible for its success.

Lucas withdraws his own name from the ballot for the upcoming election for class president, and he nominates Julio in his place. The story ends with an account of the election, which Julio wins.

After reviewing the plot of the story chronologically, Franklin asks her students which qualities Julio displayed to demonstrate that he would make a good class president. One student responds that Julio "spoke up to the principal."

"He had confidence," says another.

"He wasn't shy any more."

"He had strong feelings."

Several students offer one-word answers to the question, for example, "Brave," and "Faith." Booker raises his hand and, when Franklin calls on him, he speaks for the first time since entering the classroom that morning. "Responsible," he says.

At this point, the teacher stops to remind her students that they are going to continue to work on their "campaign speeches," which they are modeling on a sample from a work sheet that accompanies the basal reader story. "Tomorrow," she announces, "we'll go over them and decide who is going to run for office." The following day, she says, the students in the class will have their own election.

Booker yells out, "Yes! Yes! I'm gonna be president. I wanna run!" to which Mrs. Franklin replies, "Then you have to have those qualities, so your classmates will vote for you."

The teacher returns to the review of the story. She asks the class why Cricket went to the principal's office. But before she permits anyone to respond, Franklin, raising her eyebrows, comments that Cricket "had a lot to say" when she got back to the classroom. She asks why neither Cricket nor Lucas said anything in the principal's office.

"Because they were afraid," offers the first student Franklin calls on.

"Why?"

"Because he shouted at them," says Booker.

"Did he shout at them?" asks Franklin, and her fourth graders yell, in unison, "No!"

Another student raises her hand and, when called on, she paraphrases from the text: "Because he looked in their eyes like his eyes could go right through their heads." Veronica Franklin reminds the children in her class that the children in the story learned that "the principal was not so mean." In the end, he arranged for extra teachers to supervise in the playground, so that students could play soccer safely.

"Responsibility" is a central theme in Veronica Franklin's classroom, where this teacher communicates to students three inter-related, but analytically distinct messages about individual responsibility. First, she stresses in classroom lessons, and in group and one-on-one discussions with children, responsibility is a desirable personal characteristic. The responsible student fulfills the obligations associated with being a student. She acknowledges, accepts, and consistently acts to fulfill her teacher's requirements and expectations. This first message takes the form of an imperative to adopt the behaviors, values, goals, attitudes, and beliefs that make possible a neat fit between the individual child and the role of the student as defined at North End. It is invoked in response to student failures to meet teacher expectations ranging from those regarded as commonplace (for example, Franklin complains, when several children come to class without pencils to complete their work, that the problem with her fourth grade is that there are "so many irresponsible people" in it) to those regarded as exceptional, or even grave. An example of the latter is Booker's infraction described at the beginning of the above vignette. The case went to the school principal, and the boy's mother was called in later that day for a conference. What might strike some as an incongruity between the apparent triviality of this offense and the drama surrounding the event is less puzzling when considered in light of the significance teachers at North End accord to this injunction to "be responsible." In the final section of this chapter, I describe a conflict that Franklin and other teachers at the school perceive between, on the one hand, being responsible in the sense of being accountable to authorities and fulfilling expectations and obligations, and on the other, conforming to competing norms, which teachers identify with what some refer to as "the street." North End teachers, I argue, tend to perceive "responsible citizenship" and "the street" as distinct trajectories that individual lives might take, and to view the latter as harmful to those who follow it. It is likely, then, that for Franklin, Carson, and the other adults involved, the incident described above is not simply about a child bringing to school a toy that, according to school rules, should stay home. Instead, it is about a particular child – whom, as I argue below, they view as teetering precariously on the line that divides "responsibility" from the "street" – opposing the former standard by bringing to school a symbol of the latter. In the vignette above, Booker serves as a foil to Julio, the protagonist from the reading text story, who demonstrates that he is responsible by fulfilling the trust, the obligation, the duty with which his classmates charge him.

The second message Franklin regularly communicates to her fourth graders is one of responsibility as a natural fact. The individual is responsible for the outcomes her actions cause. Franklin teaches her students that, by virtue of her character, talents, desires, and capacities, combined with the choices she makes about how to use these, the individual child is the author of her future. In the story the class reviews during the lesson described above, the perceived constraints in the social environment are not real. The principal is "not so mean," and there is nothing stopping the fictional children from attaining the result that they want. What determines one's lot in life, Franklin explains to her students repeatedly, and in a variety of ways, is who one is, combined with the choices one makes. In a typical exchange, then, she attributes academic failures to her students' unwillingness to work to develop their intellectual talents and capacities. "You know what really bothers me?" she scolds her class. "You people don't want to learn. You have the ability, but," and at this point the students, familiar with their teacher's complaint, chime in, "*you don't use it.*" Students are responsible for the negative consequences of their actions ("You brought that on yourself"). They are capable of meeting their goals and fulfilling their aspirations, if only they make and act upon the appropriate choices. What are the appropriate choices? The choices made by the student who "is responsible," in the sense that she fulfills her teacher's expectations and requirements. Hence, on one of several occasions on which Booker announces that he hopes to become a lawyer when he grows up, Franklin responds by asking, "Then what do you have to do?" "Don't talk. My behavior," says the boy, eliciting from his teacher a nod of approval. As a matter of fact, Booker *is responsible* for what becomes of him. He must choose to *be responsible*, that is, willingly to conduct himself so that he fulfills the obligations associated with his role as a student at North End, if he is to achieve his goals and fulfill his aspirations.

The third message about responsibility that Franklin communicates to her students is that they should "take responsibility," in the sense of blame for personal shortcomings and failures. This injunction follows logically from the claims that students should be responsible, in the sense that they should be accountable to those in authority, and that they are responsible, in the sense that they are the agents of the outcomes caused by their actions. In order to correct one's deficiencies and thereby improve one's future, one must first own up to one's failures to meet expectations and fulfill obligations. It becomes apparent, then, during the course of the class review of the basal reader story that the least likable character is the girl named Cricket. Franklin's tone of voice is sarcastic when she comments that Cricket "had a lot to say" when she returned to the classroom. On more than one occasion during the course of the review, the teacher returns to the content of Cricket's statement: "The matter is all arranged." Cricket, like Lucas, fails to fulfill her duties. But unlike Lucas, who redeems himself, at least partially, by admitting publicly that Julio is the better candidate for class president, Cricket refuses to take responsibility for her own ineptitude. Throughout the school year, Franklin regularly urges her students to "take responsibility" in this sense: to give credit where credit is due and to acknowledge and accept blame for personal flaws and failures. This teacher stresses, in particular, that students should "take responsibility" when they fail to "be responsible." For example, every day after she takes attendance, she calls the names of her students, one by one, requiring each to state publicly whether or not she completed her homework. If the answer is "No," Franklin asks "Why not?" But she invariably rejects as unacceptable the explanation the student offers. "No excuses," she scolds one typical morning. "You are responsible."

The report cards that North End's district prints for all its elementary schools are divided into two sections: "Progress in School Subjects" and "Progress in Effort and Social Responsibility." The centrality of this theme, the reports suggest, is not unique to the North End Community

School. The latter half of the report provides space for teachers to record student grades in five categories, which are illustrated as follows:

Category	Illustration
"Behavior"	A white girl sits at a desk, raising her hand.
"Work Habits"	A white girl sits at a desk, holding a pencil in her hand and striking a pose that suggests that she is listening attentively.
"Social Habits"	A white boy and a white girl stand, a ball in mid-air between them.
"Attitudes"	A white boy stands in front of a police officer, who lifts the child by his shirt collar.
"Attendance"	(No illustration)

Here, as in Franklin's classroom, student responsibility is defined in terms of conducting oneself in ways that render one trustworthy in the eyes of school authorities. These include abiding by classroom rules, adhering to social norms when interacting with peers, demonstrating deference to authority, and showing a desire to succeed academically. The illustrations implicitly equate the standard of responsibility with dominant social groups, in particular the white middle class, and deviation from it with lawlessness or delinquency. I return to this association in the final section of the chapter, where I argue that Franklin and other adults at the North End Community School define as among their principal pedagogic aims inducing students to accept and to conform to middle-class attitudinal and behavioral norms, which they view as critical to avoiding "the street" and the threats it poses to students' security and well-being.

Before turning to a consideration of student responses to the classroom experience at North End, I want to draw attention to the fact that, in Franklin's fourth grade, it is not uncommon for particular children to fail on a consistent basis to measure up to this standard of responsibility as accountability. The composition of the student body changes during the course of the academic year, but at any given point in Franklin's classroom three to five out of approximately eighteen children are regarded as "problem students" by their teacher and by other school authorities. Booker is a paradigmatic case. He regularly fails to fulfill the academic and behavioral obligations assigned to the role of student at North End, prompting his teacher to express, on more than one occasion, her desire to "have him tested." When teachers at the school become exasperated with students who fail to "be responsible" in this sense, among the most common responses is to attempt to initiate evaluation by a team of specialists whose job is to identify and to label psychological, social, emotional, linguistic, and other developmental problems. Booker's mother refuses to grant the legally required parental permission to have her son "tested," compounding Franklin's frustration. But the teacher remains suspicious, as she explains repeatedly, both to me and to other adults at the school, that there is something profoundly wrong with Booker.

That some children are deficient in ways that render them incapable of functioning as responsible students is made evident to Franklin and her colleagues by the example of the "Learning Resource Program" (LRP) students mainstreamed into some non special-education classes for part of each school day. These children, most of whom are classified EMR (educably mentally retarded), are, in Franklin's words, "underachievers." Incapable of comprehending and fulfilling the duties of the normal student, they are by virtue of their deficits unable to conform to the standard of responsibility as accountability. "That's why you'll never move, honey, cause you can't do right," Franklin tells one LRP student who fails to follow instructions during math class. "Can't do right to save your life." When there is a persistent disparity between, on the one hand, standards of responsible performance and conduct, and on the other, the behavior of an individual child, North End teachers tend to reach for a label to explain their repeated failure to accomplish the task of inducing the child to meet expectations and fulfill obligations.

Conversations I observed among teachers in the faculty room over lunch, before and after school, and during non-instructional periods, as well as interviews I conducted with teachers and other staff members, reveal, however, that the views adults at North End hold about individual responsibility are considerably more complex than the messages they communicate to students. They suggest that neither Franklin nor her colleagues believe the simple story about human agency outlined above. As I explain in greater detail in the final section, adults at North End tend to experience school outcomes, both behavioral and academic, as, to a significant extent, socially structured. They do not unequivocally embrace the conventional morality they preach. Submissiveness to authority, obedience to imposed rules, and a proclivity to fulfill duties defined by others, I argue, are not necessarily what North End teachers ultimately want, or hope for, from the children they teach. What is more, teachers and other adults at the school do not consider children there wholly blameworthy for all, or even for most, failures to meet attitudinal, behavioral, and academic standards. Thus, on the same day that Booker brings his "gun" to school, Yvette Smith, North End's other fourth grade teacher, comments over lunch in the faculty room – eliciting expressions of agreement from Franklin as well as the other teachers present – that adults at North End need frequently to remind themselves that "what goes on at this school is not the fault of the students."

Power: action upon action

Accounts of power's various faces in the classroom suggest that pedagogic practice at North End is more than a mere anomaly. An authoritarian style of discipline not dissimilar to the one I describe has been associated at least since Bowles and Gintis's seminal study with the schooling of the working class and the poor.[32] Franklin's presentation of school knowledge approximates what Freire called the "banking model" of education.[33] And, at North End, the ideology of individual responsibility as accountability, agency, and blame functions as part of the "hidden curriculum" through which, according to critical educational theorists, teachers shape student attitudes, beliefs, values, and aspirations.[34] Does this mean that Franklin is a powerful "A" who exercises power over her students? In the next section, I take issue with the view that this teacher "has" and "uses" power over the children in her charge.

First, however, I make the case that pedagogic practices at North End define power relations that constrain students' freedom, by severely restricting their capacity to act in ways that affect classroom rules, standards, and other key boundaries to action. Granted, some constraint on this capacity to "act upon" power's mechanisms is unavoidable in any educative process, and in particular in any such process that involves young children. At North End, however, these restrictions are extreme. Students are almost completely excluded from processes of evaluating, deliberating about, and helping decide rules of conduct, as well as from processes of determining the conditions governing their work and learning. What is more, the local definition of a standard of responsibility as accountability to adults in positions of authority supports and reinforces these restrictions. In the discussion that follows, I present ethnographic as well as survey evidence suggesting that the effect of pedagogic practices at North End is, in fact, to discourage students from acting upon classroom rules and norms, and standards of academic competence and excellence. Lessons about individual responsibility, my data suggest, reinforce authoritarianism by teaching children to view accountability as a desirable personal trait, which enables people to succeed. These lessons may further limit the social capacity to act in ways that alter or otherwise affect social relations of power, by deflecting criticism from structural sources of inequality, to personal failures to "be responsible."

---

[32] Bowles and Gintis (1976). See also Anyon (1980, 1981, and 1997), Carnoy and Levin (1985), and Mickelson (1980).
[33] Freire (1970 and 1987), and Shor and Freire (1987).   [34] Bowles and Gintis (1976).

"Better schools make better tomorrows"

The subtitle above, Veronica Franklin informs me one mid-November morning, is the theme for American Education Week. North End's principal, Natalie Carson, has directed teachers to have their students write essays on the theme, and she has announced that she will award prizes for the best essays in the school. Franklin asks me to introduce the assignment to her students and to conduct a short lesson, to help get them started writing their essays.

"Better schools make better tomorrows." I begin by writing the theme on the chalkboard and telling Franklin's class about the essay contest. "What do you think of when you hear 'Better schools make better tomorrows'?" I ask, and almost every child in the class raises her hand. I call names, one by one, and copy student responses on to the board. Each response to my question, without exception, is a statement to the effect that students at North End should obey a particular rule or set of rules prescribed by teachers and other school authorities. Students should not threaten other students, for example. Children at North End should come to school wearing their uniforms every day.

"*Why* should students wear uniforms?" I ask, hoping to move the brainstorming session away from the enumeration of rules.

One girl raises her hand and, when I call her name, answers, "Because it's a uniform school."

I point out that the class has listed a lot of rules on the board, and I ask why the children think these are important. Why, I ask, would following these rules make for "better schools"? Again, the majority of Mrs. Franklin's students raise their hands, apparently eager to be called on. But the only responses my question elicits are recitations of still more school rules.

Students at the North End Community School are encouraged neither to inquire into the purposes rules serve nor to evaluate their fairness, soundness, or expediency. The emphasis teachers and other school authorities place on unquestioning obedience to imposed rules discourages these forms of critical thinking. In the time I spent at the school, I never observed a child presented with the opportunity to question or to challenge school or classroom rules, or to participate in collective processes of deliberating about, making, evaluating, or amending them.

Does this mean that the children at North End abide by rules completely or embrace them without reservation? Far from it. Franklin's students and other children at the school evince a range of the contestatory behaviors celebrated by "resistance" theorists of schooling. Student protests against school regulations and discipline are, however, restricted in patterned ways. They center almost exclusively on the facts of individual cases of alleged wrongdoing and perceived lapses in the impartiality of the administration of punishment. They take the form of denials, counter-accusations, and demonstrations of affective reactions to punishment, such as shame or anger. Typical in kind, if somewhat extreme in degree, is Charles's reaction to being punished by the music teacher for talking during class, described in the following excerpt from my field notes:

When the students are on their way back from music, there is a scene in the hallway between Charles and Franklin . . . Charles cries and bangs his fists on the wall. Franklin tells me, as I approach, that, as Charles left the music room, he walked away from her angrily toward the exit of the building, as if he were going to leave the school. She tells him sternly that there are "no babies here." I offer to stay in the hallway with Charles while Franklin escorts the rest of the students back to the classroom.

The boy continues to cry and to bang his hands against the wall. I ask him why he is upset, and he tells me that he was falsely accused. The music teacher, he says, put a check next to his name in her roll book, when not he, but James, was talking. Charles tells me that he received no star for the day's music lesson, and that he now has lost his chance to earn a prize from the teacher's prize jar.

What Franklin identifies as "babyishness" – an immature overreaction to a trivial conflict – is, no doubt, in part an expression of Charles's anger and frustration at his experience of the arbitrariness of discipline. This student attributes the misdeed of which he is accused to his classmate James, and he decries the unfairness of the punishment he received at the hands of the music teacher. He does not, however – and in this sense his response is typical – challenge the content of the rule he is said to have violated, the appropriateness of the punishment attached to the transgression, or the processes by which rule and punishment are decided and enforced.

Students at North End are not encouraged to, nor do they tend to, deliberate about the ends school and classroom rules serve, or the fit between those ends and the means employed to attain them. They are not offered opportunities in school to discuss with others or legitimately to contest the regulations and policies that govern their activities. Good children, they are told both implicitly and explicitly, accept uncritically and unconditionally rules imposed by adults.

My participant-observation data suggest that students at North End learn this lesson well. They seem to equate "better schools" with more perfect student compliance. In their day-to-day responses to the practice of classroom discipline, North End students tend to accept rules as given and to regard them as tools for the production of obedience, rather than the promotion of students' well-being or the interests of school community as a whole. When they evaluate the practice of discipline, they do so positively with circular reference to extant rules ("Because it's a uniform school") or with reference to the judgment of authorities. Alternatively, they negatively valuate disciplinary practice with reference to inconsistencies in the administration of punishment. Rarely do they criticize the content or the effect of rules with reference either to what, in their own judgment, are valuable ends or to some standard of reasonableness.

Students of power's various faces in the classroom suggest that authoritarian disciplinary practices in schools serving members of marginalized social and economic groups depart from those serving dominant groups. The former, the literature suggests, promote skills, attitudes, values, and beliefs needed for lives of "powerlessness," while the latter foster competencies required for effective participation in collective self-government.[35] In chapter 5, I present comparative participant-observation data that demonstrate that both "classroom management" and student responses to discipline at the predominantly white, affluent, suburban Fair View Elementary depart radically from disciplinary practices and student responses at North End. Patterned differences in pedagogic practice, my evidence suggests, may contribute to asymmetries in the social capacity to act in ways that affect rules and other boundaries that shape the field of the possible.

Further support can be adduced from written responses to questions about the purpose and fairness of school rules, which I posed to the universe of fourth and fifth graders at the North End Community School and fourth graders at Fair View Elementary.[36] The first question, "In school we have rules, like, 'Don't run in the hallway.' Why do you think we need rules?" was worded to suggest clear purposes for school rules: to prevent harm to students and promote their safety and well-being, and to promote order and prevent disorder in the school. At both schools, the largest group of students answer with reference to harm or order. At North End, however, a significantly larger group, 38 percent, compared with 15 percent at Fair View, offer circular explanations of the purpose rules serve, for example, "So you can follow them," or "We need rules because so we won't get in trouble"; explain their function in terms of the

---

[35] Anyon (1980, 1981, and 1997), Bowles and Gintis (1976), Carnoy and Levin (1985), and Mickelson (1980).

[36] I questioned and received responses from all North End fourth and fifth graders and Fair View fourth graders present the day I administered surveys. Respondents totaled 133: 55 at the North End Community School and 78 at Fair View Elementary (which ends at fourth grade). For exact wording, see Appendix B.

bad character of children, for example, "We need rule[s] because kids are bad and they don't give respect," or "Because some people are bad and don't want to learn anything"; or offer no explanation at all, for example, "I don't know why."[37]

I followed this question with one asking students to evaluate the fairness of rules at their school: "Are the rules at [North End/Fair View] fair? Why?" At Fair View Elementary, the majority of the students, 65 percent, answer with reference to the well-being of students. For example, "I think the rules at Fair View are fair. Because they have to do with are [our] safety and us learning." At North End, more than half offer no explanation, or explain only with reference to trust in the judgment of school authorities or the effectiveness of rules at producing conformity to a behavioral norm. For example:

Yes they are fare [fair] rules. To let you know that you have to follow rules.

I think they are fair personly [personally] to me. Everybody everywhere should have rules everywhere they go.

Yes. Because if the rules were not fair they would not have made them.

The rules at North End is fair and right to do. Because they won't tell you no wrong thing to do to make you get in more trouble.

Yes. So people won't do thing bad [bad things].

As the above responses suggest, North End students who offer no explanation for their judgment or answer with reference only to trust in authorities or the effectiveness of rules at producing conformity are, disproportionately, students who accept school rules as fair. At Fair View, by contrast, where only 26 percent fall into this category, they tend to be children who judge rules to be unfair, for example because they do not like a particular rule or rules:

Not always. Because the rule, sit at assigned talble [table] isin't [isn't] fair because some people we sit with can be discusting [disgusting] or something. And we like to sit near our friends.

or because they do not trust in the judgment of school authorities:

Most of them. [Some are not fair] because sometimes you have to do exactly what the teacher says but I think I do better doing things my way.

At North End, almost half of the students who judge rules unfair explain their judgment with reference to the inconsistent enforcement of discipline. For example:

No. If reveren [Reverend] Johnson is mad at me and I did something he would get me [but] if a person that he likes did the same thing he would not do nothing.

---

[37] For a breakdown of student responses to this question, see Appendix A, table 7.

No because if one person talking to the other person and the teacher get one of the person[s] and [the] other one do not get in trouble that's not fair.

Only 26 percent, compared with 65 percent at Fair View, make reference to student well-being in their response to this question. And only 5 percent, compared with 18 percent at Fair View, refer to a standard of reasonableness.[38]

Clearly, the above is not a causal argument. Limits to my data prevent me from advancing one. It is likely that a range of extra-school factors excluded from my study, such as disciplinary practice in families, contributes to systematic differences in student attitudes toward rules and authority at North End and Fair View. It seems plausible, however, that patterned differences in pedagogic practice contribute to the differential development of attitudes, beliefs, values, and competencies that enable and promote effective participation in helping determine, evaluate, and change collective rules and norms. The possible implications for democratic participation are troubling. Franklin and other adults at North End severely restrict the scope within which children at the school can participate in reasoning and deliberating about, and making decisions about how to govern school activities. One need not prove that differences in pedagogic practice cause the attitudinal differences described above to rouse democratic suspicions toward them. If opportunities to participate in reasoning and deliberating about, and making decisions about how to govern classroom activities are severely limited in some schools serving children of the poor and marginalized racial and ethnic groups – that is, if such opportunities are limited in public institutions that these children are required by law to attend – then the concerns voiced by critical educational theorists and others who study the role power plays in the classroom are warranted.

"I ain't doing this!"

Veronica Franklin begins the science lesson by assigning to each group of three or four students two planets, and instructing the children to use their text books and classroom encyclopedias to write reports about them.

Jocelyn announces, "I ain't doing this!" She puts her head down on her desk.

Charles says that he is not going to do the assignment, either.

"Charles said he wasn't going to do it," Tesha reports to Franklin, who has not acknowledged either child's remark.

"He better do it," she responds. "Or I'll put him out of this room."

---

[38] For a breakdown of student responses to this question, see Appendix A, table 7.

Veronica Franklin tends to define school knowledge as facts and the rules governing their use, and to require that her students demonstrate, in the way she prescribes, that they have absorbed the requisite "pieces of knowledge." The purpose of learning, this teacher implies, is to meet the expectations of school authorities, to earn rewards in the form of good grades and prizes, and to avoid punishment. During the class period that follows the above exchange, then, Franklin has her students copy paragraphs about the planets from text and reference books and demonstrate that they have performed the assigned task by reading their "reports" in front of the class and submitting them to her. The lesson is like most of this teacher's lessons in that it includes no discussion of why it is important to learn, in this instance, facts about the planets, or what purpose is served by copying from texts. Franklin requires of her students an intellectual obedience that entails accepting unquestioningly her definitions of valid knowledge and demonstrating knowledgeability in the ways she demands.

Like her strategies for classroom management, Franklin's teaching techniques fail to generate perfect student compliance. Instead, her fourth graders exhibit a range of responses, from near total embrace of the role of the learner as their teacher defines it, to occasional outright refusals to comply with her demands. Charles and Jocelyn provide examples of the latter response ("I ain't doing this!"). Candy is an example of a student who regularly falls into the former category. She follows her teacher's instructions perfectly almost all of the time and, on the rare occasion on which she fails to, becomes visibly distraught.[39] Most of the time, the majority of Franklin's students fall between these extremes, practicing less directly confrontational forms of resistance, for example, performing assigned tasks incompletely or with deliberate carelessness, or expressing disdain for particular assignments or academic subjects. Consider Jaclyn's reaction to the frustration she experiences while trying to complete an assignment, described in the following excerpt from my field notes:

Jaclyn, who is working on a science work sheet, asks me to check it for her several times. Each time, she has almost all of the answers wrong. She says, "How can I get this right?" and then writes on the top of her paper, "I hate science."

Jaclyn's response is typical in that, although she defies her teacher by expressing contempt for the knowledge she instructed her to acquire ("I

---

[39] One morning, for example, she comes to school with dark circles under her eyes, and when I ask her what is wrong, explains that she was unable to sleep the night before because she left her homework assignment in school and was worried that she would be in trouble with Mrs. Franklin.

hate science"), she accepts her definition of valid knowledge, as well as her implicit contention that the purpose of school work is to "get [it] right." Student resistance to instruction at North End takes the form of a (total or partial) withdrawal from classroom activities, a rejection of school knowledge as irrelevant, and/or a refusal to perform assigned tasks. But even those children who are willing to risk punishment by openly defying their teacher (such as Charles and Jocelyn in the above vignette) stop short of questioning or contesting her judgments about what counts as valid knowledge or what purposes school work serves. They do not, for example, challenge Franklin by asking why they should learn about the planets, or why they should do so by copying information from text and reference books. Students at North End tend to accept teacher definitions of school knowledge as isolated facts and rules, and to understand the function of learning in the classroom in terms of meeting the expectations of those in positions of authority, earning rewards, and avoiding punishment.

Comparative participant-observation data in chapter 5 paint a strikingly different picture of student attitudes toward school work at Fair View Elementary. The difference is reflected, as well, in written responses to questions about the significance of classroom learning. The majority of fourth and fifth graders at the North End Community School answer the question, "What is the most important thing you learned this year?" by naming either a subject – for example, "I learned math" – or an isolated fact or rule – for example, "I learned my time table because I had only new [known] my 2 throw [through] my 4." The second most common response is to name a rule of conduct, for example, "The most important thing is to coroll [control] my altutude [attitude]." At Fair View, by contrast, most name as the most important thing learned an integrated set of facts or cognitive, personal, or interpersonal skills, or an insight about the self or the social world. For example:

I learned about analyising [analyzing] books.

The most important thing I learned this year is how to solve problems.

Once, we made a contract to the teacher, with goals of achievements, both acedemicly [academically] and personally. This was probably the most important thing I learned, worked for goals.

The most important thing I learned this year is how to deal with difficult people.

I learned that it doesn't matter if you're good or not, we're all equal.

Only 31 percent list a subject name or an isolated fact or rule, compared with almost twice that many, 60 percent, at North End. And only 4 percent, compared with 18 percent at North End, name a behavioral norm or a rule of conduct.[40]

When asked to explain why what they name is important, the majority of students at both schools make reference to utility. They suggest that what they identified as the most important thing they learned is useful to them now, or will be useful in the future to attain some individual or collective good. At Fair View, however, a larger percentage name a specific use for what they learned, for example:

I think that probably the most important think [thing] I learned this year was when and where to put commas in a sentence. I think this is <u>very</u> important because if you didn't have commas in a sentence then not everything would sound right. You could have sentences that make you use all of your breath in one sentence, and that isn't always great.

This most important thing I learned this year was to be neat and orgainized [organized]. Neatness helps me because every thing is easyer [easier] if your [you're] neat. Because you'll be able to get things done quickly and well.

How to be a leader in a group. So everyone does the right thing, and no one gets lost in what you're working on.

More than half of those who answer with reference to utility, or 32 percent of the total of Fair View fourth graders, fall into this category. At North End, by contrast, less than a third of those who answer with reference to utility, and only 18 percent of all respondents, name a specific use. The majority simply state that what they learned is useful or make reference to a general context in which it might become useful. For example:

I learned new words and more Math. Because when [I] am in the 6th grade I will have to know some of the things.

The most important thing I learned is long divion [division]. You might have to use it when you get older.

The most important thing I learn is divison [division]. [It] is important because it's a lot of problem to do with it.

What is more, at North End 29 percent, compared with only 18 percent at Fair View, offer no explanation at all of the importance of what they learned or explain only with reference to avoiding punishment, receiving rewards, or fulfilling requirements determined by those in positions of authority. For example:

Math & Reading. Because They are important that we do them.

How to respect other's [others] and not show my temper in class. So I can keep my files say she has never been saspinded [suspended].

---

[40] For a breakdown of student responses to this question, see Appendix A, table 8.

How to do type of math. Because I'm not to [too] good in all subjects.

A lot of things like math, readen [reading], language, spelling and lots of other things. Because we have to learn about all of it.[41]

Again, this is not a causal argument. It seems far from implausible, however, that Franklin's pedagogic practices, and in particular the ways in which she defines school knowledge and the proper role of the learner, constrain her students' freedom. They likely help encourage the types of student responses described above, which range from near perfect compliance to the outright rejection of school knowledge, the refusal to complete assigned work, and withdrawal from classroom activities. They do not encourage, and seem actively to discourage, the development of beliefs, attitudes, and skills that enable and promote participation in processes of critically evaluating, making, and re-making definitions of valid knowledge, the ends of schooling, and the best means to realize those ends. An important hypothesis developed by critical educational theorists is that patterned differences in the schooling of members of dominant and marginalized groups contribute to the differential development of competencies needed for relatively autonomous professional jobs, such as self-discipline, self-motivation, and self-direction.[42] Clearly, Franklin's actions alone do not cause her students to have diminished access to professional work and to the middle-class incomes and lifestyles that accompany it. Yet a plausible interpretation of my data is that her pedagogic practices contribute to the reproduction of economic and social hierarchies by shaping students' perceptions of what school knowledge is and why one acquires it, in ways that foster cognitive capacities and habits, beliefs, attitudes, and behaviors – including forms of resistance – appropriate for low-status, low-paying work directed and controlled by others.

"Sometimes I don't like myself so much"

At dismissal, Franklin instructs her students to stand up and quietly put their chairs on top of their desks.

She then decides that they were too noisy, and so she tells them to take the chairs off their desks and sit down again. She waits for a moment. She announces that one child in the classroom is not ready to leave for the day.

"Booker!" her students shout at the prompt.

"Why you always saying 'Booker'?" responds the boy to his classmates. One of the girls answers, "Because you always doing something."

Franklin scolds Booker. She asks why he sits back in his seat looking

---

[41] For a breakdown of student responses to this question, see Appendix A, table 8.
[42] The best-known statement is Bowles and Gintis (1976).

proud of himself every time he gets in trouble. She asks if he *likes* to get in trouble. She asks if he likes the attention.

Booker answers, "Sometimes I don't like myself so much."

I argued above that Veronica Franklin teaches her students three inter-related lessons about individual responsibility. First, children should *be responsible* to school authorities. They should readily assume and fulfill the obligations associated with the role of the student at North End, by conducting themselves as required and by adopting the attitudes, values, motivations, and goals that render them trustworthy in the eyes of teachers and other adults at the school. Second, the individual student, by virtue of who she is and the choices she makes, *is responsible* for both the positive and the negative consequences of her actions. She is the author of her future. And third, the child who fails to meet the expectations of those in authority should *take responsibility* for her shortcomings as well as the consequences that follow from them. It is important to acknowledge that the source of personal failure is one's own character, combined with the choices one makes. The individual must own up to her shortcomings in order to correct her deficiencies and improve her lot in life.

As might be expected, given that Franklin, like other adults at North End, gives students few opportunities to "be responsible" and little incentive to "take responsibility" (that is, given the constant and close supervision at the school and the frequency of reprimand and punishment), these lessons fail to produce perfect conformity with local standards of responsibility. Rather than consistently "being responsible" to school authorities, the majority of Franklin's students resist fulfilling expectations and requirements when it seems likely that they can do so with impunity. Generally, pandemonium breaks out when the teacher steps out of the classroom to speak with another adult in the hallway, and when a substitute takes her place for the day, few students complete even a fraction of the work they are assigned. Nor do Franklin's fourth graders, generally, "take responsibility" as their teacher exhorts them to. Consider, for example, the common practice of denying allegations and lodging counter-accusations at fellow classmates when reprimanded for violating school and classroom rules.

My participant-observation data do, however, reveal three patterned student responses to the classroom experience at North End, which suggest that Franklin's lessons about responsibility constrain her students' freedom. First, when this teacher draws students' attention to individual failures to conform to behavioral and attitudinal requirements, or to meet academic expectations, they tend to join her in denouncing the deviant. During the class dismissal described above, Booker's classmates shout his name on cue and with apparent enthusiasm, implicitly endorsing their teacher's negative valuation of this boy who is "always doing something" that the responsible student does not do. The vignette illustrates that this devaluation of actors who fail to conform to standards of responsibility extends, at times, to intrasubjective judgments ("Sometimes I don't like myself so much"). Although, as I argue above, there is a considerable range in student response to the classroom experience at North End, no child unequivocally rejects Franklin's definition and acclamation of the responsible student. Even Booker, the class "bad boy," is at times self-critical when he fails to meet his teacher's requirements and expectations. He announces, for instance, in the wake of a minor academic failure, that he is "dumb" and "stupid." On more than one occasion he endorses Franklin's censure of his classroom conduct. Consider the following field notes excerpt:

During the math lesson, Franklin asks Kevin what eighteen minus nine is, and he hesitates before responding. Booker yells, "You should have known that since the second grade!"

Franklin turns to Booker and asks, "Then what is it?"

"Nine," he answers.

Franklin says, "Is it nice to put him down for thinking? There's a lot of things you should've known since the second grade. Like how to act."

Booker responds, "That's what I was gonna say."

Booker outsteps the role of the student, in this instance, by "yelling out," rather than waiting to be called on, by failing to be "nice" to a peer, and by passing judgment on his classmate's knowledgeability, which at North End only the teacher legitimately can do. Yet at the same time he endorses Franklin's criticism of his failure to know "how to act" and to regulate his behavior accordingly. Even if the teacher is correct in positing that Booker likes the attention he receives when he "gets in trouble," this enjoyment marks, at best, an ambivalence about his status as a "problem student." Like the majority of his classmates, Booker tends to concur with the teacher's judgment that failures to meet standards of responsible character and conduct are evidence of stupidity, a "bad attitude," or another personal defect.

Not only do Franklin's fourth graders tend to accept her definition of discrepancies between the self and the responsible student as deficiencies; they further identify these as the source of a host of difficulties ranging from immediate inconveniences to more significant and long-term problems. In the estimation of his classmates, then, the fact that Booker is "always doing something" interferes with their prompt dismissal. For many North End fourth and fifth graders, the bad character, bad attitudes, and bad actions of children at the school are the cause of its most pressing problems, including its lack of physical safety and its poor academic standing. In response to the questions, "If you could change one thing about [North End/Fair View] or your classroom, what would you change? Why?" almost a third of North End fourth and fifth graders, compared with only 4 percent of fourth graders at Fair View Elementary, answer with reference to the "badness" of students. For example:

I would change all the bad kids. If I don't they would start trouble.

I will stop the fighting and profaneity [profanity]. So the school will be safe.

I change kids from being bad! Because I want to see every bad kids have a job and [not] be hanging around on the street.[43]

As the last answer illustrates, Veronica Franklin's fourth graders and their schoolmates tend to draw a strong causal connection between, on the one hand, the degree to which an individual conforms to standards of responsibility, and on the other, what the future holds for her, in particular whether she will realize responsible goals and aspirations. Booker, for example, who announces repeatedly during the course of the school year that he hopes to become a lawyer when he grows up, because, in his words, "All I know is a lawyer is important," associates realizing this goal with changing his attitudes, conduct, and performance to match the standards defined by his teacher. To be "important," this child professes – to be a person who deserves and is accorded social recognition and respect – one must first "be responsible."

Generally, North End students hold what, in their teacher's estimation, are responsible aspirations. During class discussions, and in school projects and essays, most state that they aim to complete high school and college, hold jobs, raise families, and attain middle-class incomes and lifestyles. In response to the question, "What is a goal you have – something you hope you'll do in the future?" the majority of students at North End, as at Fair View, name a career goal (75 percent at North End and 69 percent at Fair View), and, although a higher percentage of North End students write that they aim for a clerical or service occupation (33 percent compared with 22 percent at Fair View), a larger percentage than at Fair View state that they aspire to a professional or a business management career (29 percent, compared with 22 percent at Fair View).[44] North End students tend to express optimism about their chances of attaining their goals. Although, to my knowledge, none of the parents of Franklin's students, and few North End parents overall, have completed

[43] For a breakdown of student responses to this question, see Appendix A, table 9.
[44] For a breakdown of student responses to this question, see Appendix A, table 10.

college, hold professional or management positions, earn middle-class incomes or enjoy middle-class lifestyles, the majority of North End students (93 percent, compared with 78 percent at Fair View) state they that they will, or probably will, attain their goals. The reasons they offer for their optimism are their unique talents and personal characteristics (33 percent); their responsible attitudes, values, and conduct (22 percent); the fact that they practice, or plan to practice, in order to develop the skills necessary for attaining their goals (16 percent); and the belief that they can accomplish whatever they aim to accomplish in life (13 percent). These responses depart from Fair View students' answers to the same questions primarily in their emphasis on accountability as a means to fulfilling aspirations. Almost a quarter of North End respondents, compared with only 3 percent at Fair View, state that they will achieve their goals because they meet attitudinal and behavioral expectations and requirements. For example:

My goal is beging [being] a hiar [hair] dresser, lawyer, nurse. Yes [I think I'll reach my goal]. Because I don't do bad thing.

When I grow up I would like to be a macanic [mechanic] or a basketball player. Yes I do think I going to reach my goal. Because I always bring in my work and get it done.[45]

The student responses outlined above suggest that lessons about responsibility at North End may encourage students to view as personal deficiencies failures to measure up to this particular definition of responsibility – a definition that emphasizes accountability to those in positions of authority – reinforcing restrictions on the capacity to act in ways that change or otherwise affect rules, norms, and other boundaries that shape the field of the possible. Student responses suggest, as well, a tendency to view those who are deficient in this sense (like Booker) as the cause of both personal and social problems. Lessons about responsibility may further restrict North End students' freedom, then, by deflecting criticism from structural sources of inequalities to individual failures to meet the expectations of teachers and others in positions of authority. They may contribute, what is more, to asymmetries in the social capacity for action across sites and among groups, to the extent that they reinforce social hierarchies of status based on respect, by teaching North End students that success and recognition are accorded to those who have good character and make good choices.

---

[45] For a breakdown of student responses to this question – worded, "Do you think you'll reach your goal? Why?" – see Appendix A, table 10.

Bounded fields of action: problems, possibilities, pedagogic options

No sophisticated account of power-with-a-face in the classroom would suggest that Veronica Franklin's use of power alone constrains her students' freedom. Most critical educational theorists would acknowledge, first, that the relationship between Franklin and her students takes place in the context of a larger array of power relations through which other powerful agents (such as city planners, capitalists who decide where to locate firms, and state legislators who determine social welfare access requirements and benefit levels) exercise power by shaping the present and future possibilities of these elementary school students. Accounts of power-with-a-face in the classroom are compatible, then, with a "life chances" argument according to which Franklin's exercise of power over her students in school is only one part of a complex process through which class, race, ethnicity, and place limit the prospects of these children to live safe, healthy, and satisfying lives.

Critical educational theorists likely would acknowledge, as well, that the political effects of Franklin's pedagogic practices depend upon, and are sustained by, the actions of other powerful agents, her relations with them, and the roles those relations define. Some accounts of power-with-a-face in the classroom are compatible, that is, with "structural" views of power. Franklin's exercise of power is dependent, one might argue (using Isaac's terms[46]), on social roles and relations that endow her with capacities, such as the capacity to assign grades, and dispositions, such as the disposition to teach students the skills tested by the Connecticut Mastery Test. It is dependent (in Wartenberg's terms[47]) on the use "peripheral agents" make of her actions. By this view, the North End principal, admissions officers at the local community college, and managers of nearby businesses empower Franklin and disempower students relative to her, to the extent that they regulate access to goods children need (such as academic promotion, college admission, and employment) with reference to measures of academic achievement and attainment. Individuals, groups, and institutions peripheral to the dyadic power relation play critical roles in constituting it. They "empower" "A" to exercise power over "B" via the choices she makes, such as Franklin's choice to award high grades to assignments that closely approximate text book work samples, and low or failing grades to assignments completed in an unconventional manner.

But the distinction between the powerful "A" and the powerless "B" that is central to this definition of the power relation tends to direct the atten-

---

[46] Isaac (1987a and 1987b).   [47] Wartenberg (1990 and 1992).

tion of even structural theorists of power away from the ways in which power delimits the field of what is socially possible for Veronica Franklin. As suggested in the last chapter, students of power-with-a-face likely would emphasize, if they were to analyze Franklin's pedagogy, the decisions she makes about how to act on rules and other power mechanisms in ways that affect her students, or alternatively, her relative powerlessness. Neither of these lines of explanation would be wholly misguided or irrelevant. It seems likely, for example, that Franklin adopts the pedagogic strategies she does in part because they enable her to direct students' conduct, at least to the degree necessary to maintain some order in her classroom. Access to resources, such as access to teacher-training programs, might enable and encourage Franklin to use instructional methods and approaches to discipline that depart from her "authoritarian" model.

Without denying, then, that there may be important elements of truth in accounts emphasizing Franklin's pedagogic choices and her access to educational and other resources, I want to make the case that pedagogic patterns at North End are not simply a function of the distribution of power's mechanisms and the exercise of "power over." These patterns – including the gaps and the inconsistencies in authoritarian pedagogic practice noted above – are in part the product of the ways in which social boundaries defining key practices and institutions delimit the field of the possible.

Relevant mechanisms of power include those that neither Franklin nor some other powerful "A" has, uses, or directs. They include the educational and other state institutional arrangements, the public laws and policies, and the social identities and exclusions that, together, define what some teachers at the North End Community School refer to as "the environment." North End teachers use this phrase as shorthand for the effects of concentrated urban poverty and racial discrimination in North End: for high rates of poverty, unemployment, and underemployment; low labor force participation rates and educational attainment; a lack of access to basic health care; public health problems such as high rates of HIV and AIDS infection, teen pregnancy and single parenthood, and prevalent substance abuse and addiction; high rates of violent crime and victimization; and high rates of incarceration, especially among young men.

In the discussion that follows, I draw on participant-observation, as well as interview data,[48] to argue that power shapes freedom in Franklin's

[48] At both the North End Community School and Fair View Elementary, I requested interviews with all administrators and classroom teachers (not including gym, music, and other "specials" teachers), and interviewed all those who were willing, a total of twelve out of sixteen at North End and ten out of twenty-six at Fair View. I conducted semi-structured, face-to-face interviews, which lasted roughly 45 to 60 minutes. See the discussion and interview format, Appendix B.

classroom in significant part by presenting this teacher with immediate problems, and with circumscribed possibilities and pedagogic options for responding to these problems. Power's mechanisms, which are in part the product of human action, here function as significant constraints on choice, shaping Franklin's pedagogic practice by defining the terrain within which she reasons about and arrives at the decisions that inform it.

Problems

Like every social actor, Veronica Franklin daily encounters problems, in the sense of difficult or uncertain situations, which, by virtue of her position, she must consider and to which she must respond. What this teacher, and what any social actor, perceives and defines as a problem, as well as the ways actors prioritize and respond to the problems they recognize, are in part functions of the history and culture of the various communities to which they belong, combined with their individual psychologies and the choices they make. They are also, in part, functions of material conditions and human biological need. So, for instance, on days when there is no heat at the North End Community School in the dead of a Connecticut winter, cold poses a problem to which the school principal and classroom teachers must respond before they can address other, perhaps in their estimation equally or even more important, yet less immediate concerns.

In this section, my claim is that power shapes freedom at North End in part by defining specific sets of problems that, given limits to time and human energy, produce pedagogic patterns. Specifically, I argue that among the problems most salient to teachers, administrators, and staff members at North End are those that derive from their perception – which is close to universal among those I interviewed – that children at the school stand at a point in their social development at which two life paths diverge: the path of "the street" and the path of "responsible citizenship." North End teachers tend to define their primary pedagogic aims in terms of enabling students to manage the dangers posed by the former "life path," while inducing them to reject it in favor of the latter. Thus first grade special education teacher Theresa Benton identifies as her principal goal for her students, "to realize you are a citizen, that they are a person that has responsibilities, and to get them to start thinking of the word 'choice.'"

I want to introduce teachers' understandings of what the life path of "the street" and the life path of "responsible citizenship" hold for students, as well as the dilemma this "fork in the road" poses, by quoting at length a story told to me by veteran fifth grade teacher Bernice

Henderson. In the following interview excerpt, Henderson recalls an incident involving a third grader she taught roughly twenty years earlier:

I was trying to help [this] little boy to read, and he got so aggravated. He told me, "I don't have to read."

I says, "Honey, when you grow up, you got to get a job."

He said, "I don't have to have a job. My mama don't have no job. My mother get two checks every month, on the first and fifteenth." He's in third grade.

And I said, "Is that what you want to do? Yeah, that's what, you're a young man. You got to take care of family and get that new car and all that stuff. You got to learn to read the driver's license book.". . .

And he says, "I'll get a wife who can read."

I said, "You know you might not find a wife that can read when you can't."

And this kid right at that time had that in his mind, that he could get welfare, he could get by.

"But you gotta . . . don't you want a car when you grow up? Most people would need one when they get to be an adult."

[Henderson shrugs.] He did like that, you know.

I said, "You know what? Mrs. Henderson wants to see you be the strong man, get up, fill out your application for a job . . . Education is important. You got to read and write. You may not, you know, you may go to college, you may not go to college, but now if you don't want to learn to read, you won't make it to college. This is . . . all of our aspiration, to go to school, you know. High expectations, baby. Mrs. Henderson wants you to read."

So, we got through that year. He did, I did get him to read. But I got him behind his mother, and told her exactly what he told me. And I said, "We are not about to produce a kid with this idea, that he's gonna get by.". . .

And [his mother] said, "Well I really wished I had gone to school. And he'd better stop that junk and learn his lesson."

Henderson takes up the story, which she characterizes as a "success story," roughly twenty years later:

And I met that young man last summer. I had not seen him since he'd been a man. He said, "Mrs. Henderson," he said, "You still look the same." You know . . . [he] must be about twenty-eight, twenty-eight, or twenty-nine . . . And he was at, in [nearby suburban town].

And I says, "Well, Joseph, oh my God, it's so good seeing you."

You know, and he hugged me. And he says, "Mrs. Henderson, I got a job . . . I got a job, my wife got a job, and I have two children."

I says, "They are adorable." Cute little boys.

And he said, "And I got a car."

I said, "I'm glad."

You know, he said, "Mrs. Henderson, I'll tell you, well you used to be a tough lady. But I'm just so glad I learned to read."

And that makes you feel very good, to, to hear success stories. Because he had gone to . . . to the community college . . . So, that's the way it went. But, you know, he seemed to be successful, he . . . was working at [the local airport], and so was his wife . . . They both had a job.

Henderson presents the story of Joseph's brother, however, as the obverse of this "success story." She continues:

Cause I asked him about his other brother. I was worried, cause I had seen his brother. He was drunk straight up. He's the older boy . . . Ronald. And he said, "Mrs. Henderson, Ronald, Ronald has had it. He's, he's, he's, he's on drugs . . ."

I knew him because, he was in fourth grade, now this kid was in third. But it just goes to show you. Kids are very appreciative, but yet again some of them really hit it hard. And some of them hit it really early.

It is possible that Henderson's story is less than perfectly accurate. She may modify it, as she recalls the two encounters with her student, perhaps in order to serve her narrative purposes. Nevertheless, the story captures this teacher's perception, a perception common among adults at North End, that students at the school face a choice between two courses in life represented by the paths taken by the brothers Joseph and Ronald. The path of "the street," the path followed by Ronald in Henderson's story, is the path of dependency, illiteracy, propertylessness, and immobility, both geographic and social. It is the path of "unmanliness": the life course taken by the male who fails to be a "strong man," who fails to work to "take care of family." Had the protagonist of the story been female, Henderson likely would have characterized the path of "the street" as the life course of the welfare-dependent mother, the young woman who not only fails to work to support herself, but further makes irresponsible reproductive decisions. The path of "the street" is the life track of the uneducated, the unsuccessful, the alcoholic, the drug addict, the drop-out. In following it, Ronald injudiciously attempted to bypass the educational system and "get by" outside the wage economy, which alone allows those who play by the rules to survive and to advance.

This life path, of "the street," North End teachers explain repeatedly and in a variety of ways, is very present in the community the school serves, tempting to some students, and at the same time, unquestionably undesirable. In Henderson's story there is no doubt that Ronald was wrong. He was wrong, first, in the sense that, according to prevailing moral conventions, which this teacher implicitly endorses, the choice to take illegal drugs is an unethical choice, and the failure to work for a wage, a sign of bad character. He was wrong, secondly, and more fundamentally, in the sense that he was factually mistaken. It is impossible, or nearly so, to "get by" on "the street." Although some North End teachers speak about following the path of "the street" in terms of moral weakness and unethical choice, what, for most adults at the school, renders the lure of this life path an exigent problem is not the dangers it poses for students' moral development, but the more immediate dangers it poses for their basic well-being and survival. In Franklin's classroom alone, Candy's father and Renee's mother recently died of AIDS. Jaclyn's mother was murdered, and her father and the fathers of several of her classmates are serving prison sentences. The likely recompense for trying to "get by," Franklin, Henderson, and many of their colleagues reason, based on what they know about the lives of former students, parents, and others who have attempted to, is a life all but consumed by the struggle to raise children on a below poverty-level income, or by incarceration, addiction, disease, or even violent death.

North End teachers not only view the path of "the street" as a decidedly unfortuitous one, they further view it as the default choice for many, or even for most North End students. Repeatedly adults at the school express their conviction that, absent their intervention, this is the life path many students will choose or, more precisely, the path they unreflexively will stumble upon. They offer as evidence stories about former students who became parents before they finished middle school, children who dropped out of school, students who are incarcerated, students who were murdered. And they point to children who start down the path of "the street" while still in elementary school. Reverend Johnson, for instance, tells me that some students at North End "run drugs" for local dealers "from first [grade] up." Bernice Henderson, envisioning what the near future holds for members of her current fifth grade class, speculates:

I can tell you I see some that's not going to really get out of middle school. They're gonna be drop-outs, if they get with the wrong group. I see some pushing through, forging ahead, and going to become what they want to become, because I have a few parents who really push to make the best out of their kids. I see some kid that's very bright but just does not have that push could fall right in the trap, a family tradition kind of thing, go, "I'm going to have me a baby."

The lure of "the street" is, of course, not the only problem North End teachers confront day to day in their classrooms and in the school. But even many of the more routine problems, in particular the discipline problems and problems of low academic achievement that surface repeatedly in teachers' conversations with each other, as well as in their interviews and informal conversations with me, they tend to experience as logically related to this larger problem via what many characterize as the local hegemony of "street values." Franklin and many of her colleagues perceive as a major obstacle to meeting both short- and long-term pedagogic aims the prevalence in students' homes and in the larger community of what they characterize as norms and values that conflict and compete with those that govern dominant social institutions, including the school. Hence first grade special education teacher Theresa Benton (who is white) responds as follows to the question, "What are the greatest challenges of your job?":

... the street values ... that they're told, that they deal with, and that come into the classroom. You know, mothers and fathers telling them, if somebody hits you, you beat them up, you know. You do this to them, you do that to them. They've survived by stealing, and they come in and they feel that's still the same method of operation, really. And you have to say, "Street rules, school rules." And to deal with that.

In a similar vein, Henderson, comparing the children she taught in Mississippi three decades ago with children at North End today, suggests that North End parents, themselves brought up on "street values," inculcate their children with attitudes antithetical to those needed to succeed:

back home we had more conversations with our children: what I want you to be. They had, the parents had great aspirations for their children. And they continued to tell you, "You're not going to make it as well as I've made it. And I want you to do better than I did." And I don't think our children hear enough of that here. Because it is a continuous cycle. "My moms, my mother is on welfare, the state paid for her, we made it. And if I have a baby, I can get on welfare." And it gets to be generation after generation after generation believing in that. And nobody having work ethics.

Half of the North End teachers I interviewed define the greatest challenges they face in the classroom in terms of this perceived hegemony of "street values."[49] Many tend to view the everyday problems they confront in school (for example, how to get students to walk quietly down the hallway to the cafeteria), as well as the problems that define their long-term pedagogic aims and their goals for their students (for example, how to keep Renee safe from the dangers that ultimately took her mother's life), as a battle over the definition of what is normal in social life, and what is of value. Below I elaborate what, for many North End teachers, this battle consists in. Here my claim is that power shapes freedom in the classroom and in the school, in part by defining problems that demand a response from teachers and others in positions of authority. Social boundaries to action – such as laws establishing a welfare system for poor families distinct from that which serves the non-poor, and norms stigmatizing dependence on Aid to Families with Dependent Children, yet legitimizing middle-class dependence on the welfare state – delimit the path of "the street" as well as its attendant dangers. In so doing, they shape Franklin's perception and that of her colleagues that to teach at North End is to engage in a battle against "street values," which predispose children to "hit it hard" and to "hit it ... early."

---

[49] That is, in terms of students' propensity to engage in activities devalued and punished by dominant social institutions. An additional 30 percent answer the question, "What are the greatest challenges of your job?" with reference to social problems associated with concentrated urban poverty. Forty percent answer with reference to insufficient parental support, which most view as the product of these larger social problems.

Possibilities

North End teachers' conversations with each other, as well as their reflections on their pedagogic goals and responsibilities, suggest that many view as a principal adversary in the classroom "street values," which, they maintain, define as normal, and even valorize, activities devalued and punished by dominant social institutions. These include illegal activities, such as drug use, drug dealing, and theft; "anti-social" activities, such as resorting to violence to resolve conflict; and activities widely regarded to be immoral, such as teen pregnancy and parenthood, or signs of bad character, such as welfare dependency. Thus Henderson, elaborating the above comparison between children she taught in Mississippi in the 1960s and North End students in the 1990s, stresses that the latter seem to her unable or unwilling to demonstrate respect for authority and to conform to social norms in peer interaction. Her students in Mississippi, she claims, were "obedient." They "knew how to play." North End students, by contrast, are "hyper." They "have a whole lot of fights." "It's a social thing," she explains, "and I think a whole lot of it is attributed to children having children. They never learn themselves, you understand. Therefore they cannot teach their children about respect." Teachers identify as the source of "street values," not only child-rearing practices but also, in the words of special education teacher Ursula Winters, "what [North End students] see in the neighborhood." Violence and drug use have become "normal" for her students, Winters claims, and fighting is, for most, matter-of-course, a common and acceptable means to getting what one wants.

By this view, then, "street" norms and values, which children acquire in the home and in the North End community generally, incline students to anti-authoritarian and "anti-social" behavior, influencing them to make choices antithetical to advancement in mainstream institutions, in particular the school and the workplace. "Street values" steer children toward the path of "the street" and away from the path of "responsible citizenship." If we return for a moment to Joseph and the "success story" Henderson tells about him, we recall that the critical difference between this boy and his brother was that Henderson was able to convince Joseph to want to read. She persuaded him that he should aspire to be literate, educated, and employed, that he should aim to "get that new car and all that stuff." Together with his mother who, apparently unlike most North End parents, rejected "street values" and "got . . . behind" her son, Henderson convinced Joseph to abandon the nascent idea, "that he [was] gonna get by."

Like Franklin and other teachers at North End, Henderson at times adopts the rhetoric of "urban underclass" theorists, who identify deviant, or even "pathological" norms, values, attitudes, and behaviors as the principal source of the ills of the American city.[50] It would be misleading, however, to focus exclusively on the themes most prominent in teachers' reflections about their pedagogic aims and goals. Although these reflections at times seem to mirror the urban underclass discourse, they diverge from it, or at least from more conservative variants of it, in that they are framed by references to ongoing structural sources of social and economic inequalities. Consider again the conversation with Franklin to which I alluded in the previous chapter. In explaining to me that some North End students work for local drug dealers, and that some are "in serious trouble" by the time they reach sixth grade, Franklin suggests that the root of the problem of the dangers and the lure of "the street" is "the environment." For kindergarten teacher Sandra Miller, it is the "distracting social environment." For Ursula Winters it is "a socio-economic difference" between North End students and white, middle-class children. For Natalie Carson it is the fact that North End families have become, over the past two decades, increasingly "entrenched in poverty."

It is unlikely that North End teachers, including African-American teachers, who comprise a majority of the faculty, are unaware that North End parents and graduates face racial discrimination in housing and employment. It is unlikely, as well, that a veteran teacher like Franklin, who has lived for decades and raised a family within walking distance of the school, is unaware of structural barriers to access to opportunities for education and work, which limit for North End students legitimate means to economic advancement and social recognition, and render relatively appealing, to some, illegitimate, illegal, and dangerous avenues to "success." That Franklin and many other adults at the school pepper their discussions of what they regard to be injudicious life choices made by North End students with reference to continuing economic and other structural conditions, which, they imply, shape student values, attitudes, and actions, suggests that they do not necessarily view a deficient or pathological "culture" as the most important, or even an independent cause of the relative attractiveness of "the street," or of some students' "choice" to follow this path.

They focus on this choice, none the less, and on fighting the "street" norms and values that inform it, in part because they stand a reasonable chance of influencing these. Social power shapes Franklin's field of action by defining problems that she must address before she can work to attain other pedagogic aims. It does so, as well, by limiting what she might rea-

---

[50] For recent overviews of the debate on the urban "underclass," see Fainstein (1993), Katz (1993), and Marks (1991).

sonably hope to accomplish in responding to these problems. The institutional arrangements, the social identities, the laws, the norms, the policies that, together, confine Franklin's students to a racially segregated neighborhood with relatively few safe, legal, and legitimate avenues for social and economic advancement not only help produce what this teacher calls "the street," and render it relatively attractive to her fourth grade students, they also make it highly unlikely that Franklin or any classroom teacher can affect the root causes of its appeal.

I suggested above that adults at North End tend to perceive their principal objectives in the classroom in terms of a battle over the definition of the normal, in which the antagonists are, on the one hand, "street values," and on the other, middle-class attitudinal and behavioral norms. Throughout the academic year I spent at North End, Franklin expressed repeatedly, both to me and to her fellow teachers, her sense that she cannot win this battle. Most students who enter her classroom on the path of "the street," she reasons, based on twenty-five years of experience teaching at North End, will leave it following that path. Nor can this teacher reasonably hope to change the terms of the battle. She focuses, instead, on individual victories, on helping shape "success stories" by inducing as many children as she can to opt for the path of "responsible citizenship." Her principal aim, then, is to produce students who are "literate," according to prevailing standards of literacy, students who aspire to be wage earners, propertied, "strong men" who support wives and children, responsible women who marry and bear legitimate offspring for whom they are able to provide, adults who own cars and are therefore able to work at the airport and live in the suburbs. She aims to induce the children she teaches to conform to middle-class norms and rules, to value education and wage labor as means to self-sufficiency, and to believe that they can build their own futures, successful futures, which meet "all of our aspirations."

That she does so does not necessarily mean that she considers the path of "responsible citizenship" to be ideal, that she believes it will provide her students with an equal or a fair opportunity to meet their needs and to develop their talents and potentials, or that, were she to reflect upon it, she would conclude that the path of "responsible citizenship" is the only conceivable alternative to the path of "the street." Rather, I want to suggest, Franklin, like many of her colleagues at North End, promotes the path of "responsible citizenship" in large part because she views it as the most viable escape route from "the street," and from the grave risks this life course poses.

Pedagogic options

The problem of the lure and the danger of "the street," many adults at the North End Community School believe, and the possibility of escape via the path of "responsible citizenship," call for a two-pronged pedagogic response. First, given that North End students are already exposed to the dangers of "the street," it is critical for teachers and for other school authorities that they enable students to avoid or to manage these. Helping children manage the immediate dangers they are likely to encounter involves protecting them when they are unable to protect themselves. Thus Reverend Johnson explains that when he learns that particular students are working for local drug dealers, he intervenes directly, threatening to call city police if dealers do not leave the vicinity of the school:

> I confront . . . I let them know, "Listen, these are my kids, and I'm not going to have you over there messing with my kids. And I . . . I mean it. And if push come to shove, what I'll do . . . I'll go to the police station . . . I'll go to the house. You know, but I'm not going to tolerate that."

More often, and, in the estimation of most, more importantly, enabling students to avoid danger involves imparting to them what teachers refer to as "survival skills" or "life skills," that is, basic competencies, which they judge students need in order to survive day to day. Alice Wilson explains that she teaches her pre-schoolers "If I'm hungry and Mom's not home . . ." that they should find food for themselves. She devotes class time to demonstrating and to letting students practice opening boxes of cereal. In the higher grades "survival skills" become more complex. Henderson, for example, teaches fifth graders how to read supermarket circulars, compare prices, and count change.

At all levels, however, "life skills" include the capacity, in Reverend Johnson's words (quoted below), "to grasp right from wrong" and the disposition "to do right" and thereby avoid life-threatening risks and dangers. Teaching students to "grasp right from wrong" and "to do right" is not principally, for adults at North End, a matter of helping them develop a capacity for moral reasoning that enables them to function as autonomous moral agents. Rather, it is a matter of getting children in the habit of trusting and obeying those in authority, especially school authorities, and following rules prescribed by authorities, in order to provide short-term protection against harm. There is an almost universal perception among those at North End whom I interviewed that students need discipline. They need it, both in the sense that they lack it (that they are not taught by parents or other adults outside of school to obey authority and follow rules) and in the sense that they require it, that it serves children's interests. Johnson claims:

A lot of them [North End students] don't understand . . . Some of them . . . it's hard for them to grasp right from wrong. Sometime they can to do some things and . . . they can be totally wrong, but they think it's right . . . And it's hard, you know, when you don't have a . . . mother or a father that's giving you the proper time you need. You know, and these kids are suffering.

Moments later he adds, "They're looking for somebody that's going to tell them how to do right."

Some North End teachers express ambivalence about the school's "authoritarian" disciplinary practices. Marilyn Simpson, for example, a white kindergarten special needs teacher, tells me that she cannot imagine her own child eating lunch in the North End cafeteria, and asks rhetorically if I can imagine my child eating there, where she characterizes disciplinary practice as "unfair" to students: "I can't imagine, can you imagine your child eating in that cafeteria? Screamed at, yelled at all the time? I mean, it's just unfair. I think it's very unfair to those kids." Moments later, however, she comments that she believes that there is a need for a strong and uncompromising disciplinary stance at the school because of "the way [North End students] were brought up: you know, no one's really set bedtimes . . . there's no rules." Mary Naughton also uses the example of the cafeteria to explain that she "feel[s] sorry" for her students, whom she thinks suffer from the relentless barrage of reprimands and reproaches to which they are subject: "Even when they go to lunch, I always say, God, those poor kids . . . They go there, and they're told to put their heads down, not talk, to do this, to do that. There's too many people on them." None the less, she claims that the school needs more consistent and stricter disciplinary standards, and even goes so far as to suggest that school authorities should expel children who break rules repeatedly: "You have to have a strong [disciplinary] program, where it's consistent. A child does this – I mean we almost have to have a contract – a child does this, this is what happens. You don't get a second chance. The second time you do it, you're out."

There is a near consensus among the teachers I interviewed, including among those who express distaste for some effects of authoritarian disciplinary practices at the school, that North End students need discipline, and that the school should adopt more consistent and even more severe rules and punishments. Most endorse strict disciplinary practices, not only because they believe that these help maintain order in the classroom, but also because they believe that they protect students from harm and promote their well-being. Johnson, for example, explains the importance of "knowing what to do" and "following the rules" with reference to his own experience that doing so best serves one's interests:

. . . you can deal better knowing what to do and how to do it than you can not knowing, you know. My . . . pet peeve above anything else is, is education. That's my number one. Then following the rules, you know. Because . . . it's hard, when you . . . look at all the people in jail, for not following the rules. Now if you knew how to do, you could . . . learn or go around a lot of things without getting in trouble, see. And there's a way to do things. You know, cause I know I broke rules . . . it didn't help me out any, you know. But it helped me out . . . when I was honest about things and when I did what I was told to do . . . I benefited more, you know.

Not one of the North End teachers or staff members with whom I spoke claimed, however, that "survival skills," including the skills they associate with obeying authority and knowing and following the rules, can equip a child to survive the path of "the street" in the long run. Simultaneously, then, they aim to steer students away from "the street" and toward the path of "responsible citizenship," a task that, they explain, involves at least three steps. First, it requires teaching children a set of basic skills, which teachers judge they need in order to thrive in dominant social institutions, in particular on the job market and in the workplace. These include academic skills, such as de-coding. They include a range of verbal skills. Carson, for example, states that students need to "[become] articulate and [express] themselves." Johnson emphasizes that they need "to be able to sit down and have a conversation." Many stress that students need to be proficient in standard English. These skills also include what teachers characterize as "social skills," in particular, the abilities to sit still, listen, and concentrate; to function in a group; and to resolve conflict with peers. Wilson offers as examples of "social skills" the capacity to observe rules of etiquette in public places and the ability to resolve conflict without resorting to violence:

That if they're able to go into a restaurant and they're able to sit there. Don't throw food. Put your hands on the table. Wait for the person to finish eating. That they be able to show . . . good manners as a result of social skills.
    The other thing is how to . . . conflict, how to resolve conflict. So we don't, you know, take the toy. That we don't hit. That we talk about what's going on.

When asked to explain why she views these skills as important, Wilson suggests that, without them, "you can't go anywhere in life":

You can't go anywhere in life if you don't know how to interact with others. Can't go through life fighting. You know, you have to know how to negotiate. That's what life is all about. That's important. If you can sit still and you can pay attention, then you can learn. But if you're all over the place having fun then you're not learning.

As the examples offered by Wilson suggest, leading students to the path of "responsible citizenship" is not only, by this view, a matter of helping them develop key skills and competencies, but also a matter of exposing them to, and inducing them to conform to, dominant norms and values. Many teachers at the school identify as an important part of their job clarifying for students the content of dominant social norms and rules. Reverend Johnson explains succinctly, "in order to deal with society, you got to know what society's calling for." They stress, in particular, the importance of teaching respect for property rights and teaching students to conform to social norms in peer interaction. They emphasize that they aim for children, not only to understand and as a matter of habit to conform to key social norms, but further to embrace values that they judge will enable them to thrive in the workplace and in the academic institutions (the high school, the college or community college) that regulate access to it. Many teachers name as their top priority teaching students to aspire to self-sufficiency and to value education – especially at the high school and post-secondary levels – as a means to economic betterment. Johnson says that he regularly tells children that, given that they are black in a society that discriminates against blacks, and given that they come from an inner-city community, school offers the only route out of poverty, away from "the environment":

Cause I tell the children, "You . . . have two strikes against you. One, you're black. Two, you're living . . . in an inner city. That's already two strikes. You don't need a third one. Ignorance . . . you don't need a third one. You need something that's going to help you come up from out of here."

To motivate students to develop the skills and the competencies, and to encourage them to adopt the norms and values they need in order to follow the life course of "responsible citizenship," North End teachers define a third and, in the view of many, a critical task. They must convince students that the individual authors her own future, that the choice between the successful path of "responsible citizenship" and the hopeless path of "the street" is *her* choice. They must convince the children in their charge that the difference between the two is a matter of holding high aspirations, believing that one can realize them, and working to do so. According to Smith:

I think it's very important that I try to teach them about life, period. To start setting some goals now. You don't wait until you become thirty, forty, twenty, eighteen years old. You set your goals now. And I always reflect on the fact that, and I tell, I share this with them, at ten years old, I knew where I was going to college. I had decided what area I wanted to go into. You know, so I think it's very important that we help them to see, start now, start early, setting some goals. And believe that you can become anything you want to become.

Teachers aim to convince students that the difference between, on the one hand, self-sufficiency and success, and on the other, dependency and despair, is believing in oneself, setting responsible goals, and working to realize them. Naughton names as her first priority "[to] develop self-esteem. Let them know that they can accomplish anything they want. I tell them that constantly . . . You know, encourage them to go on and let them know that, you know, they will accomplish something if they try . . ." North End teachers, my data suggest, do not fully believe that all that bars students from "becom[ing] anything [they] want to become" is a lack of high aspirations and hard work. Nor do they necessarily believe that character and choice alone determine one's life course. Nevertheless, they regard as a critical part of their job inspiring children, encouraging them to follow the path of "responsible citizenship," by convincing them that it offers – to anyone who wants them and who is willing to work to obtain them—possibilities and rewards that far exceed those which "the street" falsely promises.

The above, I want to emphasize, is not meant to suggest that pedagogic practice at the North End Community School is completely, or even largely, the product of conscious and rational deliberation. No doubt, much of what Veronica Franklin does, day to day, in her classroom, she does because, as a matter of course, it is "what is done" at North End. My claim is not, then, that she calculates the risks associated with the life path of "the street" and the most viable pedagogic means to helping students manage or avoid these, each time she reprimands a child, each time she tells a student, "You are responsible."

Nor, however, is her pedagogic practice – and in particular her tendency to require unquestioning conformity to imposed rules, to present learning as intellectual obedience, and to define the responsible student in terms of accountability, agency, and blame – the simple product of a lack of resources or a decision to "exercise power over." If Franklin does not direct her efforts in the classroom toward "politicizing" dominant norms and values, encouraging students to think critically about social relations of domination, and inspiring them to work to promote social justice in North End, this is not because she wants to reproduce political, economic, and social hierarchies; because she benefits from the *status quo*; or because she fails to understand, or does not care about, the ways power constrains her students' freedom. The pedagogic strategies she adopts are based, in part, on the pragmatic judgment that, if imperfect, they are none the less practicable means to helping students avoid dangers that threaten their well-being, and improving their chances for social and economic advancement.

5   The "world" of Fair View

The first time I hear about it is during a class meeting one mid-October morning. Monica Segal's fourth graders are writing to the state Commissioner of Education to voice their criticisms of the Connecticut Mastery Test. During the meeting, the teacher reminds her students that, after they drafted the letter, she showed it to the principal, Anita Byrne, "to make sure that it was OK with her for us to send it." Byrne, she announces, thought it was a good idea, one that "might generate some press." That afternoon the class revises the letter, which, in its final form, reads:

Hi! We are students at Fair View Elementary School in Fair View. Last week we finished taking the Fourth Grade Connecticut State Mastery Test. When we spend a lot of time on something in class we always write down our thoughts. We would like to share our thoughts about the test with you. We classified what we had to say in 3 sections: general thoughts, thoughts on directions, and suggestions.

General thoughts

The writing I had to rush a little because it was 45 minutes, not a long time.

Confusing to have two answer sheets on the same page.

The anser [answer] boklet [booklet] was difakot [difficult] to read.

I don't know why they did math twice instead of combinding [combining] it.

When the writing part came up and only 45 minutes it kind of got on my nerves and then I wrote fast enough to finish in twenty minutes.

I think that the listening comprehension is very annoying when the man says one minute left. I think it is distracting and if your [you're] trying to think it takes up your time and gets you off the topic.

First you have abcd and then abcde it was confusing because when I wanted d I would accidently [accidentally] fill in e.

Thoughts on directions

Make the directions clearer.

The directions were very confusing. For example: Questions 10, 11 in box 10 on page 14. And then there would be boxes 10 and 11 on page 12.

I thought the directions on written communication were confusing becaus [because] the question was on one page and the passage was on another.

Confusing directions.

Suggestions

Each test should start on a different page.

The 45 minute test for writing should be longer because we write so fast, sometimes we don't even know what we're writing about.

Is there any way to fix the Connecticut State Mastery Test so it makes more sense? We would like to know what you think. Thank you. Sincerely,

The letter is signed by Monica Segal and each of her students.

Roughly one month later, John Travero from the state Department of Education's Bureau of Assessment and Testing arrives at Fair View Elementary to discuss with Monica Segal's fourth graders their concerns about the test. The afternoon before, the students had rearranged their classroom for the meeting. Their work tables, normally placed in the center of the room, are lined up along its walls to form a U-shape facing the blackboard. In front of the board sits a chair intended for Travero and a second for Susan, the student Segal chose to moderate the discussion. Place cards bearing the children's names line the tables, facing the two chairs.

When Travero enters the classroom, Segal directs him to his seat and tells him that Susan will moderate the discussion. Travero does not reply. Instead, he addresses the children. He introduces himself as the Manager of Connecticut Mastery Testing. He announces that, during the meeting, he will do two things. First, he will explain to the students "what we do to make the test fair." Then, he will address the concerns they voiced in their letter. Travero launches into a lengthy discussion of the history of the CMT, the committee processes used to develop the test, and the state's aims and objectives in administering the exam. He speaks monotonously, using an inflated vocabulary. The children stare at him, blank-faced.

Several minutes into Travero's speech, Monica Segal interrupts and addresses her students. She says that Travero is using "a lot of big words that we don't usually use," words like "assessment." She asks if anyone in the class knows what "assessment" means. The children shake their heads and smile. The teacher initiates a short discussion about what it means to "assess" something or someone. When the discussion ends, Travero resumes his speech.

Meanwhile, several adults file in and take seats at the back of the classroom: the Fair View Elementary principal, the assistant superintendent of schools for the district, a local newspaper reporter, and a photographer. Travero continues. He offers a detailed explanation of the structure of the committee that designed the CMT and the committee's decision-making procedures. He emphasizes the state's effort to make the committee representative, pointing out that it includes not only teachers from "schools like Fair View" but also teachers from "schools in Bridgeport."

At this point, Monica Segal interrupts a second time. She announces that Susan will moderate the discussion. Susan will call on students who have prepared specific questions for Travero, she says, and then will "open up the floor" to any other children who have questions. Segal motions to Susan, who reads a short introductory statement welcoming Travero to the classroom, and then calls T.J.'s name.

T.J. asks why, while students are answering two-minute reading comprehension questions, a recorded voice announces that there is one minute left. He says that when he heard the announcement he "almost got off the topic." "Why do you have to do that?" he asks. "Can they say it in a lower voice or not at all?"

Travero responds that the decision as to whether or not to include this announcement was "a judgment call." He says that the announcement "does not affect testing." He adds that, if he were to poll the 35,000 children who took the test, he thinks that "most would find it more helpful than distracting."

Monica Segal asks the students in her class how many of them found the recorded announcements distracting. All of the children raise their hands.

Travero replies that the announcements are "not meant to distract you." He says that the children should not pay attention when they hear them. He adds, with more than a hint of sarcasm in his voice, that the announcements are "for those who, unlike you, need a reminder."

One by one, Susan calls the names of children chosen to read questions from the class's letter. After Travero has responded to each, she allows other students to ask additional questions. These include:

Why do we get timed?

How are we supposed to write a good story in forty-five minutes when some people are slow at writing?

Why are there two math sections, and no sections on science and other subjects?

The directions say that we can write as much as we want, but the test has three blank pages. Why can't we write on loose leaf instead of answer book sheets?

Why does it take so long to get back our grades?

Travero responds to each question with detailed explanations of logistical problems associated with what he refers to as "test building," and with scoring the CMT. For example, in response to "Why can't we write on loose leaf instead of answer book sheets?" he explains that the CMT is scored by "professional scorers" trained to grade tests according to state-determined guidelines and with reference to state-established standards. Each essay, he says, is read by two scorers. If the grades they assign vary by more than one point, then the exam is passed on to a supervisor who reads the essay and determines its score. Travero claims that short essays can receive high scores, and long essays, low scores. He stresses that children should not be concerned about length, but rather should focus on the organization and clarity of their writing. The reason students cannot staple loose leaf to answer booklets, he explains, is that the papers are sorted by machines that separate students' essays from their names and demographic data, and then bar code each, so that scorers do not know who wrote which essay. Staples, he says, would jam the machines.

Repeatedly during the course of this discussion, Monica Segal interrupts Travero, encouraging her students to challenge his replies. Thus, after the above explanation she asks Peter, the boy who asked the question that prompted it, to tell Travero what he thinks when he sees three blank pages. Peter says, "If you see three pages, you think you need to fill up at least two."

At several points during the discussion, Travero promises to takes steps to improve the Connecticut Mastery Test.

Shortly after John Travero leaves Fair View Elementary, Monica Segal conducts a class discussion about his visit. Student comments include:

> He had a lot of big words.
> He explained questions. He didn't answer them.
> He gave more excuses for why they should stay that way, instead of how to change it.
> He gave so many details that I forgot what he was saying.
> When he said he looked at it last night – he didn't take the test!
> I think he talked too much and didn't let us ask the questions.
> It's sort of like he's telling us he's older and knows better.
> Mr. Travero explains the questions and then gets off the topic.

Segal tells her students that Travero's task was not an easy one. She points out that he did read their letter and make an effort to respond to it. And she comments that Travero is not used to talking to fourth graders.

Segal's students agree that they want to write a letter to thank Travero for coming to their classroom. As they begin to discuss the content of the note they will send him, Christopher says, aloud, "I think we may have changed it."

The predominantly white, upper middle-class community of Fair View, Connecticut, with its own thriving downtown of upscale retail and commercial businesses, functions in significant part as a residential suburb for the families of upper-level managers and professionals who commute to work in New York. The town's strategic location outside one of the world's three global cities, along with the postwar local and federal policies and the real estate, mortgage lending, and other private practices that fueled urban deindustrialization and suburbanization, helped transform Fair View into one of the few apparent winners in the late twentieth-century game of attempting to capture increasingly mobile capital.

Data from the census tracts that together roughly outline the town's boundaries paint a statistical portrait of concentrated affluence, of privilege. Fair View ranks in the top 5 percent in the state for almost every measure of socio-economic status. The majority of employed residents work in managerial and professional occupations: about 55 percent, compared with 31.5 percent statewide, and only about 17 percent in the North End community. The unemployment rate is about 2 percent, compared with 5.4 percent for the state as a whole, and roughly 8 percent for North End. Median household income, median family income, and per capita income are each about double the state rate, and more than four times the rate in the North End tracts. The poverty rate of about 3.5 percent is roughly half the state rate of 6.8 percent and about one-eighth the approximately 28 percent poverty rate in North End. The majority of Fair View residents over the age of twenty-five hold bachelor's degrees, and about 94 percent have graduated from high school. The 1990 Census classifies as "white" approximately 96 percent of the town's population, although "white" persons comprise only 87 percent of the state population.[1]

Parents who live in Fair View and who elect to send their children to the local public schools send them through a district that consistently outperforms almost every other in the state according to all available measures of educational achievement. On the 1995–96 Connecticut Mastery Test, roughly 67 percent, 30 percent, and 50 percent more Fair View fourth graders than fourth graders statewide met the state goals for reading, writing, and mathematics, respectively. Roughly half of Fair View fourth graders met the state goal for all three parts of the test, compared with 28.3 percent statewide, and 0 percent – no students – at the North End Community School. The student population at Fair View Elementary is about 95 percent white. About 1 percent of the school's students qualify for free or reduced-price meals, compared with 29 percent statewide and about 80 percent at the North End Community School.[2]

A student of power-with-a-face might reasonably hypothesize that, if any public fourth grade classroom is the site of the schooling of the "powerful," Monica Segal's is. Segal's students have available to them almost

---

[1] For a detailed comparison of occupational, unemployment, labor force participation, income, poverty status, educational attainment, and racial and ethnic composition data for Fair View, North End, Connecticut, and the state's three largest cities, see Appendix A, table 1.

[2] See Appendix A, table 3 for comparative data on school racial composition, students qualifying for free or reduced-price meals, and Mastery Test achievement.

every conceivable educational resource. Fair View Elementary, housed in a modern building and surrounded by large, well-maintained athletic fields, boasts such amenities as a spacious school library furnished with rows upon rows of book stacks, and a high-ceilinged auditorium with theater-style seating and a grand piano on stage. Not only does the school have computers in every classroom, it also has a fully equipped computer lab, staffed by an instructor. Monica Segal, like other classroom teachers at Fair View, is assisted regularly by a teacher's aide, as well as by "resource teachers," that is, specialists in various academic fields who are available to give curricular advice and to present what Segal refers to as "guest lectures" in the classroom. Segal herself is a scarce educational resource. A Vassar graduate recruited by the Fair View district from one of the nation's most prestigious teacher education programs, she was one of hundreds of applicants for her position.[3] Monica Segal is also one of the best paid young teachers in the country, which partially accounts for Fair View's success at recruiting her and others like her. The district pays teachers on average about 12 percent more than other districts in Connecticut,[4] which is itself the state with the highest teachers' salaries in the United States.[5]

Clearly, however, the differences between this classroom and Veronica Franklin's classroom at the North End Community School extend beyond differences in access to educational and other resources. Segal's pedagogic practices depart radically from Franklin's, perhaps most apparently in the above vignette in that this teacher cultivates, not an unquestioning submissiveness to the authority of the state test and those who design and administer it, but rather an active, at times almost confrontational engagement with that authority. Although Segal does not encourage her students to be "critical" in the sense in which critical educational theorists use that term (she does not, for instance, initiate a class discussion of the gendered and cultural biases of standardized testing), she does actively encourage the fourth graders in her charge to use their experiences taking the CMT as grounds for judging the exam and finding fault with some aspects of its structure and content.

This teacher models for her students, and she encourages them to adopt, behaviors that challenge some of Travero's claims (such as his assertion that it is likely that "most" students find the test's recorded announcements "more helpful than distracting"), as well as the language

---

[3] According to Fair View principal Anita Byrne, the district averages between 200 and 250 applicants per position.

[4] Average teacher salaries in Fair View rank in the top 5 percent for the state. Source: Connecticut State Department of Education.

[5] In 1994–95, the average annual salary for public elementary and secondary school teachers in the US was $37,868. The average salary in Connecticut was $51,495. Connecticut ranked first for the third consecutive year (US Department of Education 1996: 85).

he uses to advance them ("a lot of big words that we don't usually use"). Segal makes it clear that she expects adults in her classroom to use language that children readily understand, and that she regards students as competent and knowledgeable participants, in this instance in the project of evaluating and working to improve the CMT. It is Susan – not the teacher, the principal, or the state official – who is formally in charge of running the meeting, and Segal helps this student assert her authority, even against Travero's efforts to take control. Children's questions and concerns provide the impetus for the meeting with the state official, and they play a significant role in determining its agenda.

What is more, the criticisms Segal's students voice and the responses these elicit from Travero are deemed sufficiently important to warrant the attention of the principal, the assistant superintendent, and the local newspaper. In Segal's classroom, students get the message that they are not only competent and knowledgeable, but also effective at eliciting a response from an important adult who visits their school to address their concerns, and who promises to make changes in a state test in response to them. These fourth graders are critical of John Travero's rhetorical strategies ("He had a lot of big words". . . "He explained questions, he didn't answer them"). They challenge the legitimacy of his claims ("It's sort of like he's telling us he's older and knows better"), asserting that their own experiences provide more valid grounds for evaluating the CMT ("When he said he looked at it last night – he didn't take the test!"). Yet they seem to experience themselves as effective, as achieving at least some of the results they aimed for ("I think we may have changed it").

The morning's events, then, might appear a skillfully orchestrated exercise in empowering the children of those who, by virtue of their social position, have power in contemporary American society. It might appear, that is, to be an effort, in large part successful, to provide the offspring of those who are privileged with the opportunities, skills, values, and attitudes they need in order to get others to do what they want them to do, or what serves their interests, "to carry out [their] own will, despite resistance."[6] In this chapter, I make the case that differences between what happens in Segal's classroom and what happens in Veronica Franklin's are real and significant. My central claim, however, is that to begin an exploration of these differences by defining Segal as a powerful teacher who chooses to use an empowering pedagogy is to overlook much of the work power performs at Fair View.

I focus, as I did in chapter 4, on classroom management, school knowledge, and the production of the responsible student. Again, I ask,

[6] Weber (1947: 152).

not "Who has power?" or "How do *A*'s choices affect *B*'s free action?" but rather "How do social boundaries to action shape the field of the possible for Segal, her students, and others at Fair View?" In the first section I argue that, although political freedom is promoted at this site in the sense that all are enabled to participate in rule-making, it is restricted along a second important dimension. The ends of local pedagogic practices are depoliticized, as are standards of knowledgeability and other forms of excellence, and definitions of social identities. This form of restriction on the social capacity for action should concern students of power relations, I argue in the second section because it can promote and legitimize the punishment of the forms of difference that ends, standards, and identities create. My claim in the third section is that the very political practices, and the municipal, educational, and other public institutions that at North End produce "the environment," cultivate domination at Fair View by enabling and encouraging teachers and other actors to experience this community as a relatively self-contained social "world." Public institutions and practices shield local ends and standards from forms of contestation that might unsettle them, while mapping distinctions between those who do and those who do not conform on to social group identities of race and ethnicity, class, and place.

Pedagogy: observations from Monica Segal's classroom

"Classroom management"

The morning of my first visit to the Fair View Elementary School, Monica Segal and I meet in the hallway outside her classroom. She extends her hand and introduces herself to me as "Monica." She looks to be in her mid- to late twenties. She has shoulder-length curly brown hair. She wears a t-shirt tucked into belted blue jeans, eye glasses, no make-up. Segal tells me that I can wait in the classroom while she goes to pick up her students from music.

Inside, I sit in an armchair near what I later learn is called "the sports center," a corner of the room in which the blue wall-to-wall carpet is covered by an area rug patterned with tennis rackets, footballs, and other athletic equipment. The sports center is where Segal's fourth graders hold their class meetings. Several times each day, the children gather here and sit on the floor, cross-legged, in no particular order. As I wait, I notice the display on the sports center wall: two poster-board squares, side by side, each surrounded on all four sides by smaller rectangles from which

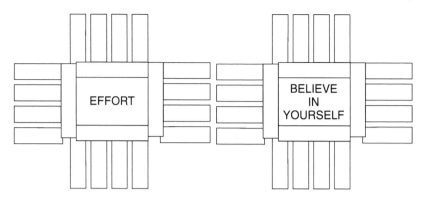

emanate, ray-like, additional quadruplets of poster-board rectangles. The square on the left reads, "Effort," its mate, "Believe in Yourself." These, Segal later explains to me, are the "central values" of her classroom. Each of the four rectangles lining the perimeter of the two large squares identifies what the teacher refers to as an "aspect of the central value" that the square represents, and each ray, a step toward realizing that "aspect." The four aspects of "Effort" are "trying your best," "thinking," "reaching out," and "working hard." The aspects of "Believe in Yourself" are "risk-taking," "not saying, 'I can't,'" "positive attitude," and "like who you are."

As Segal's fourth graders enter the classroom, their teacher instructs them to take a seat in the sports center. She adds that they should introduce themselves to me before they sit down. One by one, the children approach, shake my hand, and tell me their names. They sit on the sports center rug and talk to each other, not inordinately loudly, but not whispering.

After a few minutes, Segal approaches the seated children and announces, "I'm waiting for you to be ready."

All the students but one stop talking. Segal addresses the child by name, stating that she will wait until he is ready to begin.

"Sorry," the boy replies, and he immediately falls silent.

Disciplining students appears not to be a primary focus of attention for Monica Segal or for other adults at Fair View Elementary. Compared with Franklin's classroom, and with the hallways and other shared spaces at the North End Community School, Segal's classroom and Fair View Elementary are the sites of relatively few dramatic "classroom management" events. Only rarely do teachers at this school impose penalties upon or publicly reprimand students. When they do, they tend to do so disimpassionedly, often simply by observing aloud that a given conduct interferes with some desirable activity or end. "I'm waiting for you to be ready," Segal tells her students. And again, not raising her voice, "I'll wait until you're ready to begin."

When this teacher does "correct" a student, she tends to do so in a private, one-on-one discussion, in which she asks the child to reflect on her conduct, to think about why it is undesirable, and why she engaged in it. For instance, when Corey and Lawrence roll their eyes and make faces at a group of their classmates who have composed and performed for the class a "rap song" about multiplication, Segal takes the boys aside and speaks with them in serious, hushed tones. I hear her tell them, "I really want you to think about why you criticize people so much." Often these teacher-mandated self-evaluations take the form of letters of apology, in which the errant child must explain why what she did was inappropriate or wrong. Rarely does Segal deal in commands, public reprimands, or sanctions.

Nor does this teacher supervise her students as closely as does Veronica Franklin. Instead, Segal explains to me, she aims to give the children in her class as much leeway as practicable, to avoid superintending their work any more than she judges necessary. Thus, when a student wants to work at a computer at a time when the classroom terminals are in use, she is permitted to leave the classroom unattended in order to work on a computer in another room in the school. Students are allowed to talk to each other while they work independently, that is, throughout most of the school day, and there is no stipulation, as there is in Franklin's classroom, that children may speak only about school work. In sharp contrast with the careful policing at North End of student movement both within and to and from the classroom, Segal allows students to move freely in her classroom and permits them to travel from place to place in the school, often without lining up and almost always without maintaining silence. My observations at Fair View throughout the year suggest that Segal's policies are not unique to her classroom. Even before I meet her in the hall that first morning, I am struck by the sight – surprising after a day at the North End Community School – of pairs of children traveling throughout the hallways, unsupervised, delivering attendance sheets and other messages.

In Segal's classroom, students are actively engaged in creating and enforcing rules. Not only Segal, but also her students, are permitted to – and regularly do – get up from their work tables to turn off the classroom lights momentarily, as one child explains to me, in order to "remind us that the noise level has gotten too high for concentrating." It is not the case that this teacher and other adults in positions of authority at Fair View defer completely to student judgments about rules. To the contrary, as Segal herself points out to me on more than one occasion, it is common practice, in her words, to "manipulate" children to arrive at the decisions at which adults want them to arrive. Consider the following field notes excerpt:

Before the children go to the cafeteria, they meet in the sports center. Segal explains to them that, when she was editing their writing, she had a problem because there was not enough space on their papers for her comments and suggestions. She asks what they think the class should do about that.

One boy raises his hand and says that Segal could write comments on the back of their papers or on a separate sheet of paper.

The teacher responds that, when she wants to edit particular parts of a story, she needs to write right next to those parts.

A girl raises her hand and suggests that students skip every other line when they write.

Segal says she thinks that is a good idea, and that that is what the children should do. She reminds her students that previously they had agreed to skip lines when writing stories and other assignments.

Clearly, the purpose of the meeting described above is to remind students to follow a rule they previously agreed to follow. The conclusion is foregone. It is not the case that any solution to Segal's "problem" will suffice. In this sense, the teacher does "manipulate" her students. She steers their discussion toward a particular solution, which she determined in advance. None the less, she structures the meeting – and in doing so she handles the matter in a manner that is prototypical of her disciplinary practice – to encourage children to derive the rule themselves, to understand or to recall the purpose it serves, and to actively agree to abide by it.

On those (relatively infrequent) occasions on which a rule is prescribed or enforced by a Fair View school authority, it is, almost without fail, accompanied by an explanation of the purpose it serves. There is little trace here of the seeming arbitrariness of discipline at the North End Community School. Thus, when Segal reminds her students to lower their voices as they walk down the hallway, she adds, "so as not to disturb others' learning." Her approach to discipline is based on the assumption, not only that children should collaborate with adults in making and enforcing most rules, but also that they should understand the rationale behind all school and classroom rules, the reasons for prohibiting or discouraging some activities and requiring or encouraging others. What is more, some rules are applicable to adults as well as to children. For example, when a fire fighter who visits the classroom instructs Segal's students to check their home smoke detectors and to have an adult sign their homework pads to verify that they have completed this task, it is deemed acceptable – not an act of insolence – for a child to raise her hand and ask who will sign to indicate that Segal has checked her smoke detector. ("My roommate," the teacher replies nonchalantly.)

At Fair View Elementary, classroom management is not a matter of compelling students to demonstrate deference toward those in positions of authority by obeying, unquestioningly, their teachers' commands, so much as encouraging them to master and embrace both the rules and what Segal refers to as the "values" that govern school life. The latter, which give meaning and content to the former, consist in standards of good conduct – in particular, norms governing the ways children should approach their work and interact and communicate with others – and character – especially personal traits, beliefs about the self, and attitudes toward school and classroom activities.

Implicit in this teacher's approach to classroom management is a distinction between, on the one hand, these "values," and on the other, classroom rules. Rules, her participatory approach to discipline suggests, are the product of human judgment. Because they can be decided in more than one way, they are subject to discussion, debate, and even at times legitimate challenge or contestation.

The former are not. This teacher does not hold class meetings to debate whether or not students should "work hard," and if so, at what. She does not explain to her fourth graders why a "positive attitude" toward school work and classroom projects and activities, rather than, say, a critical attitude is desirable.

A central claim I advance in this chapter is that what Segal calls "values" regulate social action in the classroom. "Values" allow and encourage specific ways of conducting oneself and particular attitudes, beliefs, and aspirations. They disallow and discourage others. For example, they encourage working to develop the cognitive skills that promote success in dominant academic and professional institutions. They discourage exhibiting a lack of motivation to succeed, demonstrating insufficient enthusiasm about school learning, and expressing an irreverent attitude toward classroom activities and assignments. They encourage children to "reach out" to their peers by expressing their thoughts clearly and rationally, and by resolving disputes smoothly with reference to their shared interests in cultivating an environment conducive to learning. They discourage them from expressing themselves emotionally or from demonstrating uncertainty about what they think and believe.

The principal difference between classroom management at the North End Community School and at Fair View Elementary, then, is *not* that the former is characterized by firm limits to student conduct, while the latter is not. Nor is it that transgressing limits is punished at North End, but not at Fair View. Subtle expressions of disapproval and the withholding of positive attention and praise can be as effective mechanisms for punishing deviations from required behavior and performance as can public reprimands, detentions, or "punishment papers."

Instead, the principal differences are, first, the forms that limits take – not injunctions and prohibitions, but norms and standards of good conduct and character – and, second, the means by which these are policed – not by demanding that students obey, so much as by inducing them to accept and to conform willingly. Without Veronica Franklin's "authoritarianism," Segal rewards particular ways of conducting oneself, while she (gently) punishes others.

School knowledge

During the morning class meeting, Segal explains to her students that today they will continue to work on preparing their portfolios for the upcoming parent–child conferences. She walks across the classroom and turns her back to write on the board.

Mark says, softly, "No thank you."

Segal turns around. "Excuse me?" she says.

The boy looks down and responds, "I was just kidding."

Segal pauses for a moment. She then asks her fourth graders what "reflection papers" are. Corey raises his hand. He answers that they are "like 'quick-writes.'"

Segal says that reflection papers are "not quite the same thing as quick-writes." "If quick-writes were drafts," she says, "reflection papers would be good copies." A reflection paper is "not just an idea," but "a good idea," she elaborates, adding that reflection papers require time and care.

Hanging on the sports center wall behind Segal is a hand-written sign listing the contents of a completed conference portfolio. It reads:

> Self evaluation*
> Peer evaluation
> Letter from Miss Segal
> Homework Grade Graph

Reading Journal Page
Reading Book Page
Spelling Page
Writing Piece } All with a Written Reflection*
Math Paper
Explorations Paper
Free Choice Paper

* Must go through writing process (pre-write, draft, revise, edit, final copy)

Later that morning, the principal, Anita Byrne, arrives in Segal's class-room for a scheduled observation. Monica Segal is in her third year of teaching, which means that this spring either she will be dismissed from her job or she will be rehired with tenure. The principal and vice principal observe Segal, as they do all non-tenured Fair View teachers, five times during the course of the year. The principal purpose of these observations, Segal explains to me later, in an interview, is "to decide whether or not they're going to offer you a job back."

Anita Byrne does not make eye contact with Segal or speak to her or the students. She walks to a table near the back of the classroom, where she sits, a pad of paper and pen in hand. Throughout the lesson she writes continuously, not looking up from the pad.

Meanwhile, Segal gathers her students around her on the floor near the board at the front of the classroom. She uses an overhead projector to show the poem "October" by Robert Frost, and she begins to relate to the children an experience she had while teaching them the poem. The day the class first read "October," Segal says, she noticed that Peter used a word from the poem – "thy" – when he was writing his own poem. Segal explains that she keeps a journal about what the students do each day in school. On that day, she says, she wrote in her journal that she realized that reading helps students learn about writing. She initiates a short class discussion, asking students to comment on how, when she was writing in her journal, she had thought about what she had learned when teaching "October."

Next, Segal asks two students to present to the class work that they have chosen to include in their conference portfolios. Christopher, who selected a math paper on palindromes, uses the projector to show the paper to his classmates while he explains why he chose it. Jackie presents a short story she wrote about getting lost in a shopping mall. Segal ends the lesson by using her oversized pad of paper to write, with the class, a "reflection" on Christopher's math page. "What were you thinking as you worked on this paper?" she asks him. "What strategies did you use? What did you learn?" Segal, together with Christopher's classmates, helps the boy clarify his ideas about the significance of the paper and the process of working on it.

When her observation has ended, Anita Byrne stands up and leaves the classroom, again without speaking. Segal's fourth graders return to their tables to work on reflections and peer evaluations. The latter they write on photocopied forms that read "_____ is good at _____ and needs to work at _____." Each child evaluates one classmate. Typical responses are:

> (Name) is good at coming up with questions for group discussion and needs to work at being nice to people who aren't his friends.
>
> (Name) is good at expressing her ideas and needs to work at letting others speak without interrupting them.
>
> (Name) is good at listening to others and needs to work at expressing her own point of view.

These tasks occupy the rest of the morning and most of the afternoon. As they work, several children comment that time goes by quickly while they are writing.

Anita Byrne's behavior during her observation of Monica Segal's class, conduct that likely would puzzle anyone unfamiliar with the vagaries of the Connecticut teacher assessment program, mirrors that of assessors trained by the state Department of Education to evaluate new public school teachers. Herself a trained assessor, Byrne conducts observations according to state protocol. Fourth grade teacher Fiona Farley, who characterizes Byrne's observations as "very stressful," describes them as follows:

She comes in the room, you know, it's very formal . . . And, you know, I time it— she walks in precisely at the moment that the lesson is scheduled to begin, so you have to be completely . . . ready. The minute she walks in the door she sits at the back table, and you start. And she does not look up from the paper. She's scripting the entire time. And at the end of the lesson she walks out, totally stone-faced, doesn't smile. You never make eye contact. And she does it exactly, as I said, this is the way the state does.

These conditions make Monica Segal's lesson atypical in some respects, in particular in its structure, which follows Connecticut state guidelines. Segal stands in front of her class. She lectures. She begins with what, in the jargon of professional educators, is called an "anticipatory set." She ends by asking for student responses to the question "What is a reflection?": the state-prescribed format for "closure." When she is not being observed by her principal or another supervisor, it is rare for Segal to lecture even for relatively short periods of time. Several of Segal's students demonstrate during the lecture that they are unaccustomed to sitting still and listening. They fidget and stare off into space as their teacher speaks. It is more common for Segal to introduce new concepts and activities with informal class discussions. As a matter of course, this teacher reserves the majority of each class period for independent work.

The lesson is, none the less, representative in other respects. In the discussion that follows, I focus on five defining characteristics of Segal's pedagogy, which it exemplifies.

First, the lesson actively engages students as knowledgeable and competent participants. Segal involves students, most notably in this lesson Christopher and Jackie, as collaborators, not, as in Franklin's classroom, as subordinates required to follow instructions and obey orders. Monica Segal's fourth graders participate still more actively in her typical, less formally structured lessons. Several times a week, for instance, they work on "writer's workshop," composing original, usually fictional writing pieces, meeting with classmates who review and make suggestions for revising first drafts, revising their writing, and only then editing with an adult (with Segal, that is, or frequently with me). The first time this teacher explains to me how to edit student work, she emphasizes that she is not overly critical. She does not "mark the paper up too much," and she never uses red pen. Unlike Franklin, who "corrects" student work by pointing out errors and reprimanding children for their mistakes, Segal "edits" with a view to ensuring that children maintain a significant measure of control over the writing process. What is more, when introducing new material to her class, Segal often asks the advice of a student who has some expertise with the subject matter. Consider the following field notes excerpt:

Monica Segal asks the students to gather around the computers so that they can all see the screens. She gives a demonstration of several new math games, which the children will work on later today.

Since Jimmy has completed all of his math work, he already has begun to play the games, and Segal asks his advice more than once during the demonstration. She asks him which games he found to be the hardest, which he thinks are best to start with, etc.

The lesson described above is typical, secondly, in its content. In Monica Segal's classroom, learning is less a matter of mastering facts and the rules governing their use than analyzing concepts and statements and devising problem-solving strategies. Segal's class fulfills the district requirement that fourth graders complete a unit on Greek myths, for example, by reading myths, keeping personal journals in which they write questions and commentary, and using what they write in their journals to open small-group student-led discussions. Near the end of the unit, the teacher convenes a meeting of the entire class during which students collaborate to create the following list, which they entitle "Elements of a Myth":

1. Who the story is about: details about characters.
2. Explains problem or conflict. Usually involves love, task involved.
3. Something goes wrong. A lie involved or a trick.
4. Problem is fixed, maybe with the help of a god.
5. Someone dies or ends up in the skies.
6. Explain why in the sky.

Students then work independently, using the list as a starting-point, to conceive, write, and illustrate their own myths.

In Monica Segal's classroom, the aim of the study of the Greek myth is not to complete a series of tasks or to consume, and then regurgitate on command, "pieces of knowledge." Instead, it is to analyze the substance and structure of the myth; to identify its component parts, their function, and their inter-relationships; and to use the results of this examination to engage in the process of constructing an original story.

Segal takes a similar approach to instructing students in most academic subject matters, and she encourages them to apply analogous analytic techniques to their own cognitive processes. "What were you thinking as you worked on this paper?" she asks Christopher during the lesson on reflections. The question is not anomalous. In this classroom, where school knowledge is a matter of analytic facility and the ability to identify and solve problems, the focus of learning tends toward the meta-cognitive. Students keep math journals, for example, in which they complete for each exercise with math manipulatives an entry describing, in Segal's words, "what you did, what you were thinking as you did it, what you learned." A central feature of this teacher's pedagogy is her effort to cultivate among students a conscious awareness of the self as a thinker and learner.

The lesson is typical, third, in the role Monica Segal plays in directing it. In this classroom the teacher is not, as in Franklin's classroom, the "keeper of knowledge," who dispenses facts and rules and functions as the sole legitimate judge of student knowledgeability. Rather, she is a facilitator for what Segal and her colleagues refer to as "the learning process." "The learning process," a phrase Fair View teachers invoke frequently, enjoys a quasi-sacred status at the school, where safeguarding it is the stated rationale behind most rules (children should not speak loudly when walking in the hallway, then, because doing so interferes with the learning process).

"The learning process" encompasses all Fair View school activities, projects, and experiences, because, and to the extent that, these promote the development of three crucial sets of skills and capacities: analytic and problem-solving abilities; the skills and dispositions needed to work effectively with others; and the personal qualities of, in the words of fourth grade teacher Risa Hanson, "self-reliant and . . . independent learners."[7] The learning process promotes rigorous thinking. It helps develop the skills needed to negotiate, to cooperate, and to function as a leader in a group. It fosters intellectual curiosity, confidence, the ability to set goals and work to attain them, and the capacity to assess one's own strengths and weaknesses as a learner. The latter, in particular, is central to Segal's classroom, where students regularly evaluate their own work. The contents of the portfolios students prepare in the above lesson, then, are, with the exception of the "Letter from Miss Segal," composed by the children themselves. The parent–child conferences at which these will be presented are representative of Segal's approach to student assessment, in that they are premised upon the assumption that students are legitimate judges of their own performance.

Fourth, the lesson demonstrates that the good student at this site is defined, not in terms of obedience to the intellectual authority of teachers and texts, but rather in terms of her serious attitude toward her work, the effort she expends, and the initiative and care she takes as she participates in "the learning process." The good student values learning. She strives to develop her talents and realize her aspirations, and she is driven to work well and progress intellectually. She is confident and articulate, capable of presenting her ideas to others. She listens to and learns from her teachers and peers. She is capable of working with others to solve problems and complete projects, yet she never loses her independence of thought, her ability to "express her own point of view."

Recall that Veronica Franklin punishes, not only children in her class who fail to demonstrate that they have mastered the requisite facts and rules, but also those who fail to demonstrate obedience to intellectual authority, for example by asking questions or attempting to initiate inquiries during class discussions. Not so Monica Segal. Compare this teacher's reaction to student questions during a science lesson about stars with Franklin's negative response to a similar classroom incident (described in chapter 4):

While the students eat their snacks, Monica Segal reviews the meanings of words listed on the big pad. These include "meteor," "black hole," "asteroid," "planet," "nova," and "supernova." The review session is punctuated with student questions. For example, Peter asks, "When they talk about a star, is it shaped like a star?" Segal tells Peter that his question is a good one, and she answers it.

---

[7] The quote is from an interview I conducted with Hanson.

Similarly, whereas Franklin punishes, Segal rewards students who complete assignments in a novel way. Another excerpt from my field notes will illustrate:

Students work on revising and editing "Off in the Distance . . ." stories, assignments Monica Segal gave the class after its recent visit to the planetarium. Almost all of the children write stories about space, most of which involve space travel and/or aliens.

But there is one exception. Peter writes what Monica characterizes as a children's book, a story describing a series of objects which the narrator sees in the distance. The story begins "Off in the distance I saw an old, old barn." The next page reads, "Off in the distance, behind the old, old barn I saw a (name of object)." The story continues along these lines.

Peter types his story at the computer, selecting a large font for the first line (about the old, old barn), a slightly smaller font for the next phrase describing the object immediately behind the barn, etc., until the line describing the last object the narrator sees (at the end of the book) is printed in a very small font.

Monica Segal devotes a relatively long period of time to working with Peter at the computer. She praises his original approach to the story, interrupting the other students' work to draw their attention to it and to explain it to them.

Finally, the lesson on "reflections" illustrates the effort Monica Segal makes to clarify for her students the purposes that school work and classroom activities serve. Unlike Franklin, who eschews explicit discussions of the purpose of school assignments, implicitly defining their purpose in terms of "getting it right," earning high grades or other rewards, or avoiding punishment, Segal has tacked to her classroom wall a string of cut-out cardboard "Y"s, in order to remind students, in her words, to "always ask why."

"Why are we spending so much time doing graphs?" Peter wonders aloud one December morning as Segal's students work on creating graphs representing the outdoor temperature during school days in November.

Segal responds by drawing Peter's classmates' attention to his question, which, she says, is a good one. "Why *are* we spending so much time doing graphs?" she asks.

The question elicits several answers, including Kathryn's, which is that graphs help people organize information, and Corey's, which is that children will need to use graphs when they grow up. Most often, Segal and her students define the purpose of school work in terms of developing the cognitive and social skills and the personal traits that "the learning process" promotes: characteristics and competencies that, Segal's pedagogy suggests, have intrinsic worth. They acknowledge, in addition, that school work is useful for attaining extrinsic ends, in particular future academic and professional success. But the emphasis is on the former. The competencies the learning process promotes are rewarded, because they are intrinsically valuable, an important form of human excellence. "Success" is more a happy by-product of the learning process than its principal end.

Pedagogic practices at Fair View, then, promote political freedom along the participatory dimension. They encourage active and competent student participation in the learning process. This is not, however, to claim that they enable free action in the sense of promoting forms of thought and speech that are independent of social constraint. To the contrary, learning process ends and excellences themselves function as important social limits to action, boundaries that make possible and encourage certain forms of action, while discouraging others.

At Fair View these boundaries defining local pedagogic practices tend to be removed from the reach of the analytic and critical thought that Segal and others at the school valorize. Students are not permitted to express a lack of enthusiasm for school activities or projects. They are corrected if they suggest that particular lessons and assignments do not contribute to developing important personal, social, and cognitive skills. Segal generally reproaches or withholds attention and approval from children who demonstrate insufficient motivation, intellectual curiosity, or interest in school work. ("Excuse me?" is her petulant response to Mark's expressed lack of enthusiasm at the prospect of working on portfolios.)

On the relatively frequent occasions on which this teacher requires students to write "reflections" describing what they learned from school activities and assignments, she makes it clear that they must draw some educative significance from all "learning process" experiences. Thus after the class views a video on bus safety, she requires a student to re-write a reflection she submits that begins, "I didn't learn anything, but the video reminded me . . ."

Expressing irreverence toward school work or learning is an almost certain means to eliciting one of Segal's relatively rare rebukes. When, for example, during a class exercise, Corey offers a humorous response to a question the teacher poses, she does not smile. "I am not trying to be silly by playing this game," she responds sternly. "I am trying to get you to think."

The responsible student, 1

Monica Segal gathers her students together in the sports center, where she tells them that they need to decide how to organize the class library. She reviews the general categories of books in the library (picture books, chapter books, science and nature) and the types of shelving available. During the discussion, students raise their hands and offer suggestions. One girl suggests that all of the books should face spine out, so that the titles are easy to read. Segal says that is a very good idea. Another child suggests that the class divide the books by category, which Segal says is a good idea as well.

Segal then instructs her students to divide themselves into groups of four. She says that each group must include boys and girls. Some of the children have difficulty with this task. A group of three girls who want to be together negotiate until two decide to exclude the third, who grasps their hands, physically refusing to leave the group. Lawrence, a boy who recently transferred to Fair View from a core urban public school in Bridgeport, Connecticut,[8] has trouble as well. No group is willing to include him. The result of this self-sorting process is several groups of four, one group twice the size Segal specified, and Lawrence, who is not in any group.

Lawrence approaches his teacher and says, "Just forget it. They hate me."

Segal responds, "They don't hate you." She announces that the large group, plus Lawrence, is in charge of sorting picture books.

The picture book group proceeds to quarrel about the logistics of sorting. Meanwhile, members of the other groups (one in charge of chapter books, one in charge of science books, one in charge of sorting the unorganized stacks of books in the library and distributing them to the others) decide how to complete their tasks. The picture book group divides itself into two smaller groups, which begin to work at separate tables, engaging in a series of disputes over turf. Segal intervenes. She sends the entire group, both factions, to the sports center, instructing the students that they "need to" work together, and that they have to decide how to organize themselves before they may resume. Segal says that the children have more than six hundred books to organize, and that they better decide how to do it.

After a few false starts, students in the picture book group agree to organize all the books by author. Monica Segal points out to me, quietly, that since there are at most four or five books by any author, and since relatively few authors have written more than one book in the library, this arrangement will prove impossible. She says that it will probably take the children about ten minutes to figure this out.

---

[8] Lawrence transferred at the start of the school year, because his father moved in with a woman who lives in Fair View. The only child in Segal's classroom who previously attended an inner-city school, Lawrence is among the 5 percent of Fair View students not classified as "white."

In fact, it takes about five. The students agree, instead, to arrange the books according to the first letter of the author's last name. One child affixes to the table at which the group is working, and to the carpeted floor beneath, small pieces of masking tape with the letters A through Z printed on them. The others begin to sort.

Re-arranging the library occupies most of the remainder of the afternoon, a little over an hour. When the job is completed, Segal takes her students on what she calls a "tour" of their classroom library, pointing out to them how to locate, and then when they are finished reading, how to re-shelve the various categories of books.

The responsible student, 2

Monica Segal announces to her students that next week a class from the Regional Center for Handicapped Students will move into the Fair View Elementary School building. The class will consist of four or five of Fair View County's most severely physically handicapped pre-school-aged children.

Segal asks her class what the word "handicapped" means, and there follows a short discussion. Student comments include, "You should be nice to them because it isn't their fault."

Segal tells her class that, because they are fourth graders, they should set an example for the rest of the school. They should be friendly and polite. They should not stare or laugh at the children. Each student will have a full-time teacher or aide who works with her, and Segal suggests that the fourth graders offer to help the aides when they see them in the hall, for example, by opening doors for them. She says that it is okay for students to say hello to the pre-schoolers, but adds that they may not be able to talk or respond.

Segal explains that last year the same class was in a room in the basement of the school. The teachers and the students, she says, "did not feel very welcome." She picks up a pen, turns, and writes on the big pad of paper: "Welcome back! We are glad that you are here." She tells her students that they should come up, one or two at a time, and draw a picture on the sign, which they will then hang on the door of the new students' classroom.

Segal's students return to their work, taking turns getting up from their seats and coming up to the sign to draw pictures on it. They draw flowers, hearts, human faces. One boy draws what he says is an electric wheelchair.

Lawrence approaches the pad and proceeds to draw a face with eyes that have no eyeballs, a mass of curly hair, and an oversized mouth from which protrude large, pointy teeth. He announces that he has drawn "a criminally insane person."

Segal tells Lawrence, "That was a smart-assed thing to do." She instructs him to write a letter of apology. She asks several of the boy's classmates to modify Lawrence's drawing, which they do, using liquid paper and colored markers.

As Lawrence writes, I look over his shoulder and see that his letter says that he "meant it as a joke and didn't know [he] would get in trouble."

When Lawrence brings the letter to Segal, she asks him why he thinks she did not think it was funny. He says something that I cannot hear. Segal says, "Go write that down."

You are responsible. In chapter 4, I argued that this statement, this claim that students are the agents of the outcomes their actions cause, is a central component of the message about personal responsibility that Veronica Franklin communicates to her students at North End. Who you are, she teaches the children in her charge, combined with the choices you make, determines your present and future, your lot in life. At North End, this assertion translates into the claim that the responsible student – the child who follows instructions and obeys the rules – eventually will attain the material and other rewards associated with "responsible citizenship."

In Segal's classroom, as in Franklin's, personal responsibility is a central concern. But this teacher tends to make the claim *you are responsible* less directly, and in rather different circumstances. Here responsibility is not a matter of accountability so much as self-sufficiency. To "be responsible" is to take charge, to do for oneself, to be vested with a sense of ownership in the process of working, as well as in what one produces. Segal gives her students the message *you are responsible* in contexts in which she also grants them a significant measure of control over their work and the environment in which they perform it, defines them as competent and knowledgeable classroom participants, and requires them to decide for themselves how to attain given aims or ends. In the lesson described in the first vignette above, the teacher could have instructed her students about how to organize the class library. She could have divided them into groups herself. She could have mediated their disputes more actively. She could have intervened when the "picture book group" devised a strategy that she knew would fail. Alternatively, she could have asked her teacher's aide, her classroom volunteer (me), or one of the many Fair View parents who stand ready to come in and help in the classroom, to reorganize the library for her students. But she did not.

Consider Segal's claim[9] that her principal pedagogic aim is teaching students to "learn to manage freedom." In elaborating on her understanding of this goal, Segal explains to me that an important part of her strategy for realizing it is to "get the kids to take responsibility for as much as possible in the classroom." This includes grading their own homework and, generally, evaluating their own performance in school. It includes running parents' night: explaining to visiting parents how the class has organized the classroom and how they spend their school days, as well as evaluating themselves for their parents with reference to their classroom's "central values." "Managing freedom" at Fair View is largely a matter of working to conform to local pedagogic standards and to develop "learning process" skills and competencies with minimal adult supervision. Monica Segal gives students (limited) control, then, vests them with a sense of ownership, and defines them as knowledgeable and competent, in order to encourage the development of the self-discipline, the self-motivation, and the self-regulation that, at Fair View, define the responsible student.

Before turning to a consideration of student responses to pedagogic practice at Fair View, I want to draw attention to an important aspect of "responsibility" as defined at this school. A crucial assumption sustaining Segal's pedagogy is that the individual herself is capable of deciding whether or not to "be responsible" in this sense.

Students can direct their own conduct and, with insistent care, they can mold their own characters. Hence the practice of almost relentless self-evaluation in Segal's classroom, and the teacher's reliance on letters of apology as means to correcting student behavior. The aim of the latter is less to compel the child to parrot her teacher's condemnation of her actions, in order to counter an act of disobedience with a demonstration of deference to authority, than to encourage the child to derive and articulate that judgment herself, of her own accord.

Consider the strategy this teacher adopts midway through spring semester, one attempt among many to induce Lawrence to take an active role in monitoring and amending his behavior, attitudes, and values. Segal begins in late April to keep what she refers to as a "journal" with Lawrence, in which she writes notes asking him to explain why he performs specific actions that she views as inappropriate or objectionable, and to devise strategies for correcting his conduct. The entries, no more than one per day, are printed neatly in a small blue notebook bearing the name "Miss Segal" on its cover. A typical journal page reads:

[9] This statement was unsolicited. She made it during the course of one of my first days in her classroom, not during an interview, and not in response to a question.

(SEGAL'S WRITING): Why did you forget your recorder today? What can I do to
   help you remember?
(LAWRENCE'S WRITING): Maybe you could remind me. Maybe you could get
   my dad to help me remember.

Segal shows me this notebook on only one occasion. She says, making
reference to the entry by Lawrence cited above (which struck me as a reasonable response to a question asking specifically how Segal herself might
help solve the problem), that Lawrence's responses signal a persistent
refusal to "take personal responsibility." Recall that at the North End
Community School, Franklin and her colleagues voice their suspicion
that some deficiency puts responsibility as accountability beyond the
reach of "problem students." At Fair View, by contrast, whether to "be
responsible" (whether to do for oneself, to be self-sufficient, to "manage
freedom") is, itself, a choice for which the individual is responsible.

Power: action upon action

Schooling in Monica Segal's Fair View classroom is, in important ways,
enabling. It is not, however, "empowering" in the sense of granting students access to power's mechanisms so that they might act independently
or authentically. Although Segal's disciplinary practices encourage
student participation in rule-making, this rule-making itself is constrained by classroom "values," which are placed beyond students' reach.
Although Segal's methods of instruction encourage active student participation in school work and learning, they discourage children from rejecting or contesting ends and standards defining the "learning process."
And, although Segal defines responsibility not as accountability so much
as self-sufficiency – a capacity and propensity to "manage" freedom – her
definition of the responsible student is itself naturalized. "Being responsible" at Fair View is a matter of choosing to adhere to (extra-political)
values and to pursue (depoliticized) learning process ends.

   In the discussion that follows, I make the case that this depoliticization
of Fair View "values," "learning process" ends and excellences, and the
definition of responsibility as self-sufficiency constrains students' political freedom, by limiting their capacity to act upon key norms and standards governing their classroom. This form of restriction on freedom is
normatively significant, I argue, because it fosters punishing attitudes
toward, beliefs about, and treatment of actors who transgress prevailing
standards and fail to attain local pedagogic ends. This is an intra-, as well
as intersubjective phenomenon. I emphasize both self-discipline and the
punishment of individuals, like Lawrence, who tend not to discipline
themselves. By depoliticizing local standards, ends, and identities,

my account suggests, pedagogic practices at Fair View translate the differences they produce into defects. These practices thereby promote and legitimize punishment, which they implicitly define as a remedial process serving the interests of those it affects.

Mark breaks "a very giant rule"

Monica Segal is reading aloud to the class when Mark returns from using the computer in another classroom. Just after passing through the door, the boy stops suddenly and announces that he "accidentally printed in another teacher's classroom."

Segal stops reading. She says that Mark has broken "a very giant rule, because he interrupted someone else's teaching." She tells him to write a note apologizing to the teacher in whose classroom he printed his work.

Mark sits down at a table and begins to write, while Segal continues to read aloud to the rest of the class. After a few minutes, he picks up his paper and starts to walk toward the door.

"Let me see it," says Segal. Mark brings her the note. The teacher reads it to herself, looks up at the boy, and says, "Why? Because you disturbed her teaching." Again, Mark takes a seat at the table, where he adds to the note the reason for his apology.

When Mark returns from delivering the revised letter, Segal explains to the entire class that students should always print their work in their own classroom, so that the sound of the printer does not disrupt another class's lesson. "Thanks, Mark," she adds, before she resumes reading aloud.

At the North End Community School, where Veronica Franklin and other adults require students to obey rules prescribed by those in positions of authority, a significant percentage of students offer no explanation or a circular explanation of the purpose rules serve, or define that purpose with reference to the bad character or conduct of students.[10] I argued in chapter 4 that when North End students obey, they tend do so without inquiring into the purpose rules serve and without helping determine their content. And when they "resist," their resistance is limited in patterned ways. Children dispute the facts of individual cases of alleged wrong-doing and object to perceived lapses in the impartiality of the administration of punishment, but rarely if ever challenge the content of rules, the appropriateness of the sanctions attached to violations, or the processes by which rules and punishments are determined. North End

---

[10] Here 38 percent do so, compared with 15 percent at Fair View. See chapter 4, pp. 85–6.

students are not permitted or encouraged to deliberate about or to participate in making and enforcing school and classroom rules, and generally they do not.

At Fair View Elementary, by contrast, where children are permitted and encouraged to participate in making decisions about how to govern their classroom and school, they tend to define the purpose of rules as serving their collective interests, and in particular in terms of promoting the learning process. As noted in chapter 4, a higher percentage of Fair View fourth graders than North End fourth and fifth graders define the purpose of school rules in terms of preventing disorder, promoting order, preventing harm, or promoting student safety and well-being.[11] What is more, at Fair View, one-third of those who identify the purpose of rules as preventing disorder or promoting order make explicit reference to the aim of fostering an environment conducive to working and/or learning: for example, "I think we need rules because without them everything would be out of hand and no one would learn anything." By contrast, not one North End student response to this question makes reference to promoting learning or enabling students to work effectively.[12]

Fair View students regularly take part in deliberating about and making rules. Throughout the year, I observed consistently high levels of participation in class discussions centered on rule-making. And they do so with apparent ease. Meetings geared toward devising rules or regulations tend to proceed smoothly in Segal's classroom. When a matter on which students disagree comes to a vote, then, almost without fail, winners and losers accept the outcome with equanimity. Segal's students, further, actively participate in enforcing rules, even against their own transgressions. Mark's behavior, described above, is not atypical. In contrast with the North End Community School, where I never once observed a child report her own violation of a rule, here the norm is, not to deny allegations of rule-breaking, but rather to openly admit to, and even at times to voluntarily report and amend, wrong-doing.

Consider, however, two additional ways that student response to discipline in Segal's classroom departs from that in Franklin's. First, it is striking to a visitor to both sites how little "resistance" Segal's fourth graders exhibit. Here "classroom management" seems, in comparison with North End, almost effortless. Segal's students generally conduct themselves as they are expected to. On a typical day, they work independently or in small groups, they move from place to place in the school building, they retrieve and eat their lunches in the cafeteria – all without incident.

[11] In total 87 percent do so, compared with 62 percent at North End. See Appendix A, table 7.   [12] See Appendix A, table 7.

Even Mark, who is more prone than most of his classmates to deviate from the standard of responsibility as defined at Fair View, actively regulates his own conduct with reference to school rules, correcting himself when he violates them. Fair View students do not, I want to emphasize, obey classroom rules without fail. Consider the following field notes excerpt:

Segal's students speak to each other while I wait with them outside the library door. I remind them to speak in a whisper, since the door is open. All lower their voices, expect Lawrence, who replies, "What do I care?"

Yet, compared with Franklin's classroom and with the North End school generally, refusals to obey, as well as less directly confrontational forms of resistance, are markedly less prevalent.

Participant-observation data suggest, what is more, that students largely accept and embrace, not only the rules, which they participate in determining and tend to experience as serving their collective interests, but also the norms and standards that define good conduct and character at Fair View. Even when students contest a teacher's judgment, then, or question or challenge a particular rule or decision, they tend to do so with reference to these norms and standards. For instance, when the music teacher, using a lottery system to decide who will participate in a dance performance, draws Lawrence's name, several children object on the grounds that, in the words of one, Lawrence "doesn't take anything seriously."

Students use these norms and standards, as well, as grounds for adjudicating disputes among themselves. The following field notes excerpt will illustrate:

Kathryn, Susan, Simone, and Jackie are sitting, propped up on pillows, near the class library, arguing about the division of work for their group project: whether some of them have been writing too much, and some not enough. One girl says, emphatically, "Then why is Jackie complaining [that is, why is Jackie voicing criticisms of what the group has written so far] if she's not doing her part?"

As they argue, Jackie moves away from the group, toward a bookshelf, and begins to peruse the titles there. One of the other children in the group addresses her in an exasperated tone of voice. "Jackie," she says, "if you want to express your ideas, you have to come over here!" Another group member suggests that perhaps Jackie no longer wants to participate, but Jackie insists that this is not the case and rejoins the group discussion.

The argument described above is typical of one in which Segal's fourth graders air (and later settle) their differences, in that in doing so they appeal, not to their teacher's judgment, but rather to the "values" that govern the classroom. Jackie's peers find fault with her for failing to demonstrate a "positive attitude" (that is, for "complaining") and to "work hard" (that is, to "[do] her part"). They suggest that perhaps she no longer wants to be included in the group when she temporarily withdraws from the discussion, that is, when she refuses to "reach out." If Jackie wishes to remain in the group, the implication is, then she needs to come to the table with a set of shared "values" that enable its members to reach an agreement about how to work together.

Second, student response to discipline in Segal's classroom departs from that in Franklin's in that Segal's students exhibit a heightened sensitivity to punishment, whether in the form of penalty or rebuke. Again, an illustrative example:

When 3:00 arrives and it is time to get ready for dismissal, Segal sends a student to get Sam, who has signed up to use a computer in another classroom. The student returns and reports that Sam was not there. Segal has Sam paged over the school intercom. When he finally enters the classroom, she takes him aside to talk with him. Sam tells Monica Segal that he *did* go to the classroom that he told her he was going to . . . Segal replies that she is not going to argue with Sam about it and adds that "it isn't going to be an issue for a while anyway," because he is not allowed to leave the classroom on his own for one week.

Silenced, Sam returns to his table and sits down. Segal tells one of the other children to tell him what the homework assignment is. Sam is crying. He has trouble copying down the assignment through his tears. Segal goes over to him and speaks to him quietly, explaining that it is important for her to know where he is at all times.

Sam's punishment for the infraction described above is unusually severe, but his response to being punished is not. Mark is similarly reduced to tears when he learns that the "Letter from Miss Segal" in his conference portfolio says that he needs to refrain from "singing silly songs" in class. And Susan becomes visibly distraught (her voice begins to crack) when Segal does not approve the book she has selected for her book report. It is difficult to imagine comparable student responses to comparable forms of punishment at North End.

Although it is likely that the relative intensity of student response to punishment at Fair View is, in part, a function of the paucity of reprimands and imposed penalties at the school, student impressibility in the face of punishment and rebuke points, more importantly, to the ways in which depoliticizing classroom "values" alters the very calculus of discipline. At Fair View, norms and standards governing the classroom are not forms of regulation to be debated and decided upon, but rather "values": obvious, natural, timeless, and true. And whereas at North End, a child must consistently fail to conform to standards of responsibility as accountability before her capacity to do so is called into question, here the individual's character is in doubt each time she falls short of her classroom's "central values." "Singing a silly song" is more than an act of disobedience. It is a choice signaling that the child who makes it is less than completely serious about her school work, that she is the kind of person whom teachers, parents, and peers might rightly judge as undeserving of respect.

These two patterns, I want to suggest – the relatively low levels of student resistance at Fair View and the heightened responsiveness to punishment – are related not only to each other, but also to the relative ease with which Segal's students participate in making and enforcing rules. Collective decision-making at Fair View is facilitated by the depoliticization of the ends rules serve (defined in terms of students' shared interests in promoting the learning process), local standards of good conduct and character, and the identity of the responsible student as the child who chooses to realize these ends and attain these forms of excellence.

In making this claim, I do not want to imply either that Segal's students would be better off if they did *not* perceive rules as promoting ends they hold in common with others, or that it would be preferable – or even possible – for Segal to manage her classroom without reference to some norms, standards, and other boundaries. Rather, my claim is that at Fair View, "values," learning process ends, and the definition of responsibility as self-sufficiency restrict the scope of (relatively participative) decision-making, because they enjoy a status similar to that of rules at North End. Just as Franklin's students tend not to ask, *Why line up? Why line up in a boy-girl-boy-girl pattern?*, Segal's tend not to ask, *Why have a positive attitude? Why not say, "I can't"?* Much like rules at North End, "values" at Fair View are taken as given, although here not because they were made by an adult in a position of authority, so much as because they seem not to have been "made" by anyone.

Visions of success

In the morning the students read quietly and, when Monica Segal or I call their names, meet to edit the letters they have written to themselves from their "bubblegum buddies." Bubblegum buddies are animal figures made from iced gumballs, which Segal gave her students as holiday presents. She instructed the children to "listen" to the figures, which, she said, would predict to them their futures in the fifth grade. The letters the students write report these predictions. Segal says that she will mail them to the students at home in one year.

As we work, I listen to Peter and Christopher, who are talking at a nearby table. Peter says that his father's Christmas bonus was $15,000. Christopher says that his father's Christmas bonus was $20,000. The boys discuss the holiday presents they will receive.

As I edit, I notice that every student letter predicts academic success in the fifth grade, and in middle school generally. Almost all specify that the writer will receive a high score on the Connecticut Mastery Test. Kathryn's letter is unusual in that its predictions extend beyond the fifth grade: she writes that she will attend Fair View High, then Harvard University, and then (an unnamed) graduate school in Paris.

At the North End Community School, even students who "resist," for example by refusing to participate in classroom activities or to complete school assignments, tend to accept their teacher's definition of the content of school knowledge as facts and the rules governing their use, as well as her implicit contention that the purpose of mastering these is to "get it right," to avoid punishment, and to obtain rewards. I showed in chapter 4 that most North End students name as the most important thing they learned in school during the past year an academic subject, such as math; a fact or a set of facts, such as multiplication tables; or a rule of conduct. At Fair View, by contrast, most name an integrated set of skills or an insight about the self or the social world.[13] A closer look at this category of responses reveals that 39 percent of respondents who fall into this category, or 22 percent of all Fair View fourth graders, make specific reference to one or more of the central elements of "the learning process" as defined at Fair View. That is, they reference:

- analysis and problem-solving, for example, "I learned problem sloving [solving] in great detal [detail]" (11 percent, or 6 percent of total respondents);
- working effectively with others, for example, "You have to work good with others" or "How to be a leader in a group" (11 percent, or 6 percent of total respondents); and
- independent learning (confidence, goal-setting, self-motivation, and/or self-assessment), for example, "The most important thing I learned in school this year is that whatever you believe in is what you aim for. Because especially to me it seems that it builds comfidence [confidence] in me" (16 percent, or 9 percent of total respondents).

At North End, not a single respondent to the question "What is the most important thing you learned this year?" makes reference to problem-solving/analysis, working effectively with others, or independent learning.

What is more, an additional 6 percent of Fair View respondents give no

[13] See chapter 4, pp. 89–90.

specific answer to this question, on the grounds that they regard everything they learned during the past year to be important. For example,

Everything is very important. Everything is important because each thing you learn teaches you something whether it is easy or hard. It may be fun or psychologically damaging to your brain but you <u>always</u> <u>have</u> to learn from it. (Or the teachers would get sued by our parents).

No North End student responds by affirming that everything she learned is important.

I noted in chapter 4 that, in explaining why what they learned is important, a larger percentage of Fair View students than North End students name a specific use. At Fair View, where students are encouraged to "always ask why," and where the purpose of learning is defined, in part, as acquiring the intrinsically valuable competencies that the learning process promotes, 10 percent of respondents make specific reference to these skills and capacities. For example,

It helps me answer "thinking" questions, and making them.
It gives me confidence in myself because I didn't do it the way the teacher said to.
I feel it is important to work for goals, because it deals with an important emotion. Motive. In life you have to show motive, give an extra shove in the right direction.

No North End student makes reference to problem-solving/analysis, working effectively with others, or independent learning in her explanation of the significance of the most important thing learned.

Participant-observation data suggest that Monica Segal's students are actively engaged in classroom activities. During class meetings and discussions almost all are attentive almost all of the time, and there is a relatively high level of participation, even enthusiasm. It is not atypical, then, one morning when Segal asks if she should continue reading from the book that she is reading aloud to the class, that her students shout "Yes!" in response. Students exhibit enthusiasm, as well, about much of the independent work they do in school. I was surprised on one of my first visits to Segal's classroom, when a boy rushed over to explain to me, excitedly, how he had figured out a math puzzle that he had shown me earlier.

Segal's students generally seem to consider themselves knowledgeable and competent participants in "the learning process," participants who should understand, and at times question intellectual authority. For instance, during one science lesson, when the teacher states that black holes are extremely dense, Corey raises his hand and asks, "How do they know that?" The question – how "they" determine the density of black holes – suggests that, rather than accept the authority of his teacher or of scientific texts, this boy questions, and apparently believes that he can and should understand, how scientific truths or facts are determined.

Segal authorizes her students to make decisions and judgments about the work they perform in school, and they regularly exercise their right to do so. An excerpt from my field notes illustrates how Samantha asserts that she – not I – controls the process of assessing her work.

I practice parent–child conferences with Samantha and Michael N. The students run the conferences. Each shows me what (s)he chose to include in her/his portfolio and explains to me why (s)he chose the pieces (s)he did, using the "reflections" (s)he wrote to help make the presentation.

When Samantha removes from her folder the first piece she chose to present, I ask, "Can I see that?" (meaning, "Can I hold that?"). "No," she replies, and she continues with her description of the piece and her account of its significance.

Generally, Segal's fourth graders evince confidence in their own abilities to engage in the central activities of "the learning process," to perform well the tasks they are expected to perform, and to succeed academically. After the parent–child conferences, then, every student I ask (about half the children in the class) tells me that her conference went well. Lawrence specifies that his father "asked good questions." Several students, upon hearing Lawrence's comment, report that their parents did not ask any questions, because, they say, they explained everything to them clearly. That every child whose letter I edit during the lesson described in the above vignette predicts future academic success is not an anomaly. Segal's students expect to do well, even to excel in school. And CMT and other academic achievement data suggest that, for the most part, they do.

Again, limits to my data prevent me from advancing a causal argument about the relationship between Segal's pedagogic practices and the values, beliefs, and attitudes toward school and learning that her students exhibit. Yet it seems plausible that this teacher's pedagogy contributes to her students' understanding of school knowledge as integrated cognitive and social skills, including those the learning process promotes; their view of these as valuable, not only because they are useful for attaining academic and professional success, but also because they are intrinsically worthwhile; and their tendency to think of themselves as capable of making, and entitled to make, decisions and judgments about their own work.

But even if Segal's pedagogy encourages her students to develop these competencies, attitudes, values, and beliefs, which are needed for high academic attainment, and for relatively autonomous, high-status, and well-compensated jobs, this does not mean she empowers them to choose which skills and capacities to develop; that she grants them more choices, or a wider range of choice, than that which Franklin's "banking" model affords; or that she enables them to use school knowledge to fulfill true aspirations, desires, or interests. Consider two patterns in student participation in "the learning process," which parallel patterns in student response to "classroom management" at Fair View.

First, although Fair View students question those in positions of authority and assert their prerogatives as active participants in classroom learning, only rarely do they resist the learning process itself or the lore that envelops it, for example, by challenging Segal's valuation of the competencies the learning process promotes, by asserting that particular activities or projects do not help to cultivate these, or by approaching school work in a manner that demonstrates a lack of motivation or enthusiasm. In contrast with the North End Community School, where "I ain't doing this!" is not an uncommon response, at Fair View, not once during the course of the year did I observe a child refuse to participate in a school activity or complete an assignment. Occasionally, Fair View students exhibit more modest forms of resistance, along the lines of Mark's mumbled "No thank you." But even these are frowned upon, and not only by Segal and other adults, but also by the offender's classmates and peers. An example will illustrate:

In the middle of the exercise, Segal tells Mark to go take a walk in the hallway, in order to "get a new attitude that's not one of being silly or stupid but one of being serious."
Mark walks out of the classroom, grinning.
Peter says, quietly, "That's the third time."

Second, although Fair View students generally seem to regard themselves as knowledgeable, competent, and successful, when they do meet with academic failure, they become noticeably distressed. Again, a field notes excerpt:

Monica Segal returns the science tests. She begins by writing the grade distribution on the board: six As, six Bs, four Cs, four Ds, and one F . . . She tells her students to look at their tests, and then put them in their backpacks. For homework, she says, they should answer any questions they got wrong, and they should also have their parents sign their graded tests.
Mark, who received a D, says, "I feel so dirty . . . my mom's gonna be mad." Lawrence, who also got a D, says, "I'm dead."
Karen, who failed, looks at her score and says, "Oh my God." She begins to cry.
When, after everyone has put their tests in their backpacks, the class reconvenes in the sports center, Karen is still crying.

Not once at the North End Community School does a child exhibit so anguished a response to school failure.

The difference, I want to suggest, is partly the product of the sanctification of "the learning process" at Fair View. Consider again the story that Segal tells her students about the relationship between school knowledge and success. Individual ability and effort (the story goes) inserted into the learning process produce intrinsically valuable accomplishments and forms of competence, and only incidentally success, which is awarded to those who realize worthy ends and excellences. This emphasis on the intrinsic value of learning process skills, this secondary status accorded extrinsic rewards like success, is hailed by critical educational theorists writing in the tradition of Bowles and Gintis as a hallmark of "empowering" schooling. Yet it extends, rather than diminishes, the disciplinary reach of grades and other measures of achievement. This is the case because, at Fair View, grades are not merely rewards teachers assign to students who obey them. They are measures of merit.

The story Segal tells about the relationship between success and school knowledge is not the only possible such story she might tell. She might, instead, present this relationship as less uni-directional. She might acknowledge that the "learning process" includes the particular cognitive and social skills rewarded in the late twentieth-century United States in part *because* these are rewarded, because they promote "success." By this account, the competencies the learning process cultivates are not entirely different in kind from the "survival skills" that Franklin teaches at North End. At Fair View, where survival is a matter, not of avoiding dangers posed by "the environment," but of perpetuating a privileged way of life, children need to think, speak, work, and interact, both with those in positions of authority and with their peers, in ways that enable them to "survive" in the academic and professional institutions that facilitate access to the resources and opportunities available in communities like Fair View.

I do not mean to imply that the particular skills and capacities that "the learning process" promotes have no value, or that these are not taught and rewarded, partly, because they are worthwhile. The abilities to analyze concepts and statements, solve problems, work effectively with others, and learn independently are clearly useful, even indispensable, for a range of human endeavors. Rather, my claim is that these particular skills are likely taught at Fair View, at the expense of others, in part because they are rewarded. And yet, much like the values that govern Segal's classroom, they are depoliticized, enshrined in a learning process that, Segal's pedagogy suggests, itself warrants no analysis, no "reflection."

The boy who "is not from here"

During recess period on my first day at Fair View Elementary, Monica Segal and I talk while we watch her students play. Segal tells me that one of the boys in the class, Lawrence, recently moved to Fair View from Bridgeport. She says that Lawrence is having trouble adjusting, in terms of both his behavior and his school work. She says that he is "not used to the level of expectations in Fair View schools." She adds that, as she watches the class, he is the one student on whom she "has [her] eyes the whole time."

At Fair View Elementary, where responsibility is defined, not as accountability, but as self-sufficiency, to "be responsible" is to be self-motivated, to be self-disciplined. The above discussions of student responses to "classroom management," and to the expectation that children participate actively and independently in "the learning process," suggest that, for the most part, Fair View students effectively regulate their own conduct with reference to Fair View "values" and discipline themselves to work to attain the ends "the learning process" promotes.

In this section, I consider how the student fares who consistently fails to meet standards of responsibility as defined at Fair View. My focus is Lawrence, the child who best personifies the "other" of responsibility in Segal's classroom. This boy's cavalier attitude toward the behavioral and attitudinal norms and the academic standards that govern the classroom is captured in several of the field notes excerpts quoted above, such as Lawrence's response ("What do I care?") to my asking him to lower his voice to preserve quiet in the library, and his drawing of what he identifies as "a criminally insane person" on the sign welcoming handicapped pre-schoolers to Fair View. Lawrence regularly transgresses and openly challenges local pedagogic standards and ends. What is more, at times he shows signs of regarding his classmates as foolish for accepting and willingly conforming to these. For the first several weeks of the school year, for instance, this boy exasperates his teacher as well as the other students in the class by calling out, as he leaves each afternoon, "Good-bye, suckers!"

I argued in chapter 4 that Booker, like other "problem" students at North End, is routinely reprimanded and punished by adults in positions of authority, and that his classmates at times join their teacher in denouncing his "bad" conduct. At Fair View, the teacher does not, as a matter of course, impose penalties on Lawrence. Instead, she redoubles her efforts to induce him to internalize the norms and standards of the school. "I need to find a way to motivate him to do [what is expected of him]," Segal tells me during an interview. "I think that every child should make progress." Yet from the start, this teacher "has [her] eyes [on Lawrence] the whole time." As the year progresses, her suspiciousness of the boy turns to disapproval. In April, relating to me that Lawrence allegedly called a first grader who rides his school bus "urine," Segal refers to him (out of his earshot) as "a hopeless case." The following field notes excerpt illustrates this teacher's perception that the root of her student's problem is a lack of interest in his own development, a refusal to "care" whether or not he learns and progresses:

Monica Segal updates me on Lawrence's behavior. Again, she seems exasperated, almost disgusted with him. She says that he left early for the spring break, because he was going to Atlantic City. Before he left, she tells me, he again called his classmates "suckers," because they were staying until school ended.

She says that she told him that he had to finish his mystery book while he was gone. He did not.

She tells me that yesterday she "sat him down" and told him that, if he didn't care, she didn't either.

Lawrence's classmates respond to his conduct by ignoring, at times even ostracizing him. At one point, Segal tells me, the other children in her class were, in her words, "so mean to Lawrence that [she] finally had to send him out of the room" so that she could talk to the rest of the students about it. She says that she told them "not to be mean to him just because he is not from here."

At the North End school, rules are acknowledged to be limits that regulate conduct by requiring children to do certain things and prohibiting them from doing others. School work, similarly, is understood as a series of tasks students are compelled to perform. "Problem students" like Booker are suspected of having a "problem," then, because they fail to be responsible, to meet teachers' expectations and fulfill requirements, even in the face of unremitting punishment.

At Fair View, by contrast, the norms and standards that regulate student action are defined, not as limits that prohibit some activities and require others, but rather as indisputable "values" that serve students' interests. School work is not a series of assigned tasks that promote some ends and frustrate others, but rather a "learning process" that fosters human excellence and garners success.

How to respond to these values and to the learning process is, then, nothing short of obvious. Children should demonstrate "effort." They should "believe in [themselves]." They should strive for excellence and for the success that accompanies it. Lawrence's persistent refusals to embrace the "values" of Segal's classroom and to immerse himself in "the learning process" are, therefore, perplexing. Unlike Booker, who is suspected of having a deficiency that causes him to persist in behaviors for which he is punished, Lawrence is perceived as stubbornly rejecting what serves his own interests, what is right and good. His is a problem for which he is ultimately responsible: a willful refusal to "care."

Generally, at Fair View, students as well as teachers emphasize individual choice and effort, rather than accountability to those in positions of authority, as means to attaining desired ends. At both North End and Fair View, then, the most common response to the questions "Do you think you'll reach your goal? Why?" is to name a personal characteristic, such as intelligence, a particular talent, or a strong desire to attain the goal. But, in contrast with North End, where the second most common response centers on fulfilling obligations and duties (22 percent, compared with 3 percent at Fair View), at Fair View the second most common response centers on individual effort and initiative, doing one's best or "put[ting one's] mind to it" (23 percent, compared with 13 percent at the North End school). For example:

> Yes. Because I think if you have a goal and work hard you will reach your goal.
>
> I don't know. It depends on how much I work on it.
>
> Definiatly [Definitely]. I can do <u>anything</u> as long as I put my mind to it.

Unlike the North End school, where disobedient or "bad" children are named by just under 31 percent of fourth graders as the one thing they would change about their classroom or school, at Fair View only 4 percent point to student behaviors or attitudes. Twenty-four percent, compared with 13 percent at North End, respond that they would change nothing, or that they would extend Fair View into higher grades, so that they could stay longer. For example:

> Nothing. Everything is just right nothing can be wrong.
>
> Having to go to a different school for middle school. Because I don't want to leave Fair View.
>
> I wouldn't change anything. Because this school is perfect how it is.

Participant-observation data suggest, however, that for this subjective feeling of "empowerment," and for this sense that there is little at Fair View that needs to be changed, a price is paid, in the form of a heightened intolerance toward deviations from standards of responsibility, both in others and in the self, deviations that seem blatant refusals to do what is unambiguously right and good.

In Veronica Franklin's classroom at North End, Booker is the class "bad boy," the child who fails to "be responsible." Yet he is generally liked by his teachers and included in games and other activities by his peers.

Lawrence, by contrast, reports that his classmates "hate" him. Segal's perception is that the other children in the class are so "mean" to Lawrence that she needs to hold a meeting in his absence to discuss how they treat him. What is more, the teacher herself often seems to be disgusted with Lawrence.

What might account for the difference? Mechanisms of power – norms, rules, laws, and other boundaries to social action – by definition create classes of actions, attributes, and actors who exceed them. Rules at North End, for instance, proscribe some forms of conduct. Standards of knowledgeability devalue some kinds of cognitive capacity. When defined as extra-political – as, not conventional norms, but universal "values," not contingent standards, but essential human excellences – these boundaries translate the differences they create into defects in need of rectification. Discipline becomes, not a form of constraint, but a remedy that enables its subject, and punishment, even when experienced as injurious, a correction that serves her interests.

Bounded fields of action: the "world" of Fair View

On my first day at Fair View Elementary, there are two conversations in the faculty room during fourth grade lunch period. The first centers on Fair View parents, who, several teachers complain, are excessively demanding, aggressive. Fourth grade teacher Risa Hanson relates, in an exasperated tone, the story of a parent who called one of the other classroom teachers to complain about the orchestra schedule. This parent, according to Hanson, had analyzed the schedule for every class in the school and had arrived at the conclusion that the orchestra director was treating her child's class unfairly, in that the students had slightly less time for lessons than did others in the school, and were divided into some groups of four and six, rather than all groups of five.

Hanson says that the teacher pointed out to the parent that, because different children were studying different instruments, it was not practically possible to keep all groups the same size. And she explained the logistical problems that necessitated a slightly shorter music period for some classes.

Hanson announces that she is "tired of hearing such terrible things" about what Fair View parents do to teachers. She says that parents "never call just to tell teachers that they are doing a good job." She adds that, when she returns home from work in the evening and describes to her husband the problems Fair View teachers have with parents, she tells him, "That's what's wrong with education!"

Across the table, the school psychologist and the speech therapist discuss recent films. Several minutes into their conversation they move to the topic of Hollywood movies. The speech therapist announces that it has been "a wonderful summer for movies." His favorite of the summer, he says, was *In the Line of Fire*.[14] He and the psychologist proceed to list, and to comment on, movies they recently attended.

I ask if either of them saw *Menace II Society*.[15] The psychologist looks at me, blank-faced. The speech therapist says, "Oh . . . that's the black thing." He says that he does not attend movies "like that" because they are "about a whole different world" and therefore "hard to relate to." He adds that he "knows it's out there," but that "nothing can be done." "Nothing changes," he comments, and he "feel[s] like running away from it."

School success

At Fair View Elementary, talk about Fair View parents dominates teachers' conversations among themselves about school problems, as well as their reflections on the same topic in the interviews I conducted. In response to the question, "What are the greatest challenges of your job?" Monica Segal expresses a view of Fair View parents representative of that held by many of her colleagues:[16]

Dealing with the parents . . . definitely. Well, I think the parents that come in here, who yell and scream at you about everything they want, and have the attitude that, "I pay . . . my taxes. You work for me." . . .

And they, they're very good. I mean, they're very well educated parents . . . And they try to manipulate the situation.

Principal Anita Byrne responds similarly to the same question:

Pleasing the parents. Because you can't. And you just have to decide what your priorities are . . .

[On the occasions when Byrne has done something parents do not like] they've gone to the superintendent. They've written letters. Some of them get hostile. They go out and they talk in the community about you . . . They're . . . very, they try to be intimidating. And that's their big threat. "I'll go over your head," kind of thing.

Byrne characterizes Fair View parents as "hard-driving, aggressive, [and] pushy" and estimates that approximately one hundred per year request personal meetings with her to discuss classroom placement alone. In August of 1993, she tells me, after she mailed placement deci-

---

[14] Wolfgang Petersen, Director, 1993.

[15] Allen and Albert Hughes, Directors, 1993. The setting is a low-income, predominantly African-American urban neighborhood.

[16] This claim is based on regular observations of teachers' conversations, as well as interviews with 10 out of 26 Fair View teachers. See Appendix B.

sions, she catalogued thirty-five conferences in nine days, all to register
complaints about classroom placement. Generally, faculty and other
staff members characterize Fair View parents as demanding, critical, and
insufficiently trusting in teachers' judgment and competence. In their
view, parents do not "respect [the teacher] as a professional."[17] Many
associate parents' attitudes and conduct with their social status and
affluence. According to first grade teacher Karen Morris, "You get a lot
of, I've often run into the attitude of, 'Hey, I make six figures, and you
don't.'"[18]

Nearly as salient in teachers' formal and informal discussions of school
problems are those relating to professional advancement and standing.
Throughout the year, teachers, and in particular non-tenured teachers,
manifest a high level of anxiety about classroom observations. When
Fiona Farley comments over lunch in the faculty room that she is
"nervous" about her upcoming observation and "not sure what Anita
wants," she expresses a sentiment that is not uncommon among non-
tenured faculty members. And she expresses one that is not unreasonable, given her principal's expectations and the likely consequences of
failure to live up to them. In the spring of the year I spent at Fair View,
three non-tenured teachers at the school were fired.[19] What is more, two
tenured teachers in the district were fired that spring. Byrne explains to
me, during an interview, that she bases decisions to re-hire or to fire
teachers on what she observes in their classrooms. For a teacher to maintain her job at Fair View, the principal says, effective "classroom management" is crucial, as are "instilling confidence" in students and inspiring
them to "rise to" meet high "expectations."

[A] decision at the end of three years is made as to whether you would permanently hire them . . . But we don't wait three years if they're not . . . Well, classroom
management is extremely important . . . I mean if you can't get the kids' attention
and keep them on task, you could be dynamite, but no one's listening to you. So
the classroom management is really key. Rapport with children to me, especially
at the elementary level, is right up there . . . Is the teacher responding appropri-
ately to them? Is she instilling confidence? And does she have expectations for
them that they can see, that they know they need to rise to? All of that.

A third category of "problems" teachers name in both formal and
informal discussions includes time constraints; curricular "extras" such
as health, safety, and cultural programs; pressures from outside the school
deriving from the institution's accountability to the public; and obstacles
from within in the form of what Morris calls "high attention children," or

---

[17] Interview with Monica Segal.   [18] Personal interview.
[19] There were eleven teachers eligible for re-hire. Of the three fired, one was a third-year
teacher (in her tenure year) and two were second-year teachers.

students who come to school with behaviors and attitudes that teachers perceive as barriers to attaining pedagogic ends.

These pedagogic ends Fair View teachers define in terms of what some call "school success." Without exception, every Fair View teacher I interviewed named as her principal pedagogic goal or goals enabling students to meet standards of academic achievement (78 percent), teaching them to enjoy and value learning (56 percent), and/or helping them become independent learners, that is, people who can and do work on their own, regularly assess their cognitive and attitudinal strengths and weaknesses, and/or are confident in themselves and their abilities (44 percent).[20] School success comes to those who are responsible, those who, in Farley's words, "take charge [of] their own decisions and ownership for their actions." Thus, according to kindergarten teacher Cynthia Walsh, "the goal is to make them as independent in their process of learning as they can be. To feel confident enough to go and attempt the task even if it's not going to be totally correct. Then that's how . . . we learn. We learn through mistakes rather than being stepped through."

The problems with parents that Fair View teachers and other staff members discuss so frequently they tend to perceive, similarly, as obstacles to attaining the pedagogic ends they associate with "school success." The trouble with "pushy" Fair View parents, then, is *not* that they want their children to achieve – which teachers view as a legitimate concern, and one they share with their students' parents – but rather that, in failing to trust in teachers' judgments, parents interfere with their efforts and undermine their effectiveness at reaching this goal. Risa Hanson tells me, "I will be the first to say I think that parents definitely have the right to kind of look at what's being done in the schools, 'cause their kids are the most important thing to them. But they also need, I think one thing that's missing here, is the trust of the faculty on the part of many of the parents, that they know what they're doing." In a similar vein, Segal explains that she "[does] not blame [parents for wanting to be involved], they need to be their child's advocate," emphasizing that her objection is to parents who go about the job of "be[ing] their child's advocate" by "giv[ing] you [a hard] time," being "always on top of" the teacher.

Likewise, in expressing anxieties about classroom observations, and about whether they will meet their supervisors' expectations, some teachers stress that they do not object to the expectations or to the observations themselves. Farley, for example, whom I quoted above telling her colleagues that she is "nervous" about Anita Byrne's observation and "not sure what Anita wants," informs me near the end of the school year that,

---

[20] These answers were given in response to the questions, "How would you describe your responsibilities as a teacher? What are your major pedagogic and professional goals?" See Appendix B, II.

in her estimation, her five observations by the principal and vice principal were "really worthwhile." She says she received "excellent" and "very specific" feedback, and "learned a tremendous amount from [the observations]." "I think it's really to keep teachers on their toes," she adds, with apparent approval. According to Hanson, "they [the administrators] need to do that [that is, to use observations to determine whom to re-hire and whom to fire]. I mean, they definitely do. In my old school they didn't do it as much as they should have . . ."

Recall that, at North End, 90 percent of teachers interviewed defined classroom problems in terms of those posed by "the environment." Here not a single teacher mentions, either in interviews or in the interactions I observed throughout the year, a lack of parental involvement, social problems associated with poverty, or "street" values. Instead, salient problems are what teachers characterize as unreasonable and intrusive demands from Fair View parents; high, yet reasonable expectations from supervisors; and constraints in the form of limited classroom time, curricular "extras," public pressure, and "high attention" children. What renders these "problems," in Segal's view and in the view of other Fair View teachers, is that they need to consider and respond to them in order to meet the pedagogic aims they associate with "school success." Teachers tend to view these goals themselves, however, as unproblematic ends, which they share with their colleagues, supervisors, and Fair View parents.

"Total freedom"

Structural accounts of power-with-a-face in the classroom emphasized what Sharp and Green called the "social context" within which (relatively) powerful teachers exercise power over (relatively) powerless students. In their study of primary education at a working-class school governed by a progressive, child-centered pedagogic philosophy, Sharp and Green attended to constraints on classroom teachers in the form of resource scarcity, as well as the expectations of other "powerful" actors, including supervisors, colleagues, and the parents of the children enrolled in the school. Even as "powerful" teachers exercise power, by this view (and Sharp and Green argued that the rhetoric and ideology of progressive education increased the scope of teachers' "power over" their students) they are constrained by the actions of others who get them to do what they "would not otherwise," for instance, by expecting and requiring them to maintain order in the classroom.[21]

---

[21] The claim was that this expectation made it necessary for teachers to use hierarchical differentiation in classroom interactions, in order to maintain order (Sharp and Green 1975).

This structural view is not implausible. Consider two sets of pedagogic ends that Segal and other teachers at Fair View Elementary might possibly emphasize in their classrooms. Fair View teachers might, as Segal in fact does, focus on teaching children to internalize the values and motivate and discipline themselves to develop the cognitive and other learning process competencies that promote independent learning geared toward academic achievement. Alternatively, they might, as critical educational theorists recommend, stress the aims and ends of the "transformative intellectual," who "problematizes" for students social relations of power and domination in the classroom and the larger society. They might, for example, focus on teaching Fair View children to think critically about the social injustices and inequalities that make possible their own privilege, for instance by conducting classroom discussions about inequalities in access to educational opportunity.

That some teachers are aware of, and, when they reflect on them, troubled by the latter is suggested by comments they make during interviews. Segal, for one, tells me:

There are certain things here that drive me nuts. It drives me nuts that we provide pencils all year, and that in other schools they don't have money for toilet paper. And, while I really like the fact that I have an unlimited, I can get money for all kinds of different things, the inequity of what the inner cities get, per capita, per student [bothers me].

Other Fair View teachers express concerns about the school's racial and social class homogeneity. Morris, for example, names as the Fair View district's greatest weakness[22] its lack of racial and ethnic diversity, which she tells me renders the town and the school "not . . . real." "This is not a real town," she says. "It just isn't . . . I've had two black kids [in the five years] I've been in this system. It's just not the real world." Fair View kindergarten teacher Sharon Ray, whose own daughter graduated from Fair View High School, tells me that, because no one in the town's schools is "not exactly like" its, for the most part, white, upper middle-class students, Fair View children do not recognize or understand that people come from different social and economic backgrounds:

There's no one [at Fair View] that is not exactly like [Fair View students] . . . I mean the first time my daughter really had friends that weren't exactly like her . . . she went to George Washington University, which has a very diverse population. She never knew about people who ever experienced any kind of difficulty. The idea that somebody's going to have trouble going to college – can they go? can they pay for it? – this was not part of anything she ever knew.

[22] This response, during an interview, was to the question, "What about the Fair View school system – what are its biggest challenges? its greatest strengths?" See Appendix B.

Structural accounts of the role power plays in defining teachers' pedagogic aims and ends might emphasize that to "problematize" the inequi-
ties that make possible Fair View students' privilege would divert time
and other resources from teaching for "school success," which supervisors and parents require. By this view, constraints, in the form of the
expectations, actions, and anticipated actions of other, more "powerful"
agents, in the context of limits to time and other resources, induce teachers to attend first and foremost to teaching for "school success," even if,
on some level, they may want to teach children to apprehend and think
critically about social injustices.

No doubt there is truth to this view. Fair View parents, clearly, exert
pressure on their children's teachers. The Fair View principal fires three
teachers in the spring for failing to meet her expectations. But, although it
may *objectively* be the case that other, more "powerful" actors would
"exercise power over" teachers were they to emphasize pedagogic
ends and excellences that depart from those that prevail at Fair View,
teachers tend not *subjectively* to experience their pedagogic practices as
significantly constrained by parents, supervisors, or others who "have
power over" them. To the contrary, what most claim they like about Fair
View, what in their opinion distinguishes Fair View from other districts, is
that teachers here have, in Farley's words, "total freedom" in matters of
pedagogy. "And I feel very fortunate," this teacher tells me, "because
when I speak with teachers in other towns, they don't have that kind of
freedom." In a similar vein, Hanson reports: "one thing I definitely have
to say about this district is you have a lot of freedom, as to you can teach
anything, however you want to teach it."

In Fair View, as in most districts, there is in place a curriculum that
specifies subjects and skills to be taught at every grade level. Yet many
teachers emphasize that they have a wide latitude within which to choose
how to satisfy these requirements. Generally, they view Fair View's curriculum, to which Farley refers as "the framework upon which we build our
lessons," as in consonance with pedagogic aims that they choose or freely
endorse. Throughout the school year, not once during any conversation
or interview did a Fair View teacher indicate that she had any sense that
she focused on teaching Fair View students the particular skills and competencies needed for "school success," rather than some other set of competencies (such as those emphasized by critical educational theorists), as
the result of pressure or influence from supervisors, parents, or other
actors. Even those teachers who, upon reflection, are troubled by the isolation of privileged white children in a resource-rich school where they
"never [know] about people who ever experienced any kind of difficulty"
tend to experience as "free" the pedagogic choice to focus time and

energy on teaching Fair View children to esteem and work effectively to attain school success.

Many Fair View teachers report feeling pressure from "intimidating" or "aggressive" parents. Many report experiencing anxiety, due to supervisors' high expectations, and demands posed by tasks that detract from their ability to accomplish what they want to accomplish in the classroom. These are "problems" for most teachers, however, only insofar as they pose obstacles to realizing the particular ends of teaching and learning captured by the phrase "school success." Teachers exhibit little, indeed almost no, sense of intrasubjective conflict or ambivalence about these ends, or about the cognitive and attitudinal standards used to measure school success. Nor do they tend to view these ends and standards as imposed or enforced by (to recall Wartenberg's term) "peripheral social agents" such as parents, supervisors, or members of the Fair View public. To the contrary, it is difficult to find any evidence at this site, whether in the form of action or "anticipated reactions," of "A exercising power over B" with respect to the definition and adoption of local ends and excellences of teaching and learning. There seems to be a widespread sense of "total freedom," as well as an absence of debate or disagreement about "the learning process," and about the standards of character, competence, and knowledgeability that define it.

This subjective feeling of being "free," I want to suggest, is enabled by boundaries – including school districts and other educational boundaries, and zoning laws and other municipal boundaries – that make possible something close to a consensus on pedagogic ends and excellences. It is difficult to live in Fair View, to send one's child to Fair View schools, or even to teach at Fair View Elementary, without first attaining a significant measure of "school success" as defined by dominant educational and professional institutions. Power's mechanisms discourage disagreement and enable consensus, by excluding from Fair View and from Fair View Elementary individuals and groups whose interests, social experiences, and understandings of worthy ends and excellences might pose a significant challenge to those that are locally ascendant.

Participation in practices defined by uncontested ends can be accompanied by feelings of empowerment. "I can do <u>anything</u> as long as I put my mind to it," one Fair View student writes. "You can teach anything, however you want to teach it," declares a Fair View teacher. But it does have a cost: the legitimation of the (inter- and intrasubjective) punishment of actors who do not realize depoliticized ends and excellences.

A central claim in chapter 2 was that power can be exercised absent clear "connections." The effects of punishment are not necessarily confined to the sites in which punishing attitudes, beliefs, and actions are learned and expressed. Instead, punishment can – when institutionalized in laws, in stereotypical media images, in gendered and class-specific communicative norms – affect action "at a distance." It is important to probe, for this reason, in social sites where ends, excellences, and other significant boundaries are depoliticized, the implied "we" of "our values." How, specifically, do Fair View actors define those with whom they share pedagogic ends and standards? How, specifically, do they define those with whom they do *not* share important values, experiences, and affinities? Even as power's mechanisms enable something approximating a local consensus about what constitutes school success, I argue in the concluding section, they encourage the definition – via ascriptive identities of race, class, and place – of specific "others" of our ends, our standards, our identities.

"A whole different world . . . out there"

Recall Monica Segal's instruction to her students, described above, "not to be mean to [Lawrence] just because he is not from here." This statement, taken at face value, is puzzling. What might Segal mean in characterizing this particular child as "not from here"? Lawrence is from Fair View. He lives in the town with his father and his father's partner. He is enrolled at Fair View Elementary, and he attends the school regularly. Although it is true that Lawrence transferred to Fair View from another district at the start of the academic year, the same can be said of other students whom Segal keeps in the classroom and addresses in his absence. A total of three children in this fourth grade classroom are new to Fair View Elementary this year. Several have moved recently from out of state. What is more, three of Segal's students are from other countries, living in Fair View because their parents are in the United States for work-related reasons. Segal makes a point of telling me that Lauren's parents, for instance, who are British and in the US only temporarily, are concerned about preparing their daughter for the standardized tests she will have to take when she returns to school in England.

The teacher implies, however, in this discussion that she reports having with her students, that other children who are new to Fair View this year, and even children who were not born in the United States and will not remain in the United States, are "from here" in some sense in which Lawrence is not. Most likely, Segal does not explicate for the children in her class the precise meaning of this statement. Most likely, she does not need to, for them to understand that Lawrence is different from them in significant ways that extend beyond his recent transfer from a neighboring school district. Lawrence comes from the "inner city." His father is, not a New York professional, but a Bridgeport firefighter. And Lawrence is not white.

The latter difference, in particular, is not one that is frequently discussed at Fair View, where 95 percent of students are classified "white" and only about 1 percent "black." Yet evidence suggests that whether or not one is "from here" has a significant racial dimension, at least for some actors at Fair View. Hence the speech therapist, in the vignette above, characterizes the "whole different world" portrayed by *Menace II Society* as "the black thing." And a Fair View fourth grader (in a written response to the questions "What is the most important thing you learned this year? Why?") equates "blackness" with immigrant status:

I think learning about imigration [immigration]. I think learning about imigration [immigration] was very important, because what if you do if you bumbed [bumped] into a poor black imigrater [immigrant] what would you do.

Not only is Lawrence, by the view of some Fair View actors, not from "here." Where he *is* from – "inner city" Bridgeport – is about as far away as possible. Participant-observation and interview data suggest that teachers and other adults at this school tend to experience core urban neighborhoods, including some that are geographically proximate to the town, as comprising social "worlds" – domains of human experience, meaning, and activity – that are wholly distinct from the "world" of Fair View. In this, the speech therapist is not alone. Morris, in the interview excerpt quoted above, characterizes the "world" outside Fair View as more "real" than the world of Fair View: real in the sense that there people face the facts of human diversity and resource scarcity ("can they go [to college]? can they pay for it?"). But in the same interview, she tells me that this "real world" is not "real" to most people at Fair View, in that it remains outside their daily lives and routines:

The greatest weakness [in the Fair View school district] is there's no racial mix here. It's a very, very affluent, homogenous (laughs) . . .

I mean, you have to work your butt off to teach anything cultural. And I still don't think they get it, because it's not here. It's not real to them.

Nor is "it" quite "real" for Fair View teachers. For them, the legal and other boundaries that create "the environment" at North End produce, not only a physical, but also a psychic distance between the privileged communities to which they experience themselves as belonging, and urban "worlds," which they view as unfamiliar, at times even frightening. Consider the following references made by three Fair View teachers to poor, primarily minority urban schools and/or districts:

1. Second grade teacher Alice Penn, describing how she came to work at

Fair View, tells me that it was not a conscious decision. Rather, "it just kind of seemed to evolve naturally." Penn recounts the "evolution" of her decision as follows: she did her student teaching in two suburban districts in the vicinity of Fair View and then applied to a number of districts in the area, which she identifies by name. She adds, parenthetically, ". . . kind of avoiding Bridgeport at the time."

2. Farley tells me that she did her student teaching at the Lincoln-Bassett school in New Haven, a school with a national reputation for effectively implementing James Comer's School Development Program.[23] I ask Farley, if she had been offered jobs both at Lincoln-Bassett and at Fair View, which she would have chosen. She responds that it would have been a difficult choice, one that might have depended on other factors, such as the grade level of the openings. She adds: "If it had been another school in New Haven and here, I think that definitely I would have come here . . . I mean I'm strong, but I think I, that element of fear of going into that kind of community, I'm not sure." In explaining how she came to work at Fair View, she tells me, "I . . . grew up in a town that's very similar to Fair View . . . I . . . also knew I'd have no problem relating, 'cause this was my background."

3. Monica Segal, who before coming to Fair View taught for part of one academic year in an urban school in Poughkeepsie, New York, speaking of her decision to apply for a job in Fair View, comments: "My father wanted me to live here. He was like, 'Go to Fair View. Go to Connecticut.'" Later, she adds, "Now I know why he likes this kind of community. Which, he's right. This is better for me . . ."

In the above interview excerpts, much goes unsaid. Penn's aside – "kind of avoiding Bridgeport at the time" – implies that something distinguishes Bridgeport from other nearby districts, something that I (a white, Yale-affiliated researcher) should be able to discern without being told, something that would make her want to avoid it. Similarly, Farley's and Segal's oblique references to "that kind of community" and "this kind of community" suggest that there exists a clear, even an obvious, set of differences between the "world" of Fair View – the world that is their "background," to which they "have no problem relating," the world that is "better for [them]" – and the world comprising communities to which they do not belong and cannot "relate," and "going into" which provokes "that element of fear."

At Fair View, power shapes fields of action by helping delimit, and circumscribe, the "world" that teachers and other actors experience

---

[23] See Spillane (1992).

themselves as inhabiting. Power's mechanisms provide Segal and her colleagues with ready means to distinguish "this kind of community" from "that kind of community." The social limits to action that create and sustain this predominantly white, affluent, and professional municipality render foremost among teachers' pedagogic problems obstacles to helping students achieve competence in negotiating their own, privileged "world." They render Fair View inaccessible to members of marginalized social and economic groups, discouraging Segal and others here from listening to, debating, or otherwise engaging those whose definitions of important collective ends and excellences might compete or conflict with local pedagogic goals and standards. They help insulate "values" and "learning process" competencies from challenge and contestation, encouraging the definition of difference as deficiency. These boundaries help identify the "others" of "our world" with the racial, economic, and other categories that mark Lawrence *not from here*.

6   Power and freedom

The concept of freedom plays a crucial role in the above, as in most critical accounts of power relations. In this concluding chapter, I want to return to the suggestion, introduced in chapter 2 and implicit in the ethnographies of schooling at North End and Fair View, that students of power conceptualize freedom as political freedom, asking how particular power relations affect participants' social capacities to act in ways that shape them.[1] I begin by engaging what is widely regarded as among the strongest defenses of the notion of freedom implicit in accounts of power-with-a-face: Isaiah Berlin's "Two Concepts of Liberty,"[2] in which he argued, famously, that freedom is best understood as "negative."[3] It is the absence of interference by others in the form of social limits that prevent actors from doing or being what they otherwise might do or be. I take up Berlin's argument as a means to tackling the normative question my own argument begs: How might one acknowledge that social relations are necessarily implicated in relations of power, and at the same time draw distinctions among, and articulate grounds for criticizing, particular relations?

De-facing power, my claim is, requires neither retreating to a relativistic stance according to which all social relations are equivalent, nor abandoning the ambition to criticize and to inform strategies for changing specific relations of power. Instead, it draws attention to conceptual and normative links between theories of power and theories of democracy. It directs critical attention, not only to the ways power relations define the capacity for action *within* their terms, but also to how they shape the capacity for

---

[1] This is a conceptualization of freedom consonant with that of, among others, Bauman (1988), Coole (1993), Di Stefano (1996), and Hirschmann (1996).

[2] Berlin (1969: 118–72). The essay was first published in 1958.

[3] Berlin was not, of course, the first to make this claim. He was arguing in the tradition of negative liberty theorists that extends back at least as far as Hobbes's assertion that "A FREE-MAN is he, that in those things, which by his strength and wit he is able to do, is not hindred to doe what he has a will to" (Flathman and Johnston 1997:115).

action *upon* (that is, action that affects)[4] the social limits that comprise them.[5] Students of power relations, I argue, should target criticism, in particular, at relations of domination, by which I mean power relations characterized by the avoidable exclusion of some participants from processes of shaping their constitutive norms, and/or by patterned and enduring restrictions on the scope of political freedom.

Negative liberty and political freedom

Freedom, according to Isaiah Berlin, is a matter of being left alone within some social realm or space. It is the absence, within a circumscribed area, of coercion, which, anticipating the power debate, Berlin defined as "the deliberate interference of other human beings within the area in which I could otherwise act."[6] He emphasized that all human limits to action are, to some degree, coercive. Hobbes was right, he claimed, to insist that even a law that provides relief from some other, more constraining law or custom, or from the arbitrary dictates of a despot, nonetheless coerces, to the extent that it impinges on negative freedom.[7] Freedom is a space, "a field . . . without obstacles, a vacuum in which nothing obstructs me."[8]

What some call "positive liberty" – self-government, that is, a value that derives from the desire to be ruled only by laws and other political and economic arrangements that one (by some accounts, rationally) authors – is another liberal value. Berlin emphasized, however, that it is distinct from the value of freedom. Not only is self-government not identical to non-interference within the free space of negative liberty, in its various casts the former value can, and often does, conflict with freedom. Positive liberty, Berlin argued, concerns itself with the question of which actors might legitimately create or modify social constraints on the actions of which others, a question that, he underscored, is distinct from the ques-

---

[4] Included in this category are actions that change power relations by invoking, without changing the content of, extant laws, norms, and other boundaries to social action. See Walzer's argument (1987) emphasizing the strategic effectiveness of "connected" social criticism, which aims to effect political change by "invok[ing] local values," and O'Brien's (1996) discussion of "rightful resistance" as a relatively effective means to advancing claims, not by altering, but by calling for adherence to, legal norms.

[5] This is my principal disagreement with Richard Flathman, who, despite his emphasis on the situatedness of social action, endorses Berlin's argument for conceptualizing freedom as negative. Although I agree with Flathman that it is "incoherent" to criticize the existence of social boundaries to action *per se*, or to propose as an ideal independence from social constraint (1987: 88 and 169), I depart from him in regarding as relevant questions about freedom, not simply whether particular agents can act, unimpeded by others, within the terms that norms, rules, and other social boundaries to action define, but also whether these norms are themselves contestable, and whether the processes by which they are determined include all whose action they circumscribe.

[6] Berlin (1969: 122).   [7] Ibid. (123n).   [8] Ibid. (144).

tion of which forms of action legitimately may not be interfered with at all.

The principal aim of Berlin's essay was not, of course, to promote agreement among philosophers about political terminology. It was to advance a political argument. "Half our world," he asserted,[9] is governed illiberally, while liberals misapprehend what costs "nationalist, communist, authoritarian, and totalitarian"[10] government entails. Confusions about what freedom is enable and fuel what Berlin viewed as a devastating and absolute loss of freedom. The crux of the argument was the claim that to conflate negative and positive liberty can enable, and with the aid of contestable ontological assumptions historically has enabled, dictators and tyrants to legitimize coercion by labeling it freedom.

I want to draw attention to an important part of Berlin's defense of negative liberty: his claim that its "space" is demarcated, not by boundaries that might enable, yet also constrain individual and collective action, but rather by what he called "frontiers." Berlin distinguished "frontiers" from laws and other forms of social constraint by arguing that "they are accepted so widely, and are grounded so deeply in the actual nature of men as they have developed through history, as to be, by now, an essential part of what we mean by being a normal human being."[11] Only inviolable frontiers that cordon off the space of negative liberty can make a society free. And these differ from coercive limits against which one might make claims to negative liberty in that they are "defined in terms of rules so long and widely accepted that their observance has entered into the very concept of what it is to be a normal human being, and, therefore, also of what it is to act inhumanly or insanely."[12] Frontiers guarding negative liberty might be legal or conventional.[13] What matters is not the form they take, but that they function as absolute barriers to the imposition of one actor's will against that of another, barriers that, by no account, should be viewed as coercive, because to transgress them would be to cease to be normal, human, and sane.

Nor are these essential "frontiers," by this view, the only social boundaries that do not constrain freedom. In a long footnote near the beginning of the essay, Berlin asserted that the extent of an individual's freedom depends on five factors:

how many possibilities are open to me . . .; . . . how easy or difficult each of these possibilities is to actualize; . . . how important *in my plan of life, given my character and circumstances*, these possibilities are . . .; . . . how far they are closed and opened by deliberate human actions; . . . [and] *what value not merely the agent, but the general sentiment of the society in which he lives, puts on the various possibilities*.[14]

---

[9] Ibid. (141).   [10] Ibid. (144).   [11] Ibid. (165).   [12] Ibid.   [13] Ibid. (166n).
[14] Ibid. (130n; emphasis added).

One's "character," Berlin implied, one's "plan of life," the communities to which one belongs, and the ways in which these determine value and meaning are not, themselves, implicated in power relations that might constrain and coerce. Instead, the negative space of freedom is located inside these boundaries.

Recall that, in criticizing definitions of positive liberty, Berlin did not reject the value of self-government itself. Instead, his criticism hinged on the claim that, in combination with controversial assumptions about what kinds of selves humans are, and how these selves can and should be socially ordered, definitions of positive liberty can be used to legitimize coercion by naming it freedom. "[C]onceptions of freedom," he wrote, "directly derive from views of what constitutes a self, a person, a man."[15] A critical part of the argument was the claim that contestable assumptions about the self inherent in some definitions of positive freedom feed authoritarian zealotry and fuel coercive politics. In particular, Berlin was critical of political effects of the premise that the self is divided between its higher and lower elements. He stressed that, if one assumes that irrational persons (that is, those whose higher or autonomous selves do not (yet) rule their passions, or their lower selves) can and should be made rational, then the questions arise: How should we make them rational? And what should we do with them in the mean time? Answers to the former question, he suggested, tend to involve claims that we must educate the irrational. He quoted Fichte, according to whom education must function so that "you will later recognize the reasons for what I am doing now."[16] A common response to the latter question, he argued, is to require the government of the irrational by a rational elite. The point, of course, was not to reject *tout court* education, rationality, or the government of some by others. Instead it was to caution that forgetting that each of these responses rests on a vision of the self that may well not be right, can blind those who would promote "positive freedom" to its coercive potential.[17]

It seems reasonable, then, to ask of Berlin and others who adopt this definition of negative liberty what vision of the human self is presupposed by an understanding of freedom as a negative space within which one chooses actions important to one's "plan of life" and defined as valuable

---

[15] Ibid. (134).   [16] Ibid. (149).

[17] Recent positive liberty theorists, such as Christman (1991), Dworkin (1988), Gould (1988), and Lukes (1991), responded to Berlin's critique by defining freedom as *individual* autonomy, understood as critically reflective self-definition. Rejecting the holism of the version of positive liberty on which Berlin's attack centered, they labeled "free" those desires and others forms of action that are autonomous. As I argued in the last chapter, however, even norms defining rational and critical reflection are social boundaries that can promote and legitimize both inter- and intrasubjective punishment. This modified version of positive liberty remains vulnerable to Berlin's critique.

by "the general sentiment of the society in which [one] lives." Negative liberty implies a view of the self as a being that either independently chooses, or is a natural match for, its individual identity (its "character" and "life plan"), its social identity (the communities to which it belongs and the beliefs and values that define these), and entrenched definitions of a universal human identity ("frontiers" defining natural, normal, and sane human being that protect, but never constrain, human agency).

Suppose, however, that character formation itself is to some extent unavoidably coercive. Suppose that what a given individual hopes to achieve and become (her "plan of life") is always, in part, the product of actions by others that enable *and* constrain possible "beings and doings." Suppose that the processes through which people arrive at more or less stable and coherent senses of who they are and to what they aspire, although these enable them to act in ways that they and others value, also always close off possibilities in ways they do not choose. If so, then Berlin's "frontiers" not only protect people from harms that might threaten their abilities to realize some range of valued actions, they also rule out possible, and possibly valued, forms of action.

Applying the questions Berlin used to interrogate positive liberty to his own definition of negative liberty, one might ask what political risks accompany the latter definition and its attendant ontological presuppositions. If being free is a matter of being left alone to choose among a range of "normal" and socially valued possibilities, then freedom requires a character and life plan neither of which is abnormal, and both of which overlap significantly with communally held beliefs and values. If one assumes that people without such normal and respected characters and life plans can be made to realize their nature as human beings, so that they might safely be left alone in the space of negative liberty, one might ask (again following Berlin): How should we make them normal? And what should we do with them in the mean time? What to do with, say, a Lawrence who greets handicapped pre-schoolers with an artistic rendering of a "criminally insane person," who does not care if his talking disturbs others' learning, who refuses to take responsibility for himself and his actions? Minimally, the answer seems to be, one must contain the effects of this boy's abnormal character and choice. One must force him to be quiet, even if he does not care. Better still, from the point of view of the true lover of negative liberty, one must enable Lawrence to choose freely by helping him realize his nature as a human agent.

Just as Berlin did not reject self-government, rationality, or the education or government of some by others, I do not want to suggest that there is not value to being left alone by others to act within a circumscribed range of possibility. To de-face power, however, is to emphasize that the "freedom of the moderns"[18] – non-interference protected by rights – is always non-interference with socially constrained possibility. Labeling socially constructed boundaries "frontiers" can blind those who define freedom exclusively as negative to the effects of power that accompany engaging in particular social practices, being governed by communally held values, and developing a character and life plan in consonance with prevailing norms and standards.

It is a mistake, then, and a potentially costly one, for students of power relations to assume that social relations dichotomize into illegitimate relations of power and legitimate states in which action is free in Berlin's negative sense. Instead, I want to return to the claim, introduced in chapter 2, that power relations fall along a continuum, one end-point of which is a state of domination. At the other end are relations that promote participants' political freedom, that is, their capacity, enabled and constrained to varying degrees by particular relations of power, to act, not only within, but also upon, or in ways that affect, the mechanisms of power that shape their fields of possibility.

This definition takes as its starting point the basic democratic norm that people should be, not only the subjects, but also the architects of key boundaries that delimit and circumscribe their fields of action. Because power relations comprise *shared* boundaries to social action, they never enable free action in the sense implied by Berlin and political theorists of power-with-a-face. Yet, as I argue in the following two sections, power relations approximate states of non-domination – that is, they promote participants' freedom[19] – to the extent that they enable *all* participants to effectively take part in making and re-making their terms, and enable participants to act upon *all* key standards, ends, and other boundaries comprising them. Power relations approximate states of domination to the extent that they avoidably exclude some actors whom they position from the processes through which they are made and re-made, and/or impose patterned and enduring restrictions on the scope of "action upon."

---

[18] Constant (1988).

[19] Like Pettit (1996 and 1997), I equate freedom with non-domination, emphasizing the relation between freedom and power relations. His, however, are strongly faced views of domination (which he claims is always the product of the "more or less intentional" action of an agent), and freedom ("resilient" or "secure" immunity to interference *by other powerful agents*) (Pettit 1997: 52 and 69). For the reasons outlined in chapter 2, I disagree with this aspect of his argument.

Domination and freedom, I: the inclusiveness of "action on" power

When Holli McCuistion gets dressed in the morning, she rummages through the racks of Ralph Lauren clothes in the closets of her apartment near Park Avenue to pull together just the right outfit – one that has been pre-approved.

At the beginning of each season, Ms. McCuistion, who works as a saleswoman at the Polo Ralph Lauren store on Madison Avenue and 72nd Street, has to bring in her wardrobe, model each outfit for her managers, pose for Polaroids, then wait for approval of her chosen combinations of the designer's clothes.

If she wears an unapproved outfit to work, she will be asked to buy something else to wear from the store (and receives a demerit in her personnel file).[20]

Thus opens a *New York Times* article on what its author terms "glamour girls": wealthy, educated women in their twenties and early thirties who work for "image-conscious employers" such as Ralph Lauren, *Vogue*, or Sotheby's. The article's emphasis is on the fierce competition for these jobs; their low pay, relative to the cost of the designer clothing, taxicab transport, and Upper East Side rents they demand; and what is, more often than not, their ultimate end, the acquisition of wealthy husbands. The article also illustrates two key dimensions of domination, characteristics of power relations that undermine political freedom, and that are central to the critiques of schooling at North End and Fair View, respectively.

For students of power-with-a-face, what is perhaps the most immediately troubling aspect of this description of McCuistion's relationship with her store managers is the interference by the latter with what many people view as a basic personal decision. Even if they grant that dress codes may be reasonable in some circumstances, and even if they grant that this particular place of work provides one such circumstance, those who define power in terms of interference with negative freedom likely would argue that people subject to such regulation should have some minimal range or "space" within which to choose, at the start of the day, which articles of clothing, and which combinations of articles, to wear. Managers at the Ralph Lauren store, by this view, intrude into this space of negative liberty when they involve themselves intimately in what should be McCuistion's personal choice. By requiring that she and other salespeople model their outfits for them and wear only pre-approved selections, company supervisors exercise power over their employees.

De-facing power, however, requires acknowledging that decisions about what to wear in conformity with a given dress code, or even decisions about what to wear in the absence of a dress code, are never

[20] Yazigi (1998: 1).

independently made. Getting dressed for work, and more generally deciding how to present one's physical self to others in a particular cultural and historical context, is a form of social action. It is inescapably bound by conventional limits to action, such as norms defining appropriate articles of clothing, or standards of beautiful or tasteful forms of self-presentation.

It is possible, none the less, to target criticism at severe asymmetries, among those whose fields of possibility they shape, in the social capacity to act in ways that affect these mechanisms of power. If the *Times* article is accurate, in this particular place of work, not only the determination of the employee dress code, but also its interpretation, takes place wholly at or above the managerial level. McCuistion's every reading of rules and conventions governing dress is subject to review by her supervisors.

In this sense, the power relations involving McCuistion and her managers parallel those involving students and teachers at the North End Community School, relationships characterized by pronounced asymmetries in the social capacity to act upon the norms, rules, and other social boundaries to action that define local practices of teaching and learning. A central claim advanced in chapter 4 is that teachers and other adults at North End almost completely exclude students from participation in deliberating about, making, and critically evaluating decisions about how to govern school activities. Franklin and her colleagues teach obedience to rules imposed by adults in positions of authority. They do so, my account suggests, partly in response to problems posed by "the environment," which is the product of human action and amenable to change by (collective) action. Authoritarian pedagogic practices, I argue, encourage unreflective rule-following and relatively ineffectual forms of resistance, such as withdrawal from classroom activities. They discourage relatively effective forms of student participation in rule-making, such as public and principled critique.

Implicit in my account of schooling at North End is the premise that self-government should play a role in the definition and re-definition of power relations. This is a premise with apparent links to some variants of democratic theory, in particular deliberative strains that posit fair preference amalgamation as insufficient to render collective decisions legitimate. To be legitimate, deliberative democrats argue, a norm must be the product of processes of debate and deliberation that include, as free and equal participants, all whom it affects. Theorists of deliberative democracy envision, then, a paradigmatic example of a power relation that approximates what I want to suggest is one important dimension of political freedom: the relation defined by rules, laws, and other boundaries created by all whose fields of action they affect via decision-making procedures in which they participate as political equals in setting the agenda and determining both outcomes and discursive norms.[21]

Like deliberative democrats, I want to draw critical attention to the question of the relative inclusiveness of processes of making and remaking the norms defining power relations. A power relation promotes freedom along this first dimension to the extent that it endows all participants with the social capacity to participate effectively in determining, evaluating, criticizing, and changing the norms and other boundaries to action that comprise it. I want to move away from much theorizing by deliberative democrats, however, in refusing to privilege debate and discussion as the only, or the most important form of action upon norms and other boundaries to social action defining power relations. Inclusiveness is relevant not only to deliberative processes, but to all forms of social action through which conditions defining a power relation are shaped, maintained, or changed. I depart, as well, from some deliberative democrats' near-exclusive emphasis on relations shaping law, public policy, and other mechanisms of state governance. Inclusiveness is relevant to power relations defined by social practices generally, and by the institutions that sustain and govern them, because of the key role practices play in delimiting the ways people in specific contexts might act that are socially recognized, respected, and praised.

This dimension of freedom might be promoted, then, to a greater or lesser extent, by power relations defined, not only by practices of political governance and state institutions, but also by economic, cultural, and other social institutions and practices. Scientific institutions and practices, or professional or artistic and other cultural institutions and practices might promote inclusiveness in defining and re-defining key creative and productive tasks, the values assigned these tasks, and the standards of truth, or the professional or aesthetic standards used to measure performance. They do so, and thereby promote participants' freedom, to the extent that restrictions on the social capacity to act on these constitutive political mechanisms are minimal and necessary, a function, for instance, of the requirement that effective criticism be intelligible to most actors who engage in the practice. If action on standards of scientific truth requires some understanding of – but not agreement with – widely accepted scientific principles, power relations defined by scientific practices do not, for this reason alone, produce relations of domination. If action on standards governing classical violin performance requires

---

[21] See, for example, Habermas (1984, 1987a, and 1998, especially chs. 7 and 8), Benhabib (1996), and Cohen (1996).

mastering a basic repertoire and attaining technical proficiency, power relations defined by this artistic practice do not, for this reason alone, produce relations of domination.

Practices and institutions comprise social definitions of worthy ends, excellences, identities, and distributions. Together, these create insiders and outsiders, as well as internal hierarchies, which almost invariably translate into some asymmetry in the social capacity for action on norms. Domination along this first dimension occurs when such asymmetries are severe and avoidably so. Of course, whether asymmetries in the capacity to shape the terms of a given relation are avoidable or not, and whether or not they are more severe than necessary, will be, in many cases, controversial questions. History offers, however, striking examples of this form of domination: power relations defined by matrices of laws, norms, and other boundaries structured such that some actors who could be included in shaping key terms of relationships in which they participate have no hand in doing so. Power relations defined by "race" in the pre-Civil Rights Movement American South, for example, shaped the field of what was socially possible for some (African-Americans) via boundaries (Jim Crow laws) they were socially precluded from helping determine.

This dimension of domination is relevant to, not only practices of legal governance and state institutions, but also cultural and other social institutions and practices. Even if they are permitted and enabled to vote, then, to the extent that black Americans or members of other marginalized social groups are excluded from processes of determining the standards that govern dominant cultural practices, and the distributive and other institutional rules that support and regulate these practices, domination obtains, because their fields of action (in this instance, the forms of expression in which they might engage and the social capacities they might develop that are publicly recognized and rewarded) are circumscribed by mechanisms of power they do not help make and re-make.

Most power relations fall between these extremes. Many include all participants in determining some key mechanisms of power, while preventing or discouraging particular participants from acting in ways that shape other important boundaries. An example is a power relation involving workers and managers at a firm where all participate in collective bargaining about salaries, benefits, and job security, but workers are excluded from making and critically evaluating decisions about research, production, or the investment of labor power and material resources. Other power relations might formally include all participants in deciding key boundaries, while severely limiting the capacities of some to act effectively in ways that shape them. Thus, although all citizens were legally enabled to vote for delegates to the Frankfurt Constituent

Assembly of 1848, the interests of members of some groups affected by decisions the assembly made were not represented.[22]

If one aims to remain in the critical tradition of the power debate, but to jettison its implicit conceptualization of freedom, an important set of questions to ask of relations that fall short of the non-domination, or freedom-promoting end of the continuum centers on the processes through which the boundaries to action that comprise these relations are made, re-made, modified, and transformed. What restrictions are placed on deliberating about and helping decide key collective norms? Are some participants in power relations prevented or discouraged from critically evaluating, openly contesting, and/or acting effectively on their terms? What are the grounds for these restrictions and exclusions? And how might these processes be re-defined in more inclusive ways?

Domination and freedom, II: the scope of "action on" power

Imagine that the Ralph Lauren corporation were to overhaul its workplace practices, to make them more autonomous, so that McCuistion and other salespeople did not need managers' approval of their every interpretation of the company dress code, and even to make them more inclusive, so that workers could participate in deliberating about and determining the policies that affect them. Such changes would reduce, in the power relations these practices define, the aspect of domination emphasized in the discussion above. Participants would be socially enabled to act in ways that change or otherwise affect the terms of these relations. Nevertheless, the scope of action on their terms would remain restricted, and in ways that are patterned and relatively enduring. Notice a second important dimension of domination captured in the *Times* article, which continues:

Ms. McCuistion, 33, who moved to Manhattan from Houston several years ago, doesn't mind the strict dress code. Nor does she object that she must wear her long brown hair in what the company considers a "clean cut" style, or that she had to buy thousands of dollars worth of Ralph Lauren clothes for a job that started at $8 an hour.

She loves her work, in part because she is surrounded by people just like her, she says.[23]

What kind of people are "just like" Holli McCuistion? The article quotes David Koch, the prominent New York philanthropist and vice president

[22] This example is from Elster (1998: 99), who reports that the assembly included "no peasants, only a few small shopkeepers, virtually no manual workers, and no industrial workers at all."   [23] Yazigi (1998: 1).

of Koch Industries, who married a former "glamour girl" assistant to the fashion designer Adolfo, describing them as people with "the right social skills, savoir-faire, and intelligence." The publisher Charles Scribner III uses similar language when he characterizes these women as "bright, attractive, and well-educated."[24]

The above might suggest, at first glance, that McCuistion is "free" in Berlin's (negative) sense of that word. No one forces her to work at Ralph Lauren. She chooses and apparently even "loves" her job. Yet Koch's and Scribner's word choice indicates that the power relation in which she participates at her place of work is constituted in part by depoliticized social boundaries to action. The example points to a second line of critique one might target at a particular power relation: criticism focused on patterned restrictions on the scope of action upon the norms and other social boundaries defining the relation. For "glamour girls" and those "just like them," it seems, to draw on one specific fund of cultural capital is to be "intelligent." To follow a circumscribed set of Euro-American conventions prescribing how women should adorn and groom themselves is to be "attractive" and "clean-cut." And to conform to upper middle-class norms governing public conduct and speech is to have "the right social skills." McCuistion is a member of an elite social group. She is privileged. Yet the power relation in which she participates approximates a state of domination to the extent that it is delimited by gendered and culture- and class-specific definitions of intelligence, of attractiveness, of what it means to be "just like me," definitions viewed as, not the proper target of critical evaluation, debate, and possibly modification or transformation, but rather invariable, incontrovertible measures of what it is to be a successful, intelligent, beautiful, "girl."

Power relations at Polo Ralph Lauren have affinities with those at Fair View Elementary, where the scope of (relatively participatory) decision-making is restricted in patterned ways. Shielded from critical analysis and from debate in Monica Segal's classroom are the standards that govern local pedagogic practices, the ends that guide them, and the social identities of those who engage in them. I want to return, briefly, to the critical claim advanced in chapter 5, in order to highlight three key facets of this analytically distinct dimension of domination. Central to my account of power relations at Fair View is the claim that the depoliticization there of classroom "values," of "learning process" competencies, and of the social identities of those who engage in local practices of teaching and learning fosters relatively severe and unambiguously punishing attitudes toward,

[24] Ibid. (2 and 1).

beliefs about, and treatment of actors who fail to conform to reigning standards of excellence, those who do not attain "school success," and those who are, in Segal's words, "not from here." These attitudes, beliefs, and behaviors function at once intra- and intersubjectively. The intensity of self-discipline at Fair View is mirrored by ostracism, public reprobation, and aggressive efforts to cure or to redeem those, like Lawrence, who do not discipline themselves with respect to prevailing rules and norms.

This critique of power relations at Fair View draws attention, first, to the centrality of difference to both freedom and domination. Every possible matrix of social boundaries to human action (every practice, for instance) creates a class of actions (and their agents) or attributes (and their bearers) that exceed the norms and other mechanisms of power that comprise it. Whereas the first dimension of domination, emphasized in the discussion above, is a function of how – that is, through what processes – power relations are determined and changed or maintained, this second dimension is a function of how – to what extent, and in what ways – power relations enable and encourage participants to engage these forms of difference, which they necessarily produce. Power relations promote freedom to the extent that they permit and even provoke participants to acknowledge, to listen to, to debate, and more generally to engage in ways not aimed at eradicating, forms of social action that exceed and/or oppose the boundaries that comprise them. Such relations promote freedom in that they encourage those whose action they enable and constrain to view them as mechanisms of power that might be defined and ordered in other ways.

Again, this line of critique parallels arguments advanced by some democratic theorists, in particular those who draw on Nietzsche, Foucault, and Arendt to argue that, not deliberation, so much as "agonism" lies at the heart of democratic politics. Democratic government, by this view, proliferates political contests. It generates a particular, and valuable, form of conflict, one that aims at, not true or even consensually agreed upon solutions, so much as a Foucaultian "care" for difference, manifested as an openness toward long-forgotten and previously unexplored possibilities for organizing the self and social life.[25]

The account of power relations at Fair View Elementary helps clarify, second, the grounds for criticizing this particular form of restriction on freedom. The complaint in chapter 5 is not that Segal's classroom suffers

[25] See, for example, Connolly (1991, esp. ch. 6; and 1995, esp. chs. 3 and 4), Honig (1993), and Mouffe (1993).

from a dearth of politics (that at Fair View there is, generally, insufficient deliberation, debate, and collective decision-making), but rather that the particular restrictions on politics that obtain, by translating into defects the differences that pedagogic practices produce, promote and legitimize relatively severe forms of discipline. The critique is not, in other words, based on the premise that people best order their lives together when they relentlessly scrutinize, contest, and re-make every law, every convention, every social meaning and value through which they define and delimit collective possibility. Such a state of continual "structure-disturbing and structure-inventing,"[26] even if attainable, would be undesirable, because inimical to the cultivation of *any* practices and the construction and maintenance of *any* institutions, which, by definition, require some measure of stability in the form of relatively enduring rules and norms. The critique is rooted, instead, in a wariness of power relations that naturalize or universalize key social limits to action comprising them. Such relations translate the differences they produce into failures to act in ways that are, unproblematically, right and good, social disorders that should or that must be set straight. They license the punishment of groups, individuals, and aspects of the self that they define as the "other" of worthy forms of being and doing.

Power relations realize a state of domination along this dimension when the boundaries to action that constitute them are so widely accepted as extra-political (as divinely ordained or biologically given or sociologically necessary) that even injurious forms of punishment are presumed to be legitimate, because understood as serving the interests of their targets. Few, if any, power relations realize domination in this sense. But relations that come close include those defined by "sex." That "male" and "female" are widely regarded as distinct and fixed categories, induced from the facts of human biology, renders actions, attributes, and relations that fail to fit one class or the other, aberrations, pathologies, violations of nature, which must be set right for the sake of those they afflict.[27]

The Fair View case illustrates, finally, that to be privileged – to have inordinate access to scarce resources and opportunities – is not to "have

[26] Unger (1987: 4). The argument is not premised, that is to say, on a definition of humans as essentially "context-revising and context-transcending agents," where "context" means roughly what I mean by power relations: "the basic institutional arrangements and imaginative preconceptions that circumscribe our routine practical or discursive activities and conflicts and that resist their destabilizing effects" (ibid, 13 and 6–7). My view of power emphasizes that "contexts" cannot be transcended in social life, although they can sometimes be reshaped, and sometimes consciously and deliberately.

[27] The example is from Butler (1990).

power." It is not to choose how to act in ways that are exempt from social constraint, or even from relatively severe forms of social discipline. The case does *not* suggest, however, that privilege is neutral in power relations. To the contrary, domination can be reinforced when located in sites of privilege. If Holli McCuistion were to question the standards of feminine beauty that govern her workplace, then, she might be reassured by the covers of this month's fashion magazines, just as, if a student in Monica Segal's class were to entertain doubts about the value assigned to "learning process" competencies at Fair View, she might be reassured by her parents' sizable Christmas bonuses. By channeling collective resources toward those who realize the ends of particular practices (such as "glamour," Ralph Lauren-style, or "school success"), institutions (including those that comprise the media and private corporations) lend the boundaries that constitute these practices a veneer of universal public endorsement.

Privilege can extend the reach of domination, as well. Consider the depoliticization of social definitions of responsibility as self-sufficiency at Fair View. The fact that most students at this school are advantaged (that they have greater family wealth than most people in the world, as well as better access to educational and work opportunities, and to channels of political influence) means that the cultivation in Segal's classroom of punishing beliefs about, attitudes toward, and ways of treating the "others" of responsibility may well affect, not only those who engage in local pedagogic practices, but also those excluded from privileged communities like Fair View. It may affect, for instance, low-income single mothers and their children, who are not responsible in this sense, by bolstering claims that the reduction or elimination of AFDC benefits in fact helps them, by improving their character.

Most power relations fall between the extremes of promoting freedom or producing states of domination along this dimension. Many mitigate, to varying degrees, the effects of political dogmatism, by promoting toleration: that is, by encouraging participants to refrain from interfering with some forms of belief, speech, and/or conduct that transgress depoliticized social limits to action. The motto of such relations might be, *leave "them" alone*. Let the others of extant social boundaries act as they will, within limits, yet there is no need to listen to or otherwise to attend to, much less actively to engage forms of doing, being, believing, desiring that violate reigning collective norms.

Power relations tempered by toleration are not, by my view, equivalent to states of domination. Yet the gap between tolerating difference and promoting freedom – which requires a vigilance toward power's mechanisms achieved only through active engagement with those who oppose them – prompts a second set of questions that students of power de-faced should ask about specific practices and institutions. Which social limits to action defining relevant power relations are resistant or impervious to contestation, criticism, and change? Which individuals, which groups, and which aspects of the self transgress these boundaries, and how are they regarded and treated by other participants? How might these power relations be re-fashioned in ways that encourage surfacing, rather than suppressing, dissension, and in ways that promote the politicization of indurated social standards, identities, and ends?

De-facing power suggests, then, a series of conceptual and normative shifts for the critical analysis of power relations. It recommends relaxing the definitional requirement that, to count as a mechanism of power, a social boundary be determined, chosen, or directed by an agent who uses it to create desired effects on the action of others, or to produce effects from which she benefits. Students of power relations should narrow their fields of analysis by focusing, not necessarily on political mechanisms that those who seem "powerful" possess and direct, but on those that are central to the definition of relevant practices and institutions.

De-facing power challenges, as well, the implicit grounds for the critique of power-with-a-face. Because social action is, invariably, enabled and constrained by social boundaries to action, interference with independent action is insufficient grounds for criticizing power relations. The object of critique shifts from constraint on negative liberty to the more democratic focus outlined above: the avoidable exclusion of participants in power relations from participation in norm-making, and the depoliticization of key social boundaries to action.

Clearly, promoting freedom, as defined above, is a goal that can compete and at times conflict with other valued social ends, such as efficiency, security, or community. To move from criticizing a particular power relation to informing strategies for reshaping it in ways that promote freedom requires, then, attention to conflicts between the democratic commitments that inform this critique of domination, and the non-, or even anti-democratic commitments constitutive of some highly valued social practices. Democratic norms are not, any more so than other norms, "frontiers" in Berlin's sense of that word. To the extent that they promote inclusiveness in processes of determining social possibility, and a relatively expansive scope of action on power, these norms discourage a range of possible ways of ordering social life, including those supported by many religious and other traditional world views.

Minimally, however, democratic political practices (that is, practices through which members of a polity act on the legal and other limits to action that govern it) and public institutions (collectively defined rights, duties, and distributions, which are backed by the state) should be structured such that their effects on other social practices and institutions are freedom-promoting. Political practices and public institutions provide a crucial vantage point from which to consider power relations for at least two reasons. First, the state's capacity to determine and enforce rights and duties and to distribute resources and opportunities translates into a significant influence over which social practices and institutions survive and flourish, as well as the internal structure of those that do. Second, although all political practices and public institutions are influenced by forces that mitigate against the promotion of political freedom (such as global markets, which constrain states to compete for increasingly mobile capital), democratic political practices and public institutions are defined in part by social boundaries to action, including egalitarian values and norms of respect for self-determination, that promote both inclusiveness in the collective determination of social possibility and some degree of mutability in power relations. These can be invoked to draw attention to contradictions between the constitutive principles and the practical effects of these particular practices and institutions.

The North End and Fair View cases suggest, then, that some political practices in the contemporary United States (in particular, public decision-making about schooling, which takes place in significant part at the level of the local district) and public institutions (such as zoning regulations, tax and housing policies, drug laws, and municipal and educational institutional arrangements) shape power relations in Franklin's and Segal's classrooms in ways that contravene basic democratic principles. At North End, they confront teachers and other adults with immediate threats to their students' well-being, encouraging them to teach unreflective rule-following and deference to authority. At Fair View, they safeguard local pedagogic ends and excellences from forms of social engagement that might unsettle them, helping maintain distinctions between those who do and those who do not conform to depoliticized standards, while mapping these distinctions on to social group identities of race, class, and place. Reducing domination at these sites, the argument suggests, involves not simply attempting to influence local pedagogic practices (as suggested by many critical educational theories). It involves, as well, re-structuring public decision-making about schooling and re-shaping key educational and other public institutions. Those who would inform strategies for changing schooling in ways that promote freedom should engage, then, in debates about and research on re-structuring both educational decision-making processes[28] and institutional design.[29]

The distinction between, on the one hand, relations of domination, and on the other, power relations that promote freedom, enables the student of power de-faced to continue the project defined by Dahl, Gaventa, and other participants in the power debate: the project of criticizing domination and informing efforts to minimize, or at least to reduce it. It enables her to do so, however, while avoiding the conceptual flaws that plague studies of power's various faces. The practical end of the critical analysis of power relations, by this view, is not eliminating power from social life, but instead defining an inclusive and expansive politics, where politics are the processes through which people collectively delimit social possibility.

[28] This is not the place to engage in an extensive debate about changes in processes of decision-making about schooling. Examples of such changes, however, are those instituted in Chicago as a result of the Chicago School Reform Act of 1988. This act establishes in each Chicago school a Local School Council (LSC) composed of parents, community residents, teachers, and the school principal. It grants LSCs the legal authority to appoint and re-appoint principals, and to negotiate their performance contracts; to help develop and approve school improvement plans, which determine how individual schools work to realize student achievement and other academic goals; and to develop and approve school budgets. The act further specifies that compensatory education funds provided for by the Illinois General Assembly be fully allocated (which they had not been prior to 1988), and that these funds be used in the ways determined by Local School Councils. Chicago School Reform Act, P.A. 85–1418, 1988, Illinois Legislative Service. (Note, however, that the 1988 reforms were eviscerated by P.A. 85–15, passed by the Illinois State Legislature in 1995. This more recent reform transfers much budgetary and personnel decision-making authority from LSCs to a School District Management Team and Board of Trustees, both appointed by the Chicago mayor.) Students of power relations in the classroom might investigate, then, whether and how these forms of school governance affect relations among teachers, students, and other actors in Chicago's schools. If "the environment" or an analogous set of constraints defines salient problems for adults in some Chicago schools, do LSCs provide means for them to devise strategies that depart significantly from the authoritarian responses at North End?

[29] Examples of institutional change include the wide variety of "school choice" plans currently in place or under consideration in particular US states and school districts. Those who study how power shapes social possibility in the classroom might ask whether particular variants of "choice" (for instance, the program in place in New York City's District 4, which eliminates attendance zones within the district and requires parents to choose among alternative schools developed by local leaders) enable some students at schools like North End to exit pedagogic practices that define relations of domination. They might ask whether, at a school like Fair View, domination can be reduced through inter-district "controlled choice" programs (Alves and Willie, 1987 and 1990), which define as a central goal integrating, at both the school and classroom level, members of economically, culturally, and politically marginalized social groups. Can choice, if accompanied by curricular planning, and teacher recruitment and training geared toward cultivating engagement with social plurality, test the walls of Fair View's "world"? They might ask, as well, how re-structuring specific non-educational public institutions – for example, regulations governing local policing in core urban areas, municipal zoning laws, or federal tax and housing policies – can contribute to the reduction of domination in specific educational contexts.

Appendix A: Tables

Table 1 *Socio-economic characteristics of Fair View and North End in comparative perspective*

	Connec-ticut	Fair View[a]	North End[a]	Bridge-port	Hartford	New Haven
Occupation of employed persons sixteen years and over (%)						
Managerial/ professional	31.5	55.0	17.0	19.0	21.1	30.0
Technical/sales/clerical	33.2	32.0	28.0	30.6	33.3	31.2
Service occupations	11.5	6.0	27.0	17.5	19.8	16.1
Agriculture	1.2	<1.0	<1.0	0.9	<1.0	<1.0
Precision production/ craft/repair	11.2	3.0	10.0	11.9	9.0	8.2
Operators/fabricators/ laborers	11.5	3.0	19.0	20.2	15.9	14.0
Unemployment and labor force participation, persons sixteen years and over (%)						
Unemployed	5.4	2.0	8.0	10.6	10.7	9.3
Labor force participation	69.0	68.0	63.0	64.6	60.5	62.5
Income and poverty status						
Median family income ($)	49,199	95,000	22,500	33,090	24,774	31,163
Median household income ($)	41,721	83,500	18,000	28,704	22,140	25,811
Per capita income ($)	20,189	45,500	10,000	13,156	11,081	12,968
Persons below poverty level (%)	6.8	3.5	28.0	17.1	27.5	21.3
Families below poverty level (%)	5.0	1.5	26.0	15.0	25.7	18.2
Education, persons over 25 years (%)						
High school graduate	79.2	94.0	57.5	61.1	59.4	71.0
College graduate	27.2	61.0	10.0	12.3	14.4	26.7
Race and Hispanic origin (%)						
White (including Hispanic)	87.1	96.0	7.0	58.7	39.9	53.7
Black (including Hispanic)	8.3	<1.0	90.0	26.6	38.9	36.3
Hispanic	6.2	2.0	4.0	25.3	31.0	12.5

Note:
[a] Approximate values for census tracts that roughly define school neighborhoods.
Source: United States Bureau of the Census 1990.

Table 2 *Revenue sources and per pupil expenditure in Connecticut school districts, 1995–1996*

Education Reference Group[a]	Local (%)	State (%)	Federal (%)	Tuition and other (%)	Per pupil expenditure (US$)
A	95.7	2.9	0.7	0.7	9,329
B	85.7	12.5	1.0	0.7	8,401
C	69.5	28.2	1.0	1.3	8,048
D	71.1	27.0	1.2	0.8	7,749
E	57.0	40.6	1.3	1.1	8,106
F	61.4	35.5	1.8	1.3	7,785
G	43.0	53.8	1.7	1.4	7,938
H	63.5	33.4	2.7	0.5	8,069
I	27.6	66.2	5.6	0.7	8,572

Note:
[a] The Connecticut State Department of Education groups school districts according to measures of socio-economic status and student need from ERG A, which consists of those districts with the highest SES and lowest student need, to ERG I, which consists of those districts with the lowest SES and student need. See chapter 4, n. 23.
Source: Connecticut State Department of Education, *1995–96 Strategic School Profiles.*

Table 3 *Race and ethnicity, poverty, and achievement at North End and Fair View*

	State of Connecticut (%)	North End[a] (%)	Fair View[a] (%)
Student race and ethnicity			
Black	13.5	90.0	1.0
Hispanic	11.8	9.0	2.0
American Indian	0.3	0.0	0.0
Asian American	2.4	0.0	2.0
White	72.0	1.0	95.0
Students qualifying for free or reduced-price meals	29.0	80.0	1.0
Connecticut Mastery Test, grade four, met state goal for:			
Reading	47.7	3.0	80.0
Writing	46.3	10.0	60.0
Mathematics	59.3	10.0	90.0
All three tests	28.3	0.0	50.0

Notes:
[a] Approximate values.
Source: Connecticut State Department of Education, *1995–96 Strategic School Profiles.*

Table 4 *Reported AIDS cases in Connecticut and its cities, by race and ethnicity* (per 1,000 population)

	Connecticut	Bridgeport	Hartford	New Haven
Total	3.05	6.10	15.24	14.11
Black	14.80	12.00	17.40	24.61
Hispanic	1.14	9.74	19.78	18.29
American Indian	3.09	3.30	8.38	19.34
Asian American	0.43	0.00	2.36	0.62
White	1.26	2.11	5.68	5.23

Note:
Data are cumulative, from 1981 through June, 1998. Population statistics are from United States Census Bureau, 1990.
Source: State of Connecticut, Department of Public Health, AIDS Epidemiology Program.

Table 5 *Reported violent crime in Connecticut and selected municipalities, 1993–1996[a]*

	US	Connecticut	Bridgeport	Hartford	New Haven	Fair View[b]
Homicide[c]	8.53	5.58	34.57	26.58	19.89	1.00
Rape[d]	38.30	23.95	44.04	78.62	92.40	8.00
Robbery[e]	229.23	179.33	794.04	1005.73	933.51	36.75
Aggravated assault[f]	419.20	223.55	626.91	979.33	1014.94	57.75

Notes:
Crime statistics are not available for North End, because it is not a separate municipality.
[a] Values are expressed as incidents per 100,000 population, averaged across four years.
[b] Approximate values for town of Fair View.
[c] Homicide is defined as "the willful (non-negligent) killing of one human being by another." *Uniform Crime Reports 1996*, 13.
[d] Rape is defined as "the carnal knowledge of a female forcibly and against her will." It includes "assaults and attempts to commit rape by force or threat of force," but not statutory rape. Ibid.: 23.
[e] Robbery is defined as "the taking or attempting to take anything of value from the care, custody, or control of a person or persons by force or threat of force of violence and/or by putting the victim in fear." Ibid.: 26.
[f] Aggravated assault is defined as "an unlawful attack by one person upon another for the purpose of inflicting severe or aggravated bodily injury." Ibid.: 31.
Source: Federal Bureau of Investigation, US Department of Justice, *Uniform Crime Reports for the United States* (Washington, DC: US Government Printing Office), 1993–96.

Table 6 *Victims of violent crime, by race and residence, 1973–1992* (per 1,000 persons age 12 and over)[a]

	Black	White	Ratio black/white	Urban	Suburban	Ratio urban/suburban
1973	41.7	31.6	1.32	44.1	31.3	1.41
1974	40.7	31.9	1.28	45.0	32.6	1.38
1975	42.9	31.6	1.36	46.1	31.7	1.45
1976	44.4	31.1	1.43	45.9	32.3	1.42
1977	41.9	33.0	1.27	47.2	33.7	1.40
1978	40.6	33.0	1.23	45.9	34.7	1.32
1979	41.6	33.6	1.24	47.5	34.8	1.37
1980	40.6	32.2	1.26	45.0	33.2	1.36
1981	49.7	33.4	1.49	51.6	32.8	1.57
1982	43.7	33.2	1.32	47.0	32.4	1.45
1983	40.6	29.9	1.36	43.4	29.4	1.47
1984	41.6	30.2	1.38	43.6	30.3	1.44
1985	38.2	29.1	1.31	39.9	26.8	1.49
1986	33.4	27.5	1.21	36.3	23.9	1.53
1987	42.1	27.7	1.52	41.5	23.7	1.75
1988	40.4	28.2	1.43	40.7	26.6	1.53
1989	36.0	28.2	1.28	38.3	27.2	1.41
1990	39.7	28.2	1.41	41.3	25.2	1.64
1991	45.7	30.5	1.5	45.0	27.5	1.64
1992	50.4	29.9	1.69	43.2	28.2	1.53

Note:
[a] Violent crimes are homicides, rapes, robberies, and aggravated assaults. For definitions, see table 5, above.
Source: US Department of Justice, Bureau of Justice Statistics, *Criminal Victimization in the United States, 1973–1992 Trends* (Washington, DC: US Government Printing Office: 1994), 14–18.

Table 7 *Beliefs about school rules*

	North End (%[a]) n = 55		Fair View (%[a]) n = 78	
"In school we have rules like, 'Don't run in the hallway.' Why do you think we need rules?"				
Prevents disorder/ensures order	18.2		30.8	
Explicit reference to fostering environment conducive to learning	0.0		10.3	
Prevents harm/ensures well-being	43.6		56.4	
No explanation or circular explanation	27.3		12.8	
Explanation with reference to bad conduct/ character of children	10.9		2.6	
"Are the rules at [North End/Fair View] fair? Why?"				
	Yes	No	Yes	No
Answers with reference to well-being of students	14.5	5.5	55.1	10.3
Specific reference to freedom – the rules leave enough unregulated	0.0	0.0	10.3	0.0
Reference to a standard of reasonableness – the rules provide appropriate means to reaching desirable ends	1.8	3.6	9.0	9.0
No explanation	23.6	7.3	6.4	15.4
Trust in the judgment of authorities	7.3	3.6	0.0	1.3
Induces conformity to a behavioral or attitudinal norm	11.0	0.0	2.6	0.0
Answers with reference to decision-making processes	1.8	0.0	3.8	0.0
Answers with reference to enforcement	11.0	14.5	3.8	0.0

Note:

[a] Values may total more than 100 percent because some responses fall into more than one category.

Source: Survey of fourth and fifth graders at the North End Community School and fourth graders at the Fair View Elementary School.

Table 8 *Beliefs about school knowledge*

	North End (%)[a] n = 55	Fair View (%)[a] n = 78
"What is the most important thing you learned this year?"		
Isolated fact(s), rule(s), technique(s) or subject matter(s)	60.0	30.8
Integrated set of facts or cognitive skills	10.9	38.5
Specific reference to analysis or problem-solving abilities	0.0	6.4
Specific reference to capacities for working effectively with others	0.0	6.4
Specific reference to capacities for independent learning	0.0	8.5
Truth(s) about the self or the social world	1.8	10.3
Rule of conduct	18.2	3.8
Social or interpersonal skills	9.1	11.5
Personal trait(s)	3.6	10.3
Does not name most important thing learned	1.8	7.8
On the grounds that everything learned in school is important	0.0	6.4
"Why is it important?"		
Utility–simply states	38.2	26.9
Utility–draws specific significance	18.2	32.1
Self-improvement	7.3	5.1
To promote the well-being of others or the world	3.6	7.7
Because it is true or morally right	0.0	5.1
Because it is fun to learn	5.5	6.4
Specific reference to "learning process" competencies	0.0	10.3
To avoid punishment, win rewards, or fulfill requirements or expectations	18.2	10.3
No explanation	10.9	7.7

Note:
[a] Values may total more than 100 percent because some responses fall into more than one category.
Source: Survey of fourth and fifth graders at the North End Community School and fourth graders at the Fair View Elementary School.

Table 9 *What North End and Fair View students would change about school*

	North End (%)[a] n = 55	Fair View (%)[a] n = 78
"If you could change one thing about [North End/Fair View] or your classroom, what would you change? Why?"		
Student conduct or attitudes	30.9	3.8
Physical plant/maintenance/resources	25.5	24.4
Rules, organization of classroom and school day	16.4	17.9
Less work or more trips or specials	7.3	21.8
Teachers, staff, administrators	9.1	1.3
Pedagogical approach	0.0	5.1
Nothing	12.7	24.4
Don't know or no answer	5.5	2.6

Note:
[a] Values may total more than 100 percent because some responses fall into more than one category.
Source: Survey of the fourth and fifth graders at the North End Community School and fourth graders at the Fair View Elementary School.

Table 10 *Goals and aspirations*

	North End (%)[a] n = 55		Fair View (%)[a] n = 78	
"What is a goal you have – something you hope you'll do in the future?"				
Specific career goal	74.5		69.2	
Managerial, executive, or professional specialty	29.1		21.8	
Service occupation	30.9		20.5	
Technical, sales, or administrative support	1.8		1.3	
Sports, arts, or entertainment	1.8		10.3	
Manufacturing or repair	3.6		0.0	
Have a job in general	7.3		1.3	
Academic attainment or achievement	1.8		14.1	
Athletic achievement	9.1		1.3	
Social or environmental good	0.0		3.8	
Creative expression	1.8		3.8	
Family life or general happiness	3.6		2.6	
Other	1.8		3.8	
No answer or no goal	0.0		3.8	
"Do you think you'll reach your goal? Why?"				
	Yes	Maybe/no	Yes	Maybe/no
Agency/effort alone	12.7	0.0	21.8	1.3
Accountability	22.1	0.0	2.6	0.0
Personal talent, characteristic, desire	30.9	1.8	25.6	5.1
Practice or other specific steps taken	16.4	0.0	9.0	0.0
Evidence from current performance and/or past achievement	3.6	0.0	16.7	0.0
Because of factors external to me (e.g. personal contacts, luck)	5.5	1.8	2.6	6.4
No answer or no reason	5.5	3.6	2.6	9.0

Note:
[a] Values may total more than 100 percent because some responses fall into more than one category.
Source: Survey of fourth and fifth graders at the North End Community School and fourth graders at the Fair View Elementary School.

Appendix B: Research methods

Richard Fenno characterizes participant-observation research as a matter of "soaking" and "poking,"[1] or, more formally, "gathering data by watching and talking to people in their natural habitats."[2] Lofland and Lofland define it as "the process in which an investigator establishes and sustains a many-sided and relatively long-term relationship with a human association in its natural setting for the purpose of developing a scientific understanding of that association."[3] For Dewalt and Dewalt it is "a method in which an observer takes part in the daily activities, rituals, interactions, and events of the people being studied as one of the means of learning the explicit and tacit aspects of their culture."[4]

Together, these definitions highlight important features of participant-observation research. It almost always takes place in a "natural setting" or "habitat." Participant-observers generally study social phenomena directly, that is, rather than rely exclusively on participants' reports of their actions and experiences, or on experimental measures. Participant-observation research is "relatively long-term." Ethnographers spend weeks, sometimes years in the field, establishing rapport with, observing, and engaging those whose actions and experiences they seek to explain, understand, or interpret. And participant-observation generally engages the researcher simultaneously as observer and participant, seeking a balance between the roles.[5]

The method's principal advantage, and the reason I adopted it to conduct the empirical research for this study, is that it offers access to the meanings social experiences, interactions, and activities have for those who participate in them. Although such access is never perfect,[6] it is potentially less restricted than that gleaned from discrete or relatively short-term research, research situated wholly outside the setting of its subject, and purely observational research.

As Lofland and Lofland note, the aim of participant-observation, at least for many who engage in it, is a "scientific" understanding of a subject: not necessarily

---

[1] Fenno (1978: xiv). [2] Fenno (1990: 6). [3] Lofland and Lofland (1984: 12).
[4] Dewalt and Dewalt (1998: 260).
[5] As Spradley notes, however, some researchers embrace one role more than the other, at the extremes, adopting the role of the pure observer "who has no involvement with the people or activities studied," or the "complete observer" who approximates "the highest level of involvement for ethnographers" (Spradley 1980: 59, 61).
[6] See Geertz (1983: 70), for whom gaining access to "the native's point of view" is "more like grasping a proverb, catching an allusion, seeing a joke . . . or . . . reading a poem . . . than it is like achieving communion."

causal explanation of social laws,[7] but an account that is the product of relatively systematic and accurate investigation. This goal may strike some who are skeptical about the method as elusive. In the discussion that follows I address three key questions such skeptics might pose about my own research: two that center on the internal validity of participant-observation,[8] specifically on the problems of subjectiveness and reactivity, and one that centers on external validity, or the representativeness of the findings participant-observation generates.[9] I explain how each concern influenced the way I designed the project. I then turn, in the second section, to a more detailed description of the mechanics of my research: how I conducted field observations and recorded field notes, structured faculty and staff interviews, and administered student surveys.

PARTICIPANT-OBSERVATION RESEARCH: THREE CONCERNS

SUBJECTIVENESS

In "Thick Description," Clifford Geertz characterizes ethnographic writings as "fictions": fictions not in the sense that they are untrue, but in the sense that they are fabricated, "'something made,' 'something fashioned.'"[10] "[W]hat we call our data," he writes, "are really our own constructions of other people's constructions of what they and their compatriots are up to . . ."[11] Participant-observation research is, necessarily, subjective. The researcher's perceptions, thoughts, and attitudes shape which possible data she records, which possible analytic categories and themes she highlights, and how she interprets what she observes and experiences in the field. Ethnographic subjectiveness raises the question: "Does the account that a given researcher presents reflect what really happened, or alternatively, a (conscious or unconscious) distortion of what happened?"

In thinking about this problem, it is important to avoid posing a false dichotomy between wholly objective quantitative social science and subjective ethnographic research. Even quantitative social scientific analysis is, to some extent,

---

[7] Many contemporary ethnographers view the enterprise, instead, as one of interpreting and/or participating in the construction of social experience and meaning. Without abandoning the aspiration to conduct systematic investigations and to present accounts that are truthful, they challenge any ethnographic pretension to measure and represent an unmediated social reality. Thus Clifford characterizes the products of ethnography as "partial truths": *truths* in the plural, because there are always multiple possible accurate accounts of a given social phenomenon, and *partial* truths, because even accurate accounts are necessarily defined by "systematic, and contestable, exclusions." He calls, none the less, for "rigorous partiality," for ethnographies that are at once "truthful" and "realistic" (Clifford 1986: 6, 25).

[8] Some ethnographers who want to distance themselves from positivistic norms of social scientific research propose focusing on, not internal and external validity, but "critical trustworthiness," defined as a function of, first, the credibility of ethnographic accounts, to both the researcher and other participants in the activities and relations under investigation, and second, "anticipatory accommodation," or attention to relevant contextual variations (Kincheloe and McLaren 1994: 151–2).

[9] For a somewhat different approach to addressing these same concerns, see Michael Burawoy's introduction to Burawoy, et al. (1991).

[10] Geertz (1973: 15–16).   [11] Ibid. (9).

subjective. Survey researchers, for instance, rely heavily on respondents' interpretations and reports of their experiences and attitudes, and they construct categories, which they use to sort and analyze data. The concern is, none the less, a valid one. Without adopting the (unattainable) goal of a wholly objective explanation of social reality, one unaffected by my own subject position, biography, and perspective, I aimed, in recording and analyzing data, to minimize unnecessary biases and distortions.

One technique I used, especially during my first weeks in the field, was to record not only what struck me as noteworthy or unusual, but as much as possible of what I heard and saw. In so doing, I followed the advice of those who advise ethnographers to "make strange"[12] what seems commonplace, in order to reduce (without eliminating) biases produced by preconceptions. I separated this descriptive text in the field notes from analytic comments,[13] writing the latter only after returning home after a day of research.

In addition, I structured my observations to search for evidence that might disconfirm working hypotheses. For example, a hypothesis that emerged relatively early on was that students at North End and Fair View exhibit differential attitudes and behaviors with respect to school and classroom rules. At Fair View, the hypothesis was, students are active in making and enforcing rules. They tend to be reflective about the content and purpose of rules and generally to view participatory rule-making as legitimate. At North End, by contrast, students are relatively passive with respect to rules. They tend to accept them as "given" and to view teachers and other school authorities as the only people entitled to make and enforce rules.

After formulating this hypothesis, I targeted further observations at testing it, asking whether the pattern held up over time and whether it was consistent across settings (for example, in different classrooms) within each school. These observations raised important questions with respect to the original hypothesis. They highlighted at North End student resistance to authority, which (as noted in chapter 4) focuses almost exclusively on the administration of punishment. At Fair View they revealed patterned limitations to student reflectivity about rules, in particular (as argued in chapter 5) the apparent immunity of key norms of conduct and standards of character from the critical thinking that students direct at classroom rules. In this instance, then, targeted observations led me, not to discard altogether, but to modify and refine the hypothesis.

A third process I used in my efforts to reduce this form of distortion is what is often termed triangulation: checking to see whether data that originate from

[12] Hammersley and Atkinson (1995: ch. 1). Here "strange" refers to Alfred Schutz's 1964 essay, "The Stranger." Schutz argues that participants in social practices tend to apprehend local norms practically, as "recipe knowledge," which they use to negotiate "normal problems" unreflectively, and hence efficiently. Strangers, by contrast – those who "[try] to be permanently accepted or at least tolerated by the group which [they approach]" – are forced to examine norms systematically in order to solve everyday problems. Strangeness, Schutz suggests, yields a form of objectivity, in part the product of the stranger's "need to acquire full knowledge *of* the elements of the approached cultural pattern and to examine for this purpose with care and precision what seems self-explanatory to the in-group" (Schutz 1971: 91 and 104; emphasis as in original).

[13] See sample field notes excerpt, below.

different sources correspond. Direct inquiry within the participant-observation setting, faculty and staff interviews, and student surveys (discussed in detail in the second section of this appendix) enabled me to check my own observations and interpretations against participants' accounts. I did not take interview and survey data at face value. Clearly, participants' accounts do not, any more than my own understandings, offer direct access to an unproblematic social reality. Yet, when these data reinforced observational data – as when written student responses to survey questions supported the hypothesis about differential attitudes toward and beliefs about school rules – the convergence increased my confidence in my findings.

REACTIVITY

A second kind of distortion that can affect participant-observation is reactivity: the problem of data-gathering processes themselves shaping data. The very presence of a researcher who actively participates in a social setting, and who openly observes and records what happens there, can affect the ways other actors behave. What is more, so-called "observer effects" can vary systematically across sites, skewing findings. It is reasonable to expect that my presence – that is, the presence of a white, Yale-affiliated researcher – would produce differential attitudinal and behavioral effects at the predominantly white, high-SES Fair View Elementary and at the predominantly black, low-SES North End Community School. Ethnographic reactivity raises the question, "Even if a given account reflects what really happened, did it happen only because the researcher was present?"

Observer effects are a sub-species of what some term "audience effects": the fact that how a person acts is often shaped by her perceived audience. The presence of the principal in Monica Segal's classroom, then, dramatically changes the way the teacher structures her lesson.[14] Of course, when observing this classroom, I could not, and I did not aim to, eliminate the effects of the principal's presence on Segal's and her students' actions. Instead, I worked to maintain an awareness of possible audience effects as I recorded and analyzed my field notes. Similarly, part of my response to the problem of observer effects was to try to maintain a conscious awareness of them and to take them into account when analyzing data. For example, on my first day at North End, I observed Veronica Franklin pass up an opportunity to engage a student in a discussion of racial conflict. The class was discussing the upcoming Columbus Day holiday, when a boy raised his hand and stated that Christopher Columbus "had a lot of wars." Franklin asked what he meant, and the boy replied, "Because the white and the black can't get along." At this point the teacher asked if the student had confused Columbus Day with another holiday. He replied, "Oh yeah. Martin Luther King Day." She elicited from two other children the comments that Columbus "made a school" and "traveled the seas and made up places' names," at which point she ended the discussion. In a case like this, it was important for me *not* to assume that Franklin would have responded the same way in my absence. I could not draw from this observation alone the conclusion that Franklin tends to avoid politicized discussions related to race. I was a complete outsider: a brand new observer in the class-

[14] See pp. 124–6.

room, whom Franklin had just met. I was the only white person in the room. It is possible that, in my absence, the teacher might have engaged in a discussion of conflict between native Americans and European settlers and/or probed the comment that "the white and the black can't get along."

In addition to maintaining an awareness of possible observer effects and avoiding unfounded assumptions about what might have happened in my absence, I took a series of practical steps aimed at reducing this form of distortion. One was to make my note-taking as unobtrusive as possible. During most of my time at North End and Fair View, I participated in school activities (by teaching lessons, for example, or working with students individually or in small groups); wrote abbreviated notes about these activities soon after, during periods when students were also engaged in writing; and fleshed out notes upon my return home at the end of the day.[15] I recorded verbatim exchanges only when I was able to do so inconspicuously because I was grading student assignments or doing other written work in my role as teacher assistant.

More generally, I aimed to reduce as much as possible, without being deceptive about the purpose of my work in the schools, the salience of my role as a researcher. I did not initiate discussions about the research. I conducted interviews and surveys only near the end of the project. The fact that several people at each school who had been told about my research subsequently forgot why I was there, assuming that I was training to become a classroom teacher, suggests that I was at least partly successful on this count.

Finally, my concern about the problem of reactivity was one reason I planned a relatively long stay in the schools and decided to participate as a teacher's assistant, rather than simply observe. Some observer effects, I expected, might lessen with time and involvement, as people at the schools became familiar and comfortable with my presence. My experience bore out this expectation. Evidence from my field notes suggests, for example, that, with time, my race grew less salient to some North End students.[16]

LIMITED GENERALIZABILITY

A third concern centers on the external validity of participant-observation. Given that ethnographies are relatively intensive and therefore tend to rely on a small number of cases, a critic might argue that the findings the method generates cannot be generalized. "Even if a given account were an accurate reflection of what happened," she might ask, "and even if it were relatively untainted by observer effects, might it not be anomalous for another reason – the product of contingencies related to the particular setting or individuals involved – and hence of little significance for understanding social phenomena beyond its immediate scope?"

---

[15] See discusssion of field observations and notes, below.
[16] On a class trip to a *Nutcracker* production in December, for instance, one of Franklin's students asked me why the white people were sitting in the balcony and the black people were sitting below (where the North End students were seated). I pointed out that there were a few black students in the balcony, and that I was sitting below, to which the student responded that I was not white, and that the people in the balcony were "whiter" than I.

This complaint points to an important limitation to ethnographic methodologies, one I kept in mind when choosing my research strategy and designing the project. Participant-observation is not the best method for answering every question. I judged it appropriate for my particular project, however, because of the role the empirical investigation was to play in the larger argument. The ethnographies serve two main purposes. First, they illustrate one of the book's key claims, that de-facing power has methodological implications for the empirical analysis of power relations. Second, they generate, not a causal explanation generalizable to all classrooms and all schools, but rather a set of hypotheses about how specific constraints in contemporary American cities and suburbs shape pedagogic practice. Here Jeffrey Johnson's distinction between exploratory and explanatory research is relevant.[17] My ethnographies fall in the former category. It remains an open question – and one that would best be addressed with a method that permits the researcher to test a larger number of cases – whether the relations among teachers and students at North End and Fair View obtain among other, similarly situated actors.

In choosing research sites, then, I looked, not for a representative sample of schools in the United States or in the state of Connecticut, but rather for limit cases that might help illuminate the difference key environmental constraints make for teachers and students. As shown in Appendix A, North End and Fair View are at opposite ends of the spectrum in terms of a range of factors such as poverty status, educational attainment, and student achievement. I maximized the difference between sites with respect to these variables, because generalization to other sites was less important than was highlighting the ways social location can affect how people understand, reason about, and decide among possibilities for action in the classroom.

I did, however, in recording field notes and in collecting other data, aim to sample widely *within* each case. I stayed for a full school day each week at both North End and Fair View, so that my observations would cover the entire daily schedule, including academic instruction, movement to and from the classroom, and "specials," such as music and gym. I scheduled observations over the course of an academic year to capture the annual cycle, as well, from teachers' early interactions with students (for example, the ways Franklin and Segal first introduced disciplinary expectations and requirements, detailed at the start of chapter 3) to their participation in more established routines. I attended trips and special events at each school, visited classrooms other than Franklin's and Segal's, ate lunch in the faculty room and the student cafeteria, and observed recess periods. I interviewed the North End and Fair View principals, as well as all classroom teachers who were willing to grant me interviews (twelve people at North End and ten at Fair View). I conducted student surveys during class time, so that I was able to collect responses from all Fair View fourth graders and all North End fourth and fifth graders who attended school on the day of the survey (fifty-five students at North End and seventy-eight at Fair View). In other words, although I did not aim to produce findings that are generalizable to all schools, I

---

[17] Johnson (1998: 139). As Johnson notes, the concept of exploratory research parallels Glaser and Strauss's notion of "grounded theory," i.e., inductive theory-building via systematic empirical investigation (Glaser and Strauss 1967).

was concerned about, and aimed to maximize, reliability within the cases I studied.

THE RESEARCH PROCESS

FIELD OBSERVATIONS AND NOTES

From September 1993 until June 1994, I spent roughly fifty six- to seven-hour school days conducting participant-observation research in Veronica Franklin's and Monica Segal's fourth grade classrooms at the North End Community School and Fair View Elementary.

I selected school districts, and then individual schools, based on data collected and published by the state of Connecticut. I made the initial cut by using Adjusted Equalized Net Grand List (AENGL) data, which are compiled by the state to make taxable property values comparable among municipalities, as well as "need student" data, which reflect the total number of students, weighted for low income (participants in the Aid to Dependent Children program) and students scoring below the remedial level on state mastery tests. The North End district falls in the bottom 5 percent for AENGL and the top 5 percent for "need students." The district in which Fair View Elementary is located falls in the top 5 percent for AENGL and the bottom 25 percent for need students. I then examined school-level demographic data, poverty statistics, and test scores. As noted above, my aim was to choose "limit cases," in order to explore the differences urban poverty and suburban privilege might make for pedagogic practice.

After selecting the districts and schools, I contacted district-level officials to attempt to obtain permission to conduct my research. In the North End district, the official process of gaining access to the school was relatively time-consuming, and I decided to circumvent the process. I contacted the school principal directly and arranged an interview with her. I explained in rough terms my research interests and offered to act as a classroom aide during the time in which I would be in the school. The principal asked me for references (whom she did not contact) and gave me permission to come into the school as a researcher/volunteer.

In the district in which Fair View is located, the official process was for me to deal directly with the school principal. When I met with her to discuss the research and my role in the classroom, she expressed concern about my "conducting research on" individual students or using proper names in any written documents. She and I agreed that I would not use the names of the school, the district, or any individual students in written documents. We also agreed that I would, as at North End, serve as a volunteer/aide while in the classroom.

At North End, the process by which I selected the fourth grade classroom I would observe was random. I met with the facilitator (a staff member whose job is to assist teachers with curriculum, supplies, etc.). He asked the only fourth grade teacher who was in her classroom at the time of our meeting if she would like a researcher/volunteer in her classroom once a week, and she agreed. Based on subsequent observations and interviews, I am reasonably certain that, had he asked the other North End fourth grade teacher, she also would have agreed.

At Fair View Elementary, the process was not one of random selection. The principal forwarded the letter I originally sent her to the fourth grade teachers, who read and discussed it. Monica Segal was interested in having me in her classroom. She brought the letter to her students, who discussed it and voted to let me observe their classroom.[18]

When I began working in the classrooms, in the fall, I recorded my observations by taking detailed field notes. For the first three months, these were roughly fifteen single-spaced pages of observations, plus several separate pages of analysis, per day. For the reasons outlined above, I attempted, as much as possible, to keep my interpretations and analyses separate from the observations, writing the former only after returning home at the end of the day, or, if I recorded interpretive/analytic comments during the day, enclosing them in brackets.

Generally, the style of the notes is narrative. I described the environment I observed, the various actors involved, and the events that took place. I wrote rough notes while in school, attempting to record what I saw and heard without stopping to sort through, refine, or analyze data until the day had ended. By late winter and early spring, as my analyses came more clearly into focus, my notes also became more focused on particular patterns and questions that had emerged from earlier observation. The following is a sample excerpt from my notes as I recorded them:

Back in the fourth grade classroom, I find [Franklin] and her fourth grade practicing reading questions for tomorrow's portion of the Connecticut mastery tests. While the children are working by themselves, reading one of the passages and answering the questions that follow, [Franklin] starts to talk to me about the test in a normal conversational tone (i.e., not whispering). She tells me how much she dislikes the test, how it disrupts the beginning of the school year. She reprimands one of the children for listening to our conversation instead of doing his work. She says "____ (name) is working so that he can pass his test tomorrow." She turns back to me and says that "they" are always getting down on "you" about the test scores. She says that I know what she's talking about, I read the papers.

[Franklin] goes to the front of the classroom where she stands as the class goes over the practice test as a group. She has one of the girls read the question (a fill-in-the-blank question) aloud, reading "blank" when she comes to the blank. Then she asks for the answer and calls on another student. The class does four questions in this manner. Each of the four times [Franklin] calls on a girl to read the question. However, she calls on both boys and girls to give the answers. When a student gives [Franklin] the correct answer (which they do every time), she asks how (s)he figured it out. She asks what clue helped him/her to figure out the answer. She stresses reading with the correct intonation. For example, when the "blank" comes at the end of the sentence and the girl who is reading fails to lower her voice, [Franklin] stops her. She asks the class as a group what "we" do when we get to the end of a sentence, and they shout (with some enthusiasm) "lower your voice!" Students are, in general, attentive during this exercise. They seem to understand the questions and the method [Franklin] is teaching them for finding the answer.

When it seems to [Franklin] like a student ([Booker]) is not following along in his book, she stops and tells him to follow along. [Booker] seems to be eager to participate in the exercise; he raises his hand often to give answers. [Franklin] calls on him. The question is about why the birds in the reading passage fly south for the winter. [Booker] starts to answer, saying something to the effect that they fly south because there is not enough food "on the other side." Another student starts to speak over [Booker]'s voice to give the answer.

18 In both classrooms students were aware of my role as researcher. But, as noted above, I aimed to minimize the salience of my research in a number of ways, such as by taking notes as unobtrusively as possible.

[Franklin] reprimands the second student: "Give him a chance! Let him finish what he's saying!" She does not accept this answer from [Booker]; she pushes him, saying, "What other side?" [Booker] says, "The North." [Franklin] tells him he is correct, and then she and [Booker] have the following exchange:

[Franklin]: You see how bright you can be if you stop clowning and acting?

[Booker]: That's because ____ (name) keeps making faces.

[note: [Booker] spends a lot of time denying accusations.]

[Franklin]: (roughly) You just ignore him. Just because he's making faces doesn't mean you have to respond. Just ignore him. If I catch him I'll punish him. See how bright you can be if you apply yourself? Now do it every day.

During the course of this exercise, [Franklin] calls on a total of four students, all girls, to read aloud. If a girl "gets stuck" on a word [Franklin] says, "What's that word, class?" and the class reads in unison. If someone tries to interrupt the girl while she is reading, [Franklin] says, "Let her read." She tells students who interrupt that they are rude. Most of the children are attentive during this class exercise.

At the end of the exercise, [Franklin] tells the students to take the practice test home and go over it with their parents the same way that they went over it in class today. She says that if their parents do not know the answer, then they (the kids) will help their parents learn something.

During the exercise, [Franklin] reprimands the boy who is sitting in the front right of the classroom and tells him to stay back from gym. (She seems to forget about this punishment, since he ends up going to gym with the class and she says nothing.) [Franklin] tells the class to be in school on time for the test tomorrow. She reminds them that the test starts at 9:15. She tells them that tomorrow she will not be able to pronounce the words on the test for them. If they cannot read a word, she says, they should keep on reading the rest of the passage and figure out from the other words what the word that they don't know is. She reminds them to cross out wrong answers. She reminds them to get clues from the sentence before and the sentence after the one with the word they don't know.

Lining up in the back of the room to go across the hall to the gym is a big production. [Franklin] lets them line up one by one, depending whether or not they are demonstrating that they are ready [I suppose by sitting still, not talking, etc.]. She says, "If I call you, you may get up."

Gym period is a free period for [Franklin]. I follow the class across the hall and into the gym . . .

TEACHER AND STAFF INTERVIEWS

I conducted semi-structured, face-to-face interviews, in order to supplement my participant-observation data with faculty and staff members' own interpretations of what they do in school, and why they do what they do. When possible, and in almost every case, these interviews took place out of sight and earshot of colleagues, students, and others whose presence might have affected interviewees' willingness to talk about potentially sensitive topics and/or the substance of their responses. I taped the interviews and later used these tapes to create detailed outlines, as well as verbatim transcriptions of key passages.

The interviews were *semi*-structured in that I did not necessarily ask questions in the exact same order from interview to interview. If a question about classroom goals prompted a teacher to talk about her students' parents, for instance, I followed her lead and moved to questions about her relationship with parents. I also changed question wording when appropriate. For example, I asked school principals, not how they decided to become teachers, but how they decided to enter the field of education, and how they decided to become school administrators. I also asked follow-up questions if necessary to elicit a full response.

The interviews were semi-*structured*, however, in that I did ask the same basic set of questions of each respondent. They were:

A. Introduction

I describe my project, briefly, explaining that I have conducted participant-observation research in two schools, one urban and one suburban, over the course of the year. I give a brief overview of the types of questions I will ask.

B. Professional background

1. What is your title? Can you tell me what your job entails?
2. What is your educational background (undergraduate, post-graduate, teacher training)?
3. Do you have professional experience outside the school system (including teaching in other districts)?
4. How many years have you been with the [North End/Fair View] school system?
5. How many years have you been at the [North End/Fair View] school?
6. Are you tenured?
7. What grade(s) and subject(s) do you teach/have you taught?
8. Which extracurricular activities do you supervise or are involved in?
9. Have you participated in professional development activities in the past five years?

C. Professional experience

1. If you think back to when you first decided to become a teacher, how would you describe the way you made that choice? When did you make it? What was it that made you want to teach? What made you decide to teach at the elementary school level?
2. What made you want to teach in the [North End/Fair View] district, and at the [North End/Fair View] school in particular? What were your perceptions of the district and the school at that time? Do you still have the same perceptions of the school and district?
3. How would you describe your responsibilities as a teacher? What are your major pedagogic and professional goals?
4. What are the greatest challenges of your job? (Prompt, if necessary: in the classroom, in your relationships with colleagues and supervisors, in interactions with parents, in interactions with the school district and state.)
5. For your grade level, do you have a set curriculum? Who designs that curriculum? How closely do you follow it?
6. How would you characterize your relationship with administrators here at [North End/Fair View]? Do you have much contact with [the principal]? With any other administrators? or What form does that contact take?
7. How would you characterize your relationship with school district officials? Do you have much contact with school administrators? What form does that contact take?

8. Do you have regular observations by [the principal] and/or other administrators in the school or district? Can you explain how those observations are scheduled, what they usually entail, and what they accomplish?

9. What about your relationship with parents? Do you have much contact with them? In what ways are your students' parents involved in your classroom and at the school? Generally speaking, are they supportive? What sorts of problems have you had with parents, if any?

10. What about your relationship with other teachers here at [North End/Fair View]? What kind of contact do you have with them? How would you describe your relationship with them?

11. If you had a problem, for example with a student or a parent, or perhaps if you had trouble teaching a particular concept or unit, who are some of the people you might turn to for assistance or advice? Whom have you found particularly helpful in the past? Is there anyone you have turned to for help and found not helpful?

12. Over the time that you have been at [North End/Fair View], what major changes have you noticed, if any?

Principals only:

13. What are the main changes that you made/plan to make as principal? How does your administration differ from that of your predecessor?

14. How much discretion do you have in terms of hiring and firing teachers and other faculty and staff members? What criteria do you use in hiring? Can you describe to me a typical search for a new teacher? Roughly how many applicants do you have per position? How do you make decisions about renewing contracts? How do you make decisions about granting and denying tenure?

15. Do you conduct regular classroom observations? Can you explain how those observations are scheduled, what they usually entail, and what they accomplish?

D. Issues at the school and district level

1. What would you say are the biggest challenges facing [North End/Fair View] as a school in its day-to-day operations?

2. What are the school's greatest strengths? What assets does it have that make it stand apart from other schools?

3. What about the [North End/Fair View] school system – what are its biggest challenges? Its greatest strengths?

4. If you could make one or two changes in the school system, and if you had unlimited resources to do so, what would you change? Why?

STUDENT SURVEYS

I administered short, open-ended written surveys to the universe of fourth and fifth graders at the North End Community School and fourth graders at Fair View Elementary (which ends at fourth grade). Respondents totaled 133: 55 at North End and 78 at Fair View. I had a 100 percent rate of response from students who were present in school that day. The surveys were anonymous, in order to reduce students' concerns about possible reprisals for writing responses to which they thought their teachers or others might object. Before passing out the survey questions, I introduced them as follows:

I have some questions, and I'm going to ask you to answer them. You see, I want to know what you think about school. So, for example, the first question asks what is the most important thing you learned this year. Now, there are no right or wrong answers to these questions. I just want to know what you think.

When I pass out the papers, I am going to ask you *not* to put your names on them. That's a little different from what you usually do. Can anyone guess why I don't want you to put your names on the papers? (Explain:) I am not trying to find out what you, [student name] think is the most important thing you learned, but just what fourth [and fifth] graders at [North End/Fair View] think. So, when I read the answers, I won't know who wrote which one. Neither will your teacher or anybody else. So even if you want to write something that's secret, it's OK, because no one will know that you wrote it.

Now, when you're writing your answers, you don't have to worry about penmanship or spelling. These papers are like a draft. But you shouldn't talk to anyone about the questions while you're working on them. If you run out of space, you can write on the back of the paper. Or if you need more paper, raise your hand and I'll bring you a piece. Does anyone have any questions before we begin?

The questions read:
1. What is the most important thing you learned this year?
   Why is it important?
2. In school we have rules, like "Don't run in the hallway." Why do you think we need rules?
   Are the rules at [North End/Fair View] fair?
   Why?
3. What is a goal you have – something you hope you'll do in the future?
   Do you think you'll reach your goal?
   Why?
4. What do you like best about school?
   Why?
5. If you could change anything about [North End/Fair View] or your classroom, what would you change?
   Why?

References

Althusser, Louis. 1971. "Ideology and Ideological State Apparatuses," pp. 172–86 in *Lenin and Philosophy and Other Essays*. New York: Monthly Review Press.

Alves, Michael and Charles Willie. 1987. "Controlled Choice Assignments: A New Approach to School Desegregation." *The Urban Review* 19(2): 67–86.

1990. "Choice, Decentralization and Desegregation: The Boston 'Controlled Choice' Plan," pp. 17–75 in William Clune and John Witte, eds., *Choice and Control in American Education, Volume II: The Practice of Choice, Decentralization, and School Restructuring*. New York and London: The Falmer Press.

Anyon, Jean. 1979. "Ideology and United States History Textbooks." *Harvard Educational Review* 49: 361–386.

1980. "Social Class and the Hidden Curriculum of Work." *Journal of Education* 162(1): 67–92.

1981. "Social Class and School Knowledge." *Curriculum Inquiry* 11: 3–42.

1984. "Intersections of Gender and Class: Accommodation and Resistance by Working-Class and Affluent Females to Contradictory Sex Role Ideologies." *Journal of Education* 166(1): 25–48.

1997. *Ghetto Schooling: A Political Economy of Urban Educational Reform*. New York and London: Teachers College Press.

Apple, Michael. 1971. "The Hidden Curriculum and the Nature of Conflict." *Interchange* 2: 27–40.

1979. *Ideology and Curriculum*. London: Routledge & Kegan Paul.

1982. *Education and Power*. London: Routledge & Kegan Paul.

1986. *Teachers and Texts*. London: Routledge & Kegan Paul.

1993. *Official Knowledge: Democratic Education in a Conservative Age*. New York: Routledge.

Apple, Michael, and Linda Christian-Smith. 1991. *Politics of the Textbook*. New York: Routledge.

Apple, Michael and Lois Weis, eds. 1983. *Ideology and Practice in Schooling*. Philadelphia: Temple University Press.

Arendt, Hannah. 1970. *On Violence*. New York: Harcourt Brace Jovanovich.

Aronowitz, Stanley and Henry Giroux. 1991. *Postmodern Education: Politics, Culture, and Social Criticism*. Minneapolis: University of Minnesota Press.

1993. *Education Still Under Siege*, 2nd edn. Westport, CT: Bergin & Garvey.

Bachrach, Peter and Morton Baratz. 1962. "Two Faces of Power." *American Political Science Review* 56: 947–52.

1963. "Decisions and Non-decisions: An Analytical Framework." *American Political Science Review* 57: 632–42.

1970. *Power and Poverty: Theory and Practice.* New York: Oxford University Press.

1975. "Power and Its Two Faces Revisited: A Reply to Geoffrey Debnam." *American Political Science Review* 69: 900–4.

Ball, Stephen. 1981. *Beachside Comprehensive: A Case-Study of Secondary Schooling.* Cambridge: Cambridge University Press.

Ball, Terrence. 1975a. "Models of Power: Past and Present." *Journal of the History of the Behavioral Sciences* 11:3 (July 1975): 211–22.

1975b. "Power, Causation, and Explanation." *Polity* 8 (Winter): 189–214.

1978. "Two Concepts of Coercion." *Theory and Society* 5(1) (January): 97–112.

1992. "New Faces of Power," pp. 14–31 in Thomas Wartenberg, ed., *Rethinking Power.* Albany: State University of New York Press.

Barnes, Barry. 1988. *The Nature of Power.* Cambridge: Polity Press.

Barry, Brian. 1976. "Power: An Economic Analysis," pp. 67–101 in Brian Barry, ed., *Power and Political Theory: Some European Perspectives.* London: Wiley.

Bartolome, Lilia. 1994. "Beyond the Methods Fetish: Toward a Humanizing Pedagogy." *Harvard Educational Review* 64(2): 173–94.

Bastian, Ann, Norm Fruchter, Marilyn Gittell, Colin Greer, and Kenneth Haskins. 1986. *Choosing Equality: The Case for Democratic Schooling.* Philadelphia, Temple University Press.

Bauman, Zygmunt. 1988. *Freedom.* Minneapolis: University of Minnesota Press.

Benhabib, Seyla. 1996. "Toward a Deliberative Model of Democratic Legitimacy," pp. 67–94 in Benhabib, ed., *Democracy and Difference: Contesting the Boundaries of the Political.* Princeton: Princeton University Press.

Benton, Ted. 1981. "'Objective Interests' and the Sociology of Power." *Sociology* 15(2): 161–84.

Berlin, Isaiah. 1969. *Four Essays on Liberty.* Oxford and New York: Oxford University Press.

Bernstein, Basil. 1975. *Class, Codes, and Control,* vol. III. London: Routledge & Kegan Paul.

1977. "Social Class, Language and Socialisation," pp. 473–86 in Jerome Karabel and A.H. Halsey, eds., *Power and Ideology in Education.* New York: Oxford University Press.

Bhaskar, Roy. 1979. *The Possibility of Naturalism: A Philosophical Critique of the Contemporary Human Sciences.* Atlantic Highlands, NJ: Humanities Press.

Bluestone, Barry. 1990. "The Great U-Turn Revisited: Economic Restructuring, Jobs, and the Redistribution of Earnings," pp. 7–37 in John Kasarda, ed., *Jobs, Earnings, and Employment Growth Policies in the US.* Boston: Kluwer Academic Publishers.

Bluestone, Barry and Bennett Harrison. 1982. *The Deindustrialization of America: Plant Closings, Community Abandonment, and the Dismantling of Basic Industry.* New York: Basic Books.

Bourdieu, Pierre. 1974. "The School as a Conservative Force: Scholastic and Cultural Inequalities," pp. 110–17 in John Eggleston, ed., *Contemporary Research in the Sociology of Education.* London: Methuen.

1977. "Cultural Reproduction and Social Reproduction," pp. 487–510 in

Jerome Karabel and A.H. Halsey, eds., *Power and Ideology in Education*. New York: Oxford University Press.

Bourdieu, Pierre and Jean-Claude Passeron. 1977. *Reproduction in Education, Society, and Culture*. Beverly Hills, CA: Sage.

Bourgois, Philippe. 1995. *In Search of Respect: Selling Crack in El Barrio*. New York: Cambridge University Press.

Bowles, Samuel and Herbert Gintis. 1976. *Schooling in Capitalist America: Educational Reform and the Contradictions of Economic Life*. New York: Basic Books.

Bradshaw, Alan. 1976. "A Critique of Steven Lukes' 'Power: A Radical View.'" *Sociology* 10 (January): 121–7.

Braverman, Harry. 1974. *Labor and Monopoly Capital: The Degradation of Work in the Twentieth Century*. New York and London: Monthly Review Press.

Brown v. Board of Education of Topeka (1954) 347 US 483.

Brown, Joshua. 1981. "Into the Minds of Babes: A Journey Through Recent Children's History Books." *Radical History Review* 25: 127–45.

Brown, Wendy. 1995. *States of Injury: Power and Freedom in Late Modernity*. Princeton: Princeton University Press.

Burawoy, Michael, et al. 1991. *Ethnography Unbound: Power and Resistance in the Modern Metropolis*. Berkeley, CA: University of California Press.

Butler, Judith. 1990. *Gender Trouble: Feminism and the Subversion of Identity*. New York: Routledge.

1997. *The Psychic Life of Power: Theories in Subjection*. Stanford, CA: Stanford University Press.

Carnoy, Martin and Henry Levin. 1976. *The Limits of Educational Reform*. New York: McKay.

1985. *Schooling and Work in the Democratic State*. Stanford, CA: Stanford University Press.

Christman, John. 1991. "Liberalism and Positive Freedom." *Ethics* 101 (January): 343–59.

Clark, Terry. 1972. "Community Power and Decision-Making." *Current Sociology* 20(2): 6–53.

Clifford, James. 1986. "Introduction: Partial Truths," pp. 1–26 in James Clifford and George Marcus, eds., *Writing Culture: The Poetics and Politics of Ethnography*. Berkeley, CA: University of California Press.

Cohen, Joshua. 1996. "Procedure and Substance in Deliberative Democracy," pp. 95–199 in Seyla Benhabib, ed. *Democracy and Difference: Contesting the Boundaries of the Political*. Princeton: Princeton University Press.

Connecticut State Department of Education. 1997. *1995–96 Strategic School Profiles*. Hartford, CT.

Connolly, William. 1983. *The Terms of Political Discourse*, 2nd edn. Princeton: Princeton University Press.

1991. *Identity\Difference: Democratic Negotiations of Political Paradox*. Ithaca and London: Cornell University Press.

1993. "Beyond Good and Evil: The Ethical Sensibility of Michel Foucault." *Political Theory* 21(3): 365–89.

1995. *The Ethos of Pluralization*. Minneapolis and London: University of Minnesota Press.

Constant, Benjamin. 1988. "The Liberty of the Ancients Compared with that of the Moderns," pp. 309–28 in Biancamaria Fontana, ed. and transl., *Political Writings*. New York: Cambridge University Press.

Coole, Diana. 1993. "Constructing and Deconstructing Liberty: A Feminist and Poststructuralist Analysis." *Political Studies* 41: 83–95.

Cremin, Lawrence. 1970. *American Education: The Colonial Experience, 1607–1783*. New York: Harper and Row.

1980. *American Education: The National Experience, 1783–1876*. New York: Harper and Row.

Crenson, Matthew. 1971. *The Un-Politics of Air Pollution: Non-decision Making in the Cities*. Baltimore: Johns Hopkins University Press.

Curtis, James and John Petras. 1970. "Community Power, Power Studies, and the Sociology of Knowledge." *Human Organization* 29: 204–18.

Dahl, Robert. 1957. "The Concept of Power." *Behavioral Science* 2 (July): 201–15.

1958. "A Critique of the Ruling Elite Model." *American Political Science Review* 52 (June): 463–9.

1961. *Who Governs? Democracy and Power in an American City*. New Haven and London: Yale University Press.

1963. *Modern Political Analysis*. Englewood Cliffs, NJ: Prentice-Hall.

1965. "Cause and Effect in the Study of Politics," pp. 75–98 in Daniel Lerner, ed., *Cause and Effect*. New York: Free Press.

1968. "Power," pp. 405–15 in *International Encyclopedia of the Social Sciences*, vol. XII. New York: Macmillan and The Free Press.

Dalberg-Acton, John Edward Emerich. 1949. *Essays on Freedom and Power*, ed. Gertrude Himmelfarb. Glencoe, IL: The Free Press.

Debnam, Geoffrey. 1975. "Nondecisions and Power: The Two Faces of Bachrach and Baratz." *American Political Science Review* 69(1): 889–99.

Delpit, Lisa. 1988. "The Silenced Dialogue: Power and Pedagogy in Educating Other People's Children." *Harvard Educational Review* 58(3): 280–98.

Dewalt, Kathleen and Billie Dewalt. 1998. "Participant Observation," pp. 259–99 in H. Russell Bernard, ed., *Handbook of Methods in Cultural Anthropology*. Walnut Creek, CA: Sage.

Dewey, John. 1916. *Democracy and Education: An Introduction to the Philosophy of Education*. New York: The Macmillan Company.

1956. *The Child and the Curriculum and the School and Society*. Chicago and London: University of Chicago Press.

1963. *Experience and Education*. New York: Collier Books.

Digeser, Peter. 1992. "The Fourth Face of Power." *Journal of Politics* 54(4): 977–1007.

Di Stefano, Christine. 1996. "Autonomy in the Light of Difference," pp. 95–116 in Nancy Hirchmann and Christine Di Stefano, eds., *Revisioning the Political: Feminist Reconstructions of Traditional Concepts in Western Political Theory*. Boulder, CO: Westview Press.

Dworkin, Gerald. 1988. *The Theory and Practice of Autonomy*. Cambridge: Cambridge University Press.

Ellsworth, Elizabeth. 1989. "Why Doesn't This Feel Empowering? Working

Through the Repressive Myths of Critical Pedagogy." *Harvard Educational Review* 59(3):297–324.

Elster, Jon. 1998. "Deliberation and Constitution Making", pp. 97–122 in Jon Elster, ed., *Deliberative Democracy*. New York and Cambridge: Cambridge University Press.

Emmet, Dorothy. 1954. "The Concept of Power." *Proceedings of the Aristotelian Society* 53: 1–26.

Fainstein, Norman. 1993. "Race, Class, and Segregation: Discourses about African Americans." *International Journal of Urban and Regional Research* 17(3): 384–403.

1995. "Black Ghettoization and Social Mobility," in Michael Peter Smith and Joe R. Feagin, eds., *The Bubbling Cauldron: Race, Ethnicity, and the Urban Crisis*. Minneapolis: University of Minnesota Press.

Fay, Brian. 1987. *Critical Social Science: Liberation and Its Limits*. Cambridge: Polity Press.

Feagin, Joe. 1994. "A House is Not a Home: White Racism and US Housing Practices," pp. 17–48 in Robert Bullard, J. Eugene Grigsby III, and Charles Lee, eds., *Residential Apartheid: The American Legacy*. Los Angeles: CAAS Publications.

Fenno, Richard. 1978. *Home Style: House Members in their Districts*. Boston: Little, Brown.

1990. *Watching Politicians: Essays on Participant Observation*. Berkeley, CA: IGS Press.

Fine, Michelle. 1987. "Silencing in the Public Schools." *Language Arts* 64(2): 157–74.

1991. *Framing Dropouts: Notes on the Politics of an Urban Public High School*. Albany: State University of New York Press.

Flathman, Richard. 1987. *The Philosophy and Politics of Freedom*. Chicago: University of Chicago Press.

Flathman, Richard and David Johnston, eds. 1997. *Thomas Hobbes: Leviathan*. New York: W.W. Norton.

Foucault, Michel. 1970. *The Order of Things: An Archaeology of the Human Sciences*, ed. R.D. Laing. New York: Pantheon Books.

1979. *Discipline and Punish: The Birth of the Prison*, transl. Alan Sheridan. New York: Vintage Books.

1980a. *The History of Sexuality, Volume I: An Introduction*, transl. Robert Hurley. New York: Vintage Books.

1980b. *Power/Knowledge: Selected Interviews and Other Writings 1972–1977*, ed. Colin Gordon, and transl. Colin Gordon, Leo Marshall, John Mepham, and Kate Soper. New York: Pantheon Books.

1982. "The Subject and Power." *Critical Inquiry* 8 (Summer): 777–95.

1984. *The Foucault Reader*, ed. Paul Rabinow, New York: Pantheon Books.

1988. "The Ethic of Care for the Self as a Practice of Freedom," pp. 1–20 in James Bernauer and David Rasmussen, eds., *The Final Foucault*. Cambridge, MA: MIT Press.

1989. *Foucault Live: Interviews 1961–1984*, ed. Sylvere Lotringer, and transl. Lysa Hochroth and John Johnston. New York: Semiotext[e].

1990. *The Use of Pleasure: Volume II of the History of Sexuality*, transl. Robert Hurley. New York: Vintage Books.

Fraser, Nancy. 1981. "Foucault on Modern Power: Empirical Insights and Normative Confusions." *Praxis International* 1: 272–87.

1992. "Rethinking the Public Sphere," pp. 109–42 in Craig Calhoun, ed., *Habermas and the Public Sphere*. Cambridge, MA: MIT Press.

Freire, Paulo. 1970. *Pedagogy of the Oppressed*. New York: Herder and Herder.

1973. *Education for Critical Consciousness*. New York: Seabury Press.

1987. "Letter to North American Teachers," pp. 211–14 in I. Shor, ed., *Freire for the Classroom: A Sourcebook for Liberatory Teaching*. Portsmouth, NH: Heinemann.

Freire, Paulo and Henry Giroux. 1989. "Pedagogy, Popular Culture and Public Life: An Introduction," pp. vii–xii in Henry Giroux and Roger Simon, eds., *Popular Culture, Schooling, and Everyday Life*. New York: Bergin & Garvey.

Freire, Paulo and Donald Macedo. 1987. *Literacy: Reading the Word and the World*. South Hadley, MA: Bergin & Garvey.

Frey, Frederick. 1971. "Comment: On Issues and Nonissues in the Study of Power." *American Political Science Review* 65(4): 1081–101.

Friedrich, Carl. 1963. *Man and His Government: An Empirical Theory of Politics*. New York: McGraw-Hill.

Gaquin, Deidre and Mark S. Littman, eds. 1998. *1998 County and City Extra: Annual Metro, City, and County Data Book*. Lanham, MD: Bernan Press.

Gaventa, John. 1980. *Power and Powerlessness: Quiescence and Rebellion in an Appalachian Valley*. Urbana and Chicago: University of Illinois Press.

Geertz, Clifford. 1973. "Thick Description: Toward an Interpretive Theory of Culture," pp. 3–30 in *The Interpretation of Culture: Selected Essays*. New York: Basic Books.

1983. "'From the Native's Point of View': On the Nature of Anthropological Understanding," pp. 55–70 in *Local Knowledge: Further Essays in Interpretive Anthropology*. New York: Basic Books.

Giddens, Anthony. 1976. *New Rules of Sociological Method: A Critique of Interpretive Sociologies*. London: Hutchinson.

1979. *Central Problems in Social Theory*. London: Macmillan.

1981. *A Contemporary Critique of Historical Materialism: Vol. 1: Power, Property, and the State*. London: Macmillan.

1984. *The Constitution of Society*. Cambridge: Polity Press.

Giroux, Henry. 1979. "Schooling and the Culture of Positivism: Notes on the Death of History." *Educational Theory* 29:4 (1979): 263–84.

1981a. "Hegemony, Resistance, and the Paradox of Educational Reform." *Interchange* 12: 3–26.

1981b. *Ideology, Culture, and the Process of Schooling*. Philadelphia: Temple University Press.

1982. "Culture and Rationality in Frankfurt School Thought: Ideological Foundations for a Theory of Social Education." *Theory and Research in Social Education* 9(4): 22–56.

1983a. *Theory and Resistance in Education*. South Hadley, MA: Bergin & Garvey.

1983b. "Ideology and Agency in the Process of Schooling." *Journal of Education* 165(1): 12–34.

1986a. "Radical Pedagogy and the Politics of Student Voice." *Interchange* 17(1): 48–69.

1986b. "Authority, Intellectuals, and the Politics of Practical Learning." *Teachers College Record* 88 (Fall): 22–40.

1988. "Border Pedagogy in the Age of Postmodernism." *Journal of Education* 170 (3): 166–81.

1990a. "Rethinking the Boundaries of Educational Discourse: Modernism, Postmodernism, and Feminism." *College Literature* 17(2/3): 5–50.

1990b. "Reading Texts, Literacy, and Textual Authority." *Journal of Education* 172(1): 84–103.

1992. *Border Crossings: Cultural Workers and the Politics of Education.* New York: Routledge.

1993. "Disturbing the Peace: Writing in the Cultural Studies Classroom." *College Literature* 20(2): 13–26.

1994. "Insurgent Multiculturalism and the Promise of Pedagogy," pp. 325–43 in David Theo Goldberg, ed., *Multiculturalism: A Reader.* Cambridge, MA: Basil Blackwell.

1997. *Pedagogy and the Politics of Hope: Theory, Culture, and Schooling: A Critical Reader.* Boulder, CO: Westview Press.

Giroux, Henry and Peter McLaren. 1991. "Radical Pedagogy as Cultural Politics: Beyond the Discourse of Critique and Anti-Utopianism," pp. 152–186 in Donald Morton and Mas'ud Zavarzadeh, eds., *Texts for Change: Theory/Pedagogy/Politics.* Urbana and Chicago: University of Illinois Press.

Giroux, Henry and Roger I. Simon. 1989. *Popular Culture: Schooling and Everyday Life.* Granby, MA: Bergin & Garvey.

Glaser, Barney, and Anselm Strauss. 1967. *The Discovery of Grounded Theory: Strategies for Qualitative Research.* New York: Aldine.

Gould, Carol. 1988. *Rethinking Democracy: Freedom and Cooperation in Politics, Economy, and Society.* New York: Cambridge University Press.

Gutierrez, Kris and Peter McLaren. 1995. "Pedagogies of Dissent and Transformation: A Dialogue about Postmodernity, Social Context, and the Politics of Literacy," in Barry Kanpol and Peter McLaren, eds., *Critical Multiculturalism: Uncommon Voices in a Common Struggle.* Westport, CT and London: Bergin & Garvey.

Habermas, Jürgen. 1984. *The Theory of Communicative Action,* vol. I *Reason and the Rationalization of Society,* transl., Thomas McCarthy. Boston: Beacon Press.

1986. "The Genealogical Writing of History: On Some Aporias in Foucault's Theory of Power." *Canadian Journal of Political and Social Theory* 10(1–2): (1986): 1–9.

1987a. *The Theory of Communicative Action,* vol. II. *Lifeworld and System: A Critique of Functionalist Reason,* transl. Thomas McCarthy. Boston: Beacon Press.

1987b. *The Philosophical Discourse of Modernity: Twelve Lectures,* transl. Frederick Lawrence. Cambridge, MA: MIT Press.

1998. *Between Facts and Norms,* transl. William Rehg. Cambridge, MA: MIT Press.

Hall, Peter and Rosemary Taylor. 1996. "Political Science and the Three New Institutionalisms." *Political Studies* 44: 936–57.

Hammersley, Martyn and Paul Atkinson. 1995. *Ethnography: Principles in Practice*, 2nd edn. London: Routledge.

Hargreaves, David. 1967. *Social Relations in a Secondary School*. London: Routledge & Kegan Paul.

Harré, Rom. 1970. "Powers." *British Journal for the Philosophy of Science* 21(1): 81–101.

Harré, Rom and E.H. Madden. 1975. *Causal Powers: A Theory of Natural Necessity*. Totowa, NJ: Rowman & Littlefield.

Harrison, Bennett and Barry Bluestone. 1988. *The Great U-Turn: Corporate Restructuring and the Polarizing of America*. New York: Basic Books.

Hartsock, Nancy C.M. 1985. *Money, Sex, and Power: Toward a Feminist Historical Materialism*. Boston: Northeastern University Press.

Hawley, Willis and James Svara. 1972. *The Study of Community Power: A Bibliographic Review*. Santa Barbara, CA: ABC-Clio.

Hebidge, Dick. 1979. *Subculture: The Meaning of Style*. London: Methuen.

Hirschmann, Nancy J. 1996. "Toward a Feminist Theory of Freedom." *Political Theory* 24(1): 46–67.

Hobbes, Thomas. 1966. *The English Works of Thomas Hobbes of Malmesbury*, vol. I. Aalen: Scientia.

Honig, Bonnie. 1993. *Political Theory and the Displacement of Politics*. Ithaca: Cornell University Press.

Horton v. Meskill 172 Conn. 615.

Hunter, Floyd. 1953. *Community Power Structure*. Chapel Hill: University of North Carolina Press.

Isaac, Jeffrey. 1987a. *Power and Marxist Theory: A Realist View*. Ithaca and London: Cornell University Press.

1987b. "Beyond the Three Faces of Power." *Polity* 20(1): 4–30.

Jackson, Kenneth. 1985. *Crabgrass Frontier*. New York: Oxford University Press.

Johnson, Jeffrey. 1998. "Research Design and Research Strategies," pp. 131–71 in H. Russell Bernard, ed., *Handbook of Methods in Cultural Anthropology*. Walnut Creek, CA: Sage.

Karabel, Jerome and A.H. Halsey. 1977. "Educational Research: A Review and an Interpretation," pp. 1–85 in Karabel and Halsey, eds., *Power and Ideology in Education*. New York: Oxford University Press.

Katz, Michael, ed. 1993. *The "Underclass" Debate*. Princeton: Princeton University Press.

Keddie, Nell. 1971. "Classroom Knowledge," pp. 133–160 in M.F.D. Young, ed., *Knowledge and Control: New Directions for the Sociology of Education*. London: Collier-Macmillan.

Keyes v. Denver School District (1972) 413 US 189.

Kincheloe, Joe and Peter McLaren. 1994. "Rethinking Critical Theory and Qualitative Research," pp. 138–57 in Norman Denzin and Yvonna Lincoln, eds., *Handbook of Qualitative Research*. Thousand Oaks, CA: Sage.

Kozol, Jonathan. 1991. *Savage Inequalities: Children in America's Schools*. New York: Crown Publishers.

Kramer-Dahl, Anneliese. 1996. "Reconsidering the Notions of Voice and Experience in Critical Pedagogy," pp. 242–62 in Carmen Luke, ed., *Feminisms and Pedagogies of Everyday Life*. Albany: State University of New York Press.

Kreisberg, Seth. 1992. *Transforming Power: Domination, Empowerment, and Education*. Albany: State University of New York Press.

Laclau, Ernesto and Chantal Mouffe. 1985. *Hegemony and Socialist Strategy: Towards a Radical Democratic Politics*. New York and London: Verso.

Lasswell, Harold and Abraham Kaplan. 1950. *Power and Society: A Framework for Political Inquiry*. New Haven: Yale University Press.

Leif, Irving. 1972. "Bibliography." *Current Sociology* 20(2): 58–131.

Levy, Frank and Richard Michel. 1991. *The Economic Future of American Families: Income and Wealth Trends*. Washington, DC: Urban Institute Press.

Levy, Frank and Richard Murname. 1992. "US Earnings Levels and Earnings Inequality: A Review of Recent Trends and Proposed Explanations." *Journal of Economic Literature* 30: 1333–81.

Locke, John. 1961. *An Essay Concerning Human Understanding*, vol. I. New York: E.P. Dutton.

Lofland, John and Lyn Lofland. 1984. *Analyzing Social Settings: A Guide to Qualitative Observation and Analysis*, 2nd edn. Belmont, CA: Wadsworth.

Lorence, Jon and Joel Nelson. 1993. "Industrial Restructuring and Metropolitan Earnings Inequality, 1970–1980," pp. 154–84 in Robert Althauser and Michael Wallace, eds., *Research in Social Stratification and Mobility*, vol. XII. Greenwich, CT: JAI.

Luke, Allan. 1988. *Literacy, Textbooks, and Ideology: Postwar Literacy Instruction and the Mythology of Dick and Jane*. New York: The Falmer Press.

Lukes, Steven. 1974. *Power: A Radical View*. London: Macmillan.

1976. "Reply to Bradshaw." *Sociology* 10(1): 129–32.

1991. "Equality and Liberty: Must They Conflict?" pp. 48–66 in David Held, ed., *Political Theory Today*. Stanford, CA: Stanford University Press.

MacIntyre, Alasdair. 1984. *After Virtue: A Study in Moral Theory*, 2nd edn. Notre Dame, IN: University of Notre Dame Press.

McLaren, Peter. 1985. "The Ritual Dimensions of Resistance: Clowning and Symbolic Inversion." *Journal of Education* 167(2): 84–97.

1989. *Life in Schools: An Introduction to Critical Pedagogy in the Foundations of Education*. Toronto: Irwin.

1991. "Critical Pedagogy: Constructing an Arch of Social Dreaming and a Doorway to Hope." *Journal of Education* 173(1): 9–34.

1995. *Critical Pedagogy and Predatory Culture: Oppositional Politics in a Postmodern Era*. New York: Routledge.

MacLeod, Jay. 1987. *Ain't No Makin' It: Leveled Aspirations in a Low-income Neighborhood*. Boulder, CO: Westview Press.

McRobbie, Angela. 1980. "Settling Accounts with Subcultures." *Screen Education* 34: 37–49.

Mann, Coramae. 1993. *Unequal Justice: A Question of Color*. Bloomington: Indiana University Press.

March, James G. 1955. "An Introduction to the Theory and Measurement of Influence." *American Political Science Review* 59: 431–55.

Marks, Carole. 1991. "The Urban Underclass." *Annual Review of Sociology* 17: 445–66.

Massey, Douglas and Nancy Denton. 1993. *American Apartheid: Segregation and the Making of the Underclass*. Cambridge, MA: Harvard University Press.

Merelman, Richard. 1968. "On the Neo-Elitist Critique of Community Power." *American Political Science Review* 62(2): 451–60.

Mickelson, Roslyn. 1980. "The Secondary School's Role in Social Stratification: A Comparison of Beverly Hills High School and Morningside High School." *Journal of Education* 162: 83–112.

Milliken v. Bradley (1974) 418 US 717.

Mills, C. Wright. 1956. *The Power Elite*. Oxford: Oxford University Press.

Mollenkopf, John. 1983. *The Contested City*. Princeton: Princeton University Press.

Morris, Martina, Annette Bernhardt, and Mark Handcock. 1992. "Economic Inequality: New Methods for New Trends." *American Sociological Review* 59: 205–19.

Mouffe, Chantal. 1993. *The Return of the Political*. New York: Verso.

Nagel, Jack. 1975. *The Descriptive Analysis of Power*. New Haven and London: Yale University Press.

Nietzsche, Friedrich. 1954. *The Portable Nietzsche*, transl. W. Kaufmann. New York: Viking.

O'Brien, Kevin. 1996. "Rightful Resistance." *World Politics* 49 (October): 31–55.

Ogbu, John. 1974. *The Next Generation: An Ethnography of Education in an Urban Neighborhood*. New York: Academic Press.

Orfield, Gary. 1983. *The Growth of Segregation in American Schools: Changing Patterns of Separation and Poverty Since 1968*. Report of the Harvard Project on School Desegregation to the National School Boards Association.

Parsons, Talcott. 1969. "On the Concept of Political Power," pp. 251–85 in Roderick Bell, David V. Edwards, and R. Harrison Wagner, eds., *Political Power: A Reader in Theory and Research*. New York: The Free Press.

Pettit, Philip. 1996. "Freedom as Antipower." *Ethics* 106:576–604.

1997. *Republicanism: A Theory of Freedom and Government*. Oxford: Clarendon Press.

Pierce v. Society of Sisters (1925) 268 US 510.

Polsby, Nelson. 1960. "How to Study Community Power." *Journal of Politics* 22: 474–84.

1968. "Study of Community Power." *International Encyclopedia of the Social Sciences*, vol. III: 157–63. New York: Macmillan and The Free Press.

1980. *Community Power and Political Theory: A Further Look at Problems of Evidence and Inference*. 2nd edn. New Haven: Yale University Press.

Poulantzas, Nicos. 1968. *Political Power and Social Classes*. Atlantic Highlands: Humanities Press.

Rae, Douglas. 1988. "Knowing Power: A Working Paper," pp. 17–49 in Ian Shapiro and Grant Reeher, eds., *Power, Inequality, and Democratic Politics*. Boulder, CO: Westview Press.

Ricci, David. 1980. "Receiving Ideas in Political Analysis: The Case of the Community Power Studies, 1950–1970." *Western Political Quarterly* 33: 451–75.

Russell, Bertrand. 1938. *Power: A New Social Analysis*. London: George Allen & Unwin.

San Antonio Independent School District v. Rodriguez (1973) 411 US 1.

Schattschneider, E.E. 1960. *The Semi-Sovereign People: A Realist's View of Democracy in America*. New York: Holt, Rinehart, & Winston.

Scholes, Robert. 1985. *Textual Power: Literary Theory and the Teaching of English*. New Haven and London: Yale University Press.

Schram, Sanford. 1995. *Words of Welfare: The Poverty of Social Science and the Social Science of Poverty*. Minneapolis and London: University of Minnesota Press.

Schutz, Alfred. 1964. "The Stranger: An Essay in Social Psychology," in *Collected Papers II: Studies in Social Theory*. The Hague: Martinus Nijhoff.

Scott, James. 1985. *Weapons of the Weak: Everyday Forms of Peasant Resistance*. New Haven: Yale University Press.

1990. *Domination and the Arts of Resistance: Hidden Transcripts*. New Haven: Yale University Press.

Shapiro, Ian. 1990. *Political Criticism*. Berkeley, CA: University of California Press.

Shapiro, Ian and Alexander Wendt. 1992. "The Difference that Realism Makes: Social Science and the Politics of Consent." *Politics and Society* 20(2): 197–223.

Sharp, Rachel and Anthony Green. 1975. *Education and Social Control: A Study in Progressive Primary Education*. London, Henley, and Boston: Routledge & Kegan Paul.

Sheff v. O'Neill 238 Conn. 1.

Shor, Ira and Paulo Freire. 1987. "What is the 'Dialogic Method' of Teaching?" *Journal of Education* 169(3): 11–31.

Simon, Herbert. 1953. "Notes on the Observation and Measurement of Political Power." *Journal of Politics* 15: 500–16.

Simon, Roger. 1987a. "Empowerment as a Pedagogy of Possibility." *Language Arts* 64(4): 370–82.

1987b. "Work Experience as the Production of Subjectivity," in D. Livingstone, ed., *Critical Pedagogy and Cultural Power*. South Hadley, MA: Bergin & Garvey.

1992. *Teaching Against the Grain: Texts for a Pedagogy of Possibility*. New York: Bergin & Garvey.

Skinner, Quentin. 1973. "The Empirical Theorists of Democracy and Their Critics: A Plague on Both Their Houses." *Political Theory* 1(3): 289–306.

Smith, Rogers. 1992. "If Politics Matters: Implications for a 'New Institutionalism.'" *Studies in American Political Development* 6: 1–36.

Spillane, Margaret. 1992. "A Tale of Two Schools II: Newhallville Turns it Around." *Nation* (September 21): 290–2.

Spradley, James. 1980. *Participant Observation*. New York: Holt, Rinehart, & Winston.

Squires, Gregory. 1994. *Capital and Communities in Black and White: The Intersection of Race, Class, and Uneven Development*. Albany: State University of New York Press.

Squires, Gregory and William Velez. 1987. "Insurance Redlining and the Transformation of an Urban Metropolis." *Urban Affairs Quarterly* 23(1): 63–83.

Stone, Clarence. 1980. "Systemic Power in Community Decision Making: A

Restatement of Stratification Theory." *American Political Science Review* 74(4): 978–90.

Tonry, Michael. 1995. *Malign Neglect: Race, Crime, and Punishment in America.* New York and Oxford: Oxford University Press.

Turner, Margery, Raymond Struyk, and John Yinger. 1991. *Housing Discrimination Study: Synthesis.* Washington, DC: US Department of Housing and Urban Development.

Unger, Roberto. 1987. *False Necessity: Anti-Necessitarian Social Theory in the Service of Radical Democracy,* Part I of *Politics: A Work in Constructive Social Theory.* New York and Cambridge: Cambridge University Press.

United States Bureau of the Census. *1990 Census of Population and Housing.* Summary Tape File 3A.

United States Department of Education, National Center for Education Statistics. 1996. *Digest of Education Statistics,* NCES 96-133. Washington, DC.

United States Department of Justice, Bureau of Justice Statistics. 1994. *Criminal Victimization in the United States: 1973–1992 Trends.* NCJ-147006.

1996. *Correctional Populations in the US, 1994.* NCJ 160091.

United States Department of Justice, Federal Bureau of Investigation. 1994. *Uniform Crime Reports for the United States, 1993.* Washington, DC: US Government Printing Offices.

1995. *Uniform Crime Reports for the United States, 1994.* Washington, DC: US Government Printing Offices.

1996. *Uniform Crime Reports for the United States, 1995.* Washington, DC: US Government Printing Offices.

1997. *Uniform Crime Reports for the United States, 1996.* Washington, DC: US Government Printing Offices.

Walzer, Michael. 1983. "The Politics of Michel Foucault." *Dissent* 30(4): 481–90.

1987. *Interpretation and Social Criticism.* Cambridge, MA: Harvard University Press.

Wartenberg, Thomas. 1990. *The Forms of Power: From Domination to Transformation.* Philadelphia: Temple University Press.

1992. "Situated Social Power," pp. 79–101 in Wartenberg, ed., *Rethinking Power.* Albany: State University of New York Press.

Weber, Max. 1947. *The Theory of Social and Economic Organization,* transl. A.M. Henderson. Glencoe, IL: The Free Press.

1968. *Economy and Society: An Outline of Interpretive Sociology,* vol. III. New York: Bedminster Press.

Weiler, Kathleen. 1988. *Women Teaching for Change.* South Hadley, MA: Bergin & Garvey.

Weis, Lois, ed. 1988. *Class, Race, and Gender in American Education.* Albany: State University of New York Press.

Weis, Lois and Michelle Fine, eds. 1993. *Beyond Silenced Voices: Class, Race, and Gender in US Schools.* Albany: State University of New York Press.

White, D.M. 1971. "Power and Intention." *American Political Science Review* 65(3): 749–59.

Wienk, Ronald, Clifford Reid, John Simonson, and Frederick Eggers. 1979.

Housing Markets Practices Survey. Washington, DC: US Department of Housing and Urban Development.

Wilcox, Kathleen. 1982. "Differential Socialization in Classrooms," pp. 268–309 in George Spindler, ed., *Doing the Ethnography of Schooling*. New York: Holt.

Willis, Paul E. 1977. *Learning to Labor: How Working Class Kids Get Working Class Jobs*. Farnborough: Saxon House.

Wolfinger, Raymond. 1971. "Nondecisions and the Study of Local Politics." *American Political Science Review* 65(4): 1063–80.

Wolin, Sheldon. 1996. "Fugitive Democracy," pp. 31–45 in Seyla Benhabib, ed., *Democracy and Difference: Contesting the Boundaries of the Political*. Princeton: Princeton University Press.

Wrong, Dennis. 1980. *Power: Its Forms, Bases, and Uses*. New York: Harper Colophon Books.

Yazigi, Monique. 1998. "The Glamour Girl's Guide to Life." *New York Times* April 5, 9: 1–2.

Young, Iris. 1996. "Communication and the Other: Beyond Deliberative Democracy," pp. 120–35 in Seyla Benhabib, ed., *Democracy and Difference: Contesting the Boundaries of the Political*. Princeton: Princeton University Press.

Young, M.F.D. 1971. "An Approach to the Study of Curricula as Socially Organized Knowledge," pp. 19–46 in M.F.D. Young, ed., *Knowledge and Control: New Directions for the Sociology of Education*. London: Collier-Macmillan.

Index

achievement ideology, 51
Acton, Lord, 33
Adolfo, 172
agonistic democracy, 173
Aid to Families with Dependent Children
    (AFDC), 58, 58–9 n6, 175
AIDS, 63, n28, 181
Althusser, Louis, 46–7, n18
anticipated reactions, 15, 15 n22
Apple, Michael, 51, n42
archaeology, 6, 6 n12
Arendt, Hannah, 32 n76, 173
Atkinson, Paul, 189 n12
authoritarianism, 40–2, 44–5, 45 n8, 65–70,
    82, 85, 106–8, 110, 136–7, 168

Bachrach, Peter, 15–16, 16 n25, 17–18, 18
    n35, 19
"banking model" of education, 82, 144
Baratz, Morton, 15–16, 16 n25, 17–18, 18
    n35, 19
Barnes, Barry, 22, 25–6, 33
Bartolme, Lilia, 49
Bauman, Zygmunt, 161 n1
behavioralism, 12–14
Benton, Ted, 22, 24 n61
Berlin, Isaiah, 162–6
Bernstein, Basil, 48, 48 n25
Bhaskar, Roy, 22
Bourdieu, Pierre, 47 n21, 47–8, 48 n24
Bourgois, Philippe, 59 n8
Bowles, Samuel, 44–5 n7, 46–7 n18, 82, 145
Braverman, Harry, 51 n42
Bridgeport, Connecticut, 59, 63 n28, n29,
    and n31, 112, 131, 146, 158, 159, 179,
    181
Brown v. Board of Education of Topeka, 60 n15
Burawoy, Michael, 188 n9
Butler, Judith, 174 n27

Chicago School Reform Act of 1988, 178 n28
Christman, John, 164 n17

Civil Rights Act of 1964, 60 n15
Clifford, James, 188 n7
Comer, James, 159
communicative action, 6
Connecticut State Department of
    Education, 62 n23 and n25, 111–14
    teacher assessment, 125
Connecticut State Mastery Test, 40, 40 n1,
    62, 62 n27, 111–14, 115, 115 n2, 143,
    180
Connolly, William, 20–1, 21 n51
Coole, Diana, 161 n1
Cremin, Lawrence, 60 n11, n12, and n13
crime, violent, 63 n29, 181
critical educational theory, 8, 45–56, 87, 91
    critical postmodern theories, 50 n39, 51
    reproduction theories, 51
    resistance theories, 47 n21, 51
    structural accounts, 49–50, 50 n38, 96,
    153, 155
critical pedagogy
    see critical educational theory
cultural capital, 47–8, 48 n24
culture of silence, 218–19
Curtis, James, 14 n17

Dahl, Robert, 11 n2, 11–12, 12–14, 13 n16,
    18–19, 30 n72, 32 n75, 178
Debnam, Geoffrey, 16 n28, 19 n41
deindustrialization, 37, 57–9, 58 n3, 114–15
deliberative democracy, 7, 168–9
Delpit, Lisa, 45 n8
Dewalt, Kathleen and Billie DeWalt, 187
Dewey, John, 45–6 n10
discourse principle, 7
domination, 39, 38 n90, 39 n91, 162, 170–1,
    172–6
Di Stefano, Christine, 161 n1
Dworkin, Gerald, 164 n17

Ellsworth, Elizabeth, 54 n51
Elster, Jon, 171 n22

"environment, the", 9, 65, 97, 104, 145, 153, 168

Fair Housing Act, 58, 58 n5
Fair View, Connecticut, 114–15, 179, 181
   see also "world" of Fair View
Fair View Elementary
   demographic and achievement data, 115, 180
   resources, 115–16
   see also "learning process"; participatory rule-making; peer evaluations; reflection papers; responsibility as self-sufficiency; "school knowledge"; "school success"; teacher observations; values, depoliticization of; the "world" of Fair View; writer's workshop
Fenno, Richard, 187
Fichte, Johann Gottlieb, 164
Flathman, Richard, 164 n5
Foucault, Michel, 5–7, 6 n12, 6 n13, 10, 30, 35 n85, 39, 39 n92, 173
Frankfurt Constituent Assembly of 1848, 171
freedom
   negative, 8, 14, 20–2, 27–30, 38, 48–9, 161, 162–6, 167, 172, 176
   political, 8, 31, 39, 117–18, 135–6, 161, 168–71, 173–6
   positive, 162–4, 164 n17
Freire, Paulo,
Frost, Robert, 129
functionalism, 35 n84

Gaventa, John, 17, 32, 33–4, 178
Geertz, Clifford, 187 n6, 188
genealogy, 6, 6 n13
Giddens, Anthony, 5–6, 22, 39 n91
Gintis, Herbert, 44–5 n7, 46–7 n18, 82, 145
Giroux, Henry, 49, 49 n34, 50 n39, 53
Glaser, Barney, 192 n17
globalization, 37, 57, 114–15
Gould, Carol, 164 n17
Green, Anthony, 50, 50 n38, 153, 153 n21
grounded theory, 192 n17

Habermas, Jürgen, 6–7, 10
Hammersley, Martyn, 189 n12
Harré, Rom, 22, 23
Hartford, Connecticut, 59, 63 n28, n29 and n31, 179, 181
hegemonic intellectuals, 49, 53
hidden curriculum, 82
Hirschmann, Nancy, 161 n1

Hobbes, Thomas, 12 n6, 161 n3, 162
Horton v. Meskill, 61 n19

In the Line of Fire, 150, 150 n14
incarceration, 63 n31
institutions, 37–8, 38 n90, 52, 52–5, 169–70, 176
   democratic public institutions, 177–8
interviews, teacher and staff, 195–7
Isaac, Jeffrey, 22, 23 n56, 24, 24 n61, 28, 30

Jim Crow laws, 170
Johnson, Jeffrey, 192, 192 n17

Kincheloe, Joe, 188 n8
Koch, David, 171–2
Kramer-Dahl, Anneliese, 54 n51

Lauren, Ralph, 167, 171–2, 175
"learning process", 9, 127–30, 135, 141–5, 147–8, 172
liberty
   see freedom
Lincoln-Bassett school, 159
Lofland, John and Lyn Lofland, 187
logical empiricism, 13, 22–3
Lukes, Steven, 16–17, 17 n29, 20, 27–8, 164 n17

MacIntyre, Alasdair, 38 n90
MacLeod, Jay, 53 n48
McLaren, Peter, 50 n39, 188 n8
Madden, E.H., 22
Menace II Society, 150, 150 n15, 158
Merelman, Richard, 16 n26
Milliken v. Bradley, 61 n17
mobilization of bias, 15, 15 n23, 16 n25

Nagel, Jack, 19
New Haven, Connecticut, 59, 63 n28, n29 and n31, 159, 179, 181
new institutionalism, 4–5
Nietzsche, Friedrich, 5–6, 173
North End, Connecticut, 57–9, 179–80
   see also "the environment"; "the street"; "street values"
North End Community School
   demographic and achievement data, 62–3, 180
   see also authoritarianism; "banking model" of education; responsibility as accountability; "responsible citizenship"; "school knowledge"; "street values"; "survival skills"

O'Brien, Kevin, 162 n4
Ogbu, John, 48 n26
Orfield, Gary, 60 n15

Parsons, Talcott, 18 n36, 35 n84
participant-observation
    and gaining access, 193–4
    and generalizability, 191–3
    note-taking, 194–5
    and reactivity, 190–1
    and subjectiveness, 188–90
    see also interviews, teacher and staff;
        surveys, student; triangulation
participatory rule-making, 42–3, 118–23,
    136–40, 172–3
pedagogy, 46 n13
peer evaluations, 125
Petras, John, 14 n17
Pettit, Philip, 14 n17
pluralism, 14
Polsby, Nelson, 15 n20
poststructuralism, 5–6
Poughkeepsie, New York, 159
Poulantzas, Nicos, 18 n36
power
    community power studies, 13–14
    de-faced, 26–38
    and difference, 149, 156–60, 172–6
    intention, conscious knowledge, and
        volition in the exercise of, 18–22
    and privilege, 175
    structural theories of, 22–6, 28–9
    three faces of, 15–18
    with-a-face, 12–26
practices, 37–8, 38 n90, 52, 54–5, 169–70,
    176
    democratic political practices, 177–8

reflection papers, 123–5, 127, 129, 130
resources, educational, 51, 60–2, 115–16, 180
responsibility
    as accountability at North End, 75–81,
        91–5
    as self-sufficiency at Fair View, 130–5,
        146–9, 175
"responsible citizenship", 48–9, 103, 105,
    108–10, 133
Russell, Bertrand, 18–19

San Antonio Independent School District v.
    Rodriguez, 61 n18
Schattschneider, E.E., 15 n23
school choice, 178 n29

"school knowledge", 70–5, 123–30, 143
"school success", 152–3, 155–6, 172
schooling, US public
    constitutional decisions about, 60–2
    funding, 60–2
    local control over, 59–60, 60 n12
Schram, Sanford, 58–9 n6
Schutz, Alfred, 189 n12
scientific realism, 22–4, 28
Scribner, Charles, III, 172
segregation, racial, 57–8, 57 n1, 58 n4–5, 62
    n26, 179
Shapiro, Ian, 23 n56
Sharp, Rachel, 50, 50 n38, 153, 153 n21
Skinner, Quentin, 14 n19
Spradley, James, 187 n15
Stone, Clarence, 20 n46
Strauss, Anselm, 92 n17
"street, the", 98–101, 106, 108, 110
"street values", 102–5, 102 n49, 152
structural Marxist theories of schooling,
    46–8
structuration, 5, 22
surveys, student, 197–8
"survival skills", 106, 108 145

teacher observations, 124–5, 151, 152–3
toleration, 175–6
transformative intellectuals, 49, 49 n34, 154
triangulation, 189–90

underclass, urban, 103–4
Unger, Roberto, 174 n26
United States Department of Housing and
    Urban Development, 58 n5

values, depoliticization of (Fair View),
    122–3, 140, 172
victimization, 63 n30, 182

Walzer, Michael, 162 n4
Wartenberg, Thomas, 24–5, 32 n77, 156
Weber, Max, 12 n6, 39, 39 n91
Wendt, Alex, 23 n26
White, D.M., 20, 34–5
Willis, Paul, 217 n22, 48 n26
Wolfinger, Raymond, 16 n26 and 27, 19
    n41, 34, 34 n83
"world" of Fair View, the, 118, 158–60
writer's workshop, 126
Wrong, Dennis, 19, 19 n40

zoning, 57–8